CRITICAL PERSPECTIVES ON NEOLIBERAL GLOBALIZATION, DEVELOPMENT AND
EDUCATION IN AFRICA AND ASIA

Critical Perspectives on Neoliberal Globalization, Development and Education in Africa and Asia

Edited by

Dip Kapoor
University of Alberta, Canada

SENSE PUBLISHERS
ROTTERDAM / BOSTON / TAIPEI

A C.I.P. record for this book is available from the Library of Congress.

ISBN 978-94-6091-559-8 (paperback)
ISBN 978-94-6091-560-4 (hardback)
ISBN 978-94-6091-561-1 (e-book)

Published by: Sense Publishers,
P.O. Box 21858, 3001 AW Rotterdam, The Netherlands
www.sensepublishers.com

Printed on acid-free paper

TABLE OF CONTENTS

Contexts of Adult Learning/Education, Community Development and/or Social Action

ACKNOWLEDGMENTS

A collection of readings on any subject is only possible through the willing effort of several contributors – I am extremely grateful to the colleagues and friends who have seen fit to share their research and reflections on the subject at hand in this joint contribution. Your prompt attention, enthusiasm and critical commentary are greatly appreciated and I sincerely hope that each of you is pleased with the results.

I am also grateful to Otto von Feigenblatt, Editor in Chief, of the *Journal of Alternative Perspectives in the Social Sciences* for the initial impetus and confidence in a project to advance scholars and critical scholarship from/about the African and Asian regions. In the process of developing these chapters, several colleagues/professors have had a part to play in reviewing manuscripts and I wish to acknowledge them, while taking final responsibility for these inclusions: Dr. Steven Jordan (McGill University, Canada), Dr. Njoki Wane (Ontario Institute for Studies in Education, University of Toronto, Canada), Dr. Anthony Paré (McGill University, Canada), Dr. Aziz Choudry (McGill University, Canada), Dr. Sourayan Mookerjea (University of Alberta, Canada), Dr. Bijoy Barua (East West University, Bangladesh), Dr. Edward Shizha (Wilfred Laurier University, Canada) Dr. Samuel Veissière (University College of the North, Canada), Dr. Amin Alhassan (York University, Canada), Dr. Farid Panjwani (Aga Khan University, Pakistan), Dr. Dia DaCosta (Queens University, Canada), Dr. Brenda Spencer (University of Alberta), Dr. Janice Wallace (University of Alberta) and Dr. David Smith (University of Alberta).

After the publication of *Education, Decolonization and Development in Africa, Asia and the Americas* in 2009, it has been a pleasure to work with Peter de Liefde and Sense Publishers once again – Peter's personable approach, quiet encouragement and reasoned-flexibility are hard to come by in the publishing business. Thanks again Peter. Last but not least, I am extremely grateful but again to Alison Crump (Doctoral Student, Department of Integrated Studies in Education, McGill University, Canada) for her vigilant editorial support and for literally making herself instantly available for this project at all times. Thanks Alison!

Dip

INTRODUCTION

*Dip Kapoor, Associate Professor, Department of Educational Policy
Studies, University of Alberta, Canada*

The global re-structuring of education or the globalization of an Euro-American modernizing-education wedded to and shaped by the neocolonial political-economic and cultural interests of capital reproduced by the UN (including the World Bank), corporatized-states and dominant civil society actors (educational international non-governmental organizations or INGOs) has been variously acknowledged and referenced in the scholarship addressing globalization and education in the field of comparative and international education (for an overview of perspectives and dominant literatures, see for example, Joel Spring, 2009).

This collection of readings is a modest contribution towards *critical* scholarship that acknowledges the colonial and imperial trajectories (Dirlik, 2004; Escobar, 1995; Fanon, 1963; Guha, 1997; McMichael, 2009; Mignolo, 2000; Mudimbe, 1988; Nandy, 1983, 1987; Quijano, 2008) that constitute what are now described as the globalization and development projects (McMichael, 2007) of the 20th and 21st century and their attendant education/learning interventions (the globalization of education or World Education Inc.), i.e., the on-going reproduction of "the global designs of Euro-American local histories" (Mignolo, 2007, p.159). Given the post-independence foundational project of inter/national development (in the "post-colonial Third World") and the most recent wave of globalization (i.e., the globalization of capitalism or neoliberal globalization), contributors to this collection have attempted to give due consideration to examining education/learning in relation to the social, political, religio-cultural and/or economic trajectories unleashed by these global projects and their neo/colonial, internal colonial and imperial implications for the peoples of these regions, including related resistances, reformulations or alternatives for renewal and local continuity. We examine these trends and their implications for and in the African and Asian regional contexts with the view to augment and compound similar and recent critical analyses focused on globalization, development and education/learning concerning these locations (Abdi, Puplampu & Dei, 2006; Abdi & Kapoor, 2008; Kapoor, 2009; Kapoor & Shizha, 2010).

The decision to bring African and Asian-specific analyses together was prompted by: (i) a dearth of critical scholarship (especially in terms of critical-colonial analysis) addressing education and globalization/development in these regions; (ii) the need to continue to develop critical education-centered scholarship of this ilk pertaining to both these regions simultaneously (introductory cross-regional research that still requires treatment), with the possibility that readers might begin to decipher similar trends and tendencies in both regions, while recognizing differences and specificities peculiar to the regions, cultures, colonial histories and micro-settings; and (iii) to address multiple spaces and types of education/learning (not restricting the analysis to formal settings alone), especially given that school/formal spaces are often hegemonic domains (and constitutive of colonial/imperial hegemonic projects) (Mayo, 2010), arguably with relatively muted/constrained radical potential in addressing the imbrications of colonial and imperial domination. The approach adopted by the various contributors is predictably multi and/or interdisciplinary as discussions on education in relation to multi-dimensional macro-phenomena (concerning political-economy, culture, society, histories, and ecology) such as *globalization* and *development* by definition, require scrutiny from a variety of disciplinary locations. This said, adopting a critical colonial/imperial analytical standpoint lends some degree of coherence to the collection and to potential contributions to critical scholarship and practice in comparative/international education and the sociology of education.

Key questions addressed in the collection include (but are not limited to) some of the following:

i. What are some of the identifiable colonial/imperial vectors embedded in *development* and *neoliberal globalization* or compulsory modernization projects in Africa and Asia today (e.g., IMF/World Bank imposed Structural Adjustment Programs in Africa; Free Trade Agreements with implications for the Asia/Pacific, for instance; exploitation of subalterns and the multitude in India; neoliberal globalization as a gendered process and associated gender-disproportionate impacts in Africa; dispossession of rural/tribal communities in Ghana, Bangladesh and Thailand)?

ii. What are some of the internal trajectories that cohere, compound, and/or co-exist with these external impositions (e.g., Saffron/religious fundamentalism in India or ZANU-PF authoritarian nationalism in Zimbabwe – the imbrications of external-internal colonizations)?

iii. How do these colonial/imperial ambitions (external-internal) define education and learning and vice versa in multiple spaces (e.g. Combined impacts of the privatization of education and ZANU-PF authoritarianism in Zimbabwe; cultural/epistemic colonization of science curricula in Africa; the re-negotiation of student identities in Pakistan; the individuation/behavioral compulsions of World Bank/IFI-determined HIV/AIDs education in South Africa)?

iv. What are some of the responses, resistances and possibilities (e.g., in/through movement activism, practice, policy, different theoretical/knowledge projects) spawned by colonial and imperial control (via development and neoliberal globalization) in education (and beyond) (e.g., renewed/ community-determined development/ educative engagements in Senegal; anti-FTA movement learning; community resistance in Bangladesh and Thailand; social movement learning in Ghana)?

v. How does/can education/learning contribute towards the shape of these counter/anti-hegemonic projects (e.g., indigenous science curricula in Africa; critical theoretical research/knowledge projects enhancing Dalit prospects in India; learning in/through struggle against FTAs; resource capture in Ghana or political pedagogies of mobilization among the multitude-subaltern in India)? Who are/ should be the agents of these projects and where are they located (e.g., critically-engaged academics in Africa/Asia/diaspora; potentially new subaltern-multitude class-formations in India; rural/tribal social groups/peasant classes in Bangladesh/Thailand/Ghana; anti-globalization/global justice constituencies and activists in the Asia/Pacific and in transnational spaces)?

The chapters include a mix of critical-analytical reflections utilizing pertinent educational and inter-disciplinary social science literatures, primary/critical-interpretive research-based reports/analyses and/or analyses that are informed by direct experience. The range of actors/spaces of education/learning considered include: schools, institutions of higher education, NGOs, social movements/struggles and local community action, subsequently embracing education/learning in all its garbs/ compartments – formal, nonformal, informal/ incidental, popular and indigenous/local.

In keeping with these emphases, "Policy/Theoretical Perspectives" are considered in Part I (chapters 1 to 6), while Part II (chapters 7 to 12) provides examples of closer examinations ("Case Studies") in formal education/schooling and higher education and in social movement/action, NGO and community contexts. In committing to a critical colonial/imperial political and analytical standpoint, the collection is limited to what this perspective might help illuminate with the conscious recognition that this is both necessary and is very likely, a partial but significant understanding of the complex and interactive socio-educational phenomena under scrutiny here on multiple scales and in various spaces.

In chapter 1, *Gloria Emeagwali* introduces the historical and contemporary impacts of Africa's encounter with neoliberal globalization as re-colonization and imperialism through the International Monetary Fund (IMF) and World Bank (WB) imposed Structural Adjustment Programs (SAPs) and conditionalities; policy mechanisms which were the product of Wall Street and a supportive Reagan-Bush neo-conservative ascendancy between 1980-89. Among other stated possibilities, the author suggests that the implicit goals embedded in the design of the SAPs included affecting a Marshall Plan in reverse as South subsidized North (e.g.in the late 1980s, Somalia transferred 47.4% of export earnings to Northern debtors), not to mention the socialization of debt through the removal of subsidies which hurt women and children the most (a theme taken up in chapter 6 by *Alenuma-Nimoh and Gerstbauer*). *Emeagwali* predicts that "the current financial meltdown will continue to expose many of the irrationalities of IMF interventions of the 1980s and 90s".

Edward Shizha (chapter 2) reminds readers about the potential and real impacts of neoliberal globalization (introduced by *Emeagwali*) and the concomitant penetration and epistemic colonization of the place of indigenous science education in Africa. His chapter speaks to the cultural-educational dissonance generated by such impositions while pointing out the value and contribution of the historical and contemporary legacy of indigenous science to Africa and beyond. *Shizha* suggests that "Africa can succeed in implementing indigenous sciences if academics in African schools act proactively and show interest in indigenous research that can facilitate indigenous peoples' struggles against the ravages of colonialism and neoliberal globalisation".

Moving away from the formal spaces of science education and schooling in Africa, *Aziz Choudry* (chapter 3) addresses bilateral Free Trade Agreements (FTAs) and their colonial/imperial implications for the Asia/Pacific (including brief references to Latin America) regions, while sketching the contours of adult learning and knowledge sharing in the process of building resistance to bilateral FTAs. He suggests that while considerable research has gone into examining popular struggles against capitalist globalization, including campaigns against the World Bank, the International Monetary Fund (IMF), the WTO and the Free Trade Area of the Americas (FTAA), relatively little attention has been paid to newer movements against bilateral free trade and investment agreements (FTAs). Informed by his activist engagements and research in these movements (e.g., GATT Watchdog), *Choudry* suggests that there has been a disconnection between major mobilizations against FTAs and established NGO networks distracted by the state of WTO talks (which might give the impression that neoliberalism is on the defensive), which completely ignores/misses the commitments now being made in bilateral free trade negotiations. However, as he states, "connections are slowly being made between movement activists fighting FTAs, and an important feature of such linkages is the production and sharing of knowledge arising from social movements themselves. It illustrates the importance of building upon, learning from, and sharing knowledge produced incrementally in social struggles against global capitalism".

Sourayan Mookerjea (chapter 4) bridges the discussion from trade to the sphere of production (exploitation) and social categories referenced by the *multitude* and the *subaltern*; two figures of political agency he suggests that are "today unavoidable points of departure for critical scholarship and leftist political engagement with global inequality and injustice". After establishing some of the theoretical space for the emergence of these "characters", the chapter dwells on a software technology park in the suburbs of Kolkata, India called Sector Five (or more officially, Rajarhat New Town), in order to locate both figures of multitude and subaltern at a specific site of production and its politics. *Mookerjea* examines the international and local division of labour through which middle class software professionals and information technology enabled service clerks are articulated to a transnational ruling class, on the one hand, and a large, informalized, marginal subsistence sector of petty manufacturing and services on the other. "The focus here is on a description of the complex structure of exploitation on which Kolkata's articulation with the world economy rests via Sector Five and on the conjunctural processes through which these arrangements were put into place". He proposes "that multitude and subaltern, as mediatory figures, pose a narrative form problem without generic solution. Rather, for the experimental social movement learning processes the Left today needs to undergo, the encounter of multitude and subaltern demands a kind of storytelling and cultural production where each character mediates the other as its symptomatic imposter or problematic allegorical double". This "encounter" is all the more pertinent given the "historically unprecedented quantum leap in inequality and in the imbalance of power between the transnational ruling classes and the multitude that has emerged over the neoliberal decades into what Samir Amin calls *global apartheid*".

In keeping with the theme of subalterity in India, *Dip Kapoor* considers the role of deploying (making productive) theory/academic perspective, research and scholarship in a politics of caste expositions and related prospects for a politics of social change that addresses the caste-class nexus of power and inequality in India. It is suggested that such an endeavour could benefit from a macro-scoping of the emergent imbrications and impacts of neoliberal globalization (i.e., the globalization of capitalism and market fundamentalism post-1991 liberalization of the Indian economy) and saffronization (post-Mandal in the 1980s and after the 1992 demolition of the Babri Masjid and the concomitant rise of the party-political Hindu right) and their implications for Dalit poverty, educational prospects and assertion. *Kapoor* suggests that "this in turn (or simultaneously) requires a re-negotiation of theoretical/perspectival discourses that have guided caste scholarship; a re-negotiation that begins to priviledge (or makes more space for) "critical sociological deployments" than has typically been the case to date". A *critical-indigenous Gramscian-Marxism* is proposed as an example of one possibility that would continue to help build momentum in this direction.

After considering caste/ism in India, gendered globalization in Africa (chapter 6) is the subject of the final contribution to this section on "Policy/Theoretical Perspectives". *Sidonia Jessie Alenuma-Nimoh* and *Loramy Gerstbauer* discuss the "gendered nature of neoliberal hegemonic globalization", addressing questions such as: "do women benefit from globalization? Are some women empowered by globalization? Addressing these questions helps to develop an analysis of the changing role of women and how women navigate their encounters with globalization". The authors "take a clear stance that neoliberal globalization is a gendered process and by its very nature eludes uniform analyses and rather deserves to be analysed through multiple lenses". After providing a brief overview of the gendered nature of globalization, they elaborate on "globalization as a double-edged sword", suggesting that African "women are very resilient and capable of subverting the very system that marginalizes them in very innovative and creative ways that ultimately work toward their advantage. Women are navigating their economic marginalization ushered in by neoliberal globalization in ways that can best be described as complex and paradoxical". They "emphasize the fact that both devotees and critics of globalization need to pay heed to the complexities of the ways African women participate in, become drawn into, are affected by, and negotiate their encounters with contemporary forms of global economic restructuring. It is only by acknowledging these complexities that we can offer analyses which will yield a deeper understanding of the phenomenon in question".

In the first case study considered in Part II (Formal Contexts of Education), a section devoted to a more detailed and close-up analysis of a particular context and line/focus of inquiry (e.g., a school, a university/education sector, a program/project/intervention, a social movement, a community or a community-development initiative/partnership), *Munyaradzi Hwami* (chapter 6) considers the crisis in Zimbabwe's public universities. Unlike previous explanations for the crisis that are either anti-Mugabe or pro-Mugabe, the author claims that "Zimbabwe is a victim of a double tragedy of radical capitalism and radical nationalism" and proceeds to examine "the crisis-making impacts of neoliberalism and ZANU-PF radical nationalism. Noting that neither neoliberalism nor nationalism are of indigenous cultural origin or meaning, *Hwami* calls for an "honest analysis of external and internal colonial explanations for the crises and the need for new approaches to address this situation; approaches that need to *critically* consider local/indigenous approaches (traditional wisdoms) to ways out of crises – a directional proposition that will no doubt require continued engagement, elaboration and political commitment on the part of concerned students, faculty and administration, if not all Zimbabweans".

Moving to neighboring South Africa, *Faisal Islam* and *Claudia Mitchell*, (chapter 8) based on their own work in HIV and AIDs education in rural schools in the country (including teacher training in relation to the same) and a review of the programmatic literature on HIV and AIDS education initiatives being undertaken by multilateral development actors and international financial institutions, suggest that "the educational contribution to HIV and AIDS prevention being advanced by many multi-lateral agencies has been inadequate as framed within a neoliberal globalization agenda, and has fallen short of its potential for addressing the epidemic". They argue that "It is important to understand the role of the corporate sector, especially the pharmaceutical companies and the failed policies of IFIs, which have played a critical role in spreading HIV and AIDS in Africa" and "suggest shifting HIV and AIDS prevention education from narrowly-focused individual fixations as imposed by agency-led development to local collective responses in accordance with community needs, initiatives and culture". They hope that their analysis "can prove to be instructive for educational initiatives undertaken by agents of the state (including schools), civil society actors and even progressive elements within these dominant development institutions (or their funded partners) who are concerned with the links between the need for greater political-economic democratization and the struggle against the epidemic".

Drawing from an ethnographic study of a group of urban high school going Pakistani youth living in Karachi (a metropolis of Pakistan, with a population of 18 million people from diverse ethnic and linguistics backgrounds) and their engagement with the global media and their responses to it, especially with respect to Bollywood and other global news channels, *Al-Karim Datoo* (chapter 9) examines questions of youth identity and the globalization of values, while exploring youth strategies to address *disjuncture* encouraged in such encounters with media. His study concludes that "being active consumers of media and other forms of information technology, youth are likely developing a transnational subjectivity, which in turn is placing them 'betwixt and between' the global and the local, between the world out there, and the world at home/family". The study also suggests that "the globalization of values is one of the most contested zones within processes of cultural globalization, where local is universalized through a re-invention of tradition or the traditional (for example, Islamic history and the role of women). In addition, 'value paradoxes' are sites of cultural production and a field of inquiry vis-à-vis the other aspects of global/colonial inquiry (political-economic, for instance) along with the various discourses related to globalization". The values-related paradoxes studied in this exploration also suggest "that the audience/youth agency is reconstructing media to use the medium to carry out their own projects of self/identity. In this way, the very tools of globalization (e.g. media) are used to counter global/hegemonic narratives of norms and being (competing narratives of self)...deploying a *disjuncture* which has emerged as a result of cultural globalization to rejuvenate local conceptions".

The next three case studies/chapters focus on adult learning and education in social movement, community action and NGO-community development spaces. *Jonathan Langdon* (chapter 10) draws upon his primary research with a rural movement in Ada, Ghana defending communal access to a salt-producing lagoon to demonstrate that: (i) "neoliberal globalization has been devastating for rural populations pushed off their lands in order to make way for extractive industries, export-oriented cash crops, and/or national development plans, while encouraging a burgeoning 'planet of slums' in urban centers", (ii) that "neoliberal globalization is most vulnerable to resistance in rural contexts" such as in Ada given that the strength and veracity of these movements lies in, both, the material (livelihood) and the epistemic (and cultural) value of these resources to the movement communities and (iii) that "the way movements are organized, led, and learn is critical to their regeneration, as well as towards ensuring that this regeneration remains rooted in the material/livelihood and epistemic/cultural critique of neoliberal globalization".

Bijoy Barua (chapter 11) advances a "critique of conventional assumptions about dominant imported development models and approaches that have dislocated ethnic communities, local knowledge, and livelihoods in parts of southeastern Bangladesh and northern Thailand". Based on his practical observation(s) and field research experience(s) in the region, he attempts to "construct knowledge from the socio-cultural perspective of a Buddhist society as the people of these regions practice *Theravada* Buddhism"; a perspective which "does not advocate *pseudo-desire* and *unbridled desire* (*tanha*) among the people or material and cultural aspirations that are central to the market model promulgated in contemporary dominant development interventions". The analytical perspective/discourse of the "Buddhist notion of development as one that promotes an *eco-centric* development approach which nurtures diversity for sustainable livelihoods is what is deployed here to critically assess the dominant modernization-oriented development interventions in these regions". *Barua* notes that "Buddhist traditions, in fact, grew as a spiritual power against social injustice and oppression (including oppression in the name of modern developmentalism) and emerged as a "movement of renouncers" in ancient India". The discussion in this chapter is limited to the issues and problematics "raised by Buddhist analytical perspectives and related postcolonial development discourses/debates pertaining to peoples' knowledge, dams, forests and livelihoods, development interventions, and socio-cultural concerns"; a juxtaposition of a Buddhist "people-centered development" in these regions and "eurocentric development".

Blane Harvey (chapter 12) augments *Barua's* critique of eurocentric-development (albeit towards projects of radical reform of development or a *rethinking of development* in the interests of community/individual agency) by deploying a Foucauldian analysis of networks, institutions and power in development partnerships between progressive environmental NGOs (Environment and Development Action in the Third World- ENDA-TM) and community-based organizations/groups (Federation of organic cotton growing farmers) in Senegal. The role of collective learning and critical analysis (relying on the work of Paulo Freire and Grif Foley) in these development relationships is emphasized. The chapter highlights the links between an ethnographic account of the influence of power on networks of development actors and institutions, and the call for contextualised ethnographic accounts of learning in social action to explore the opportunities and conditions for drawing on collective learning "to contest the subjugating power of development." By relying on the case of an NGO with a stated commitment to challenging relations that marginalise communities in the South, *Harvey* states that he has "sought to illustrate the complexity of negotiating these relations, demonstrating how individuals and institutions are constantly engaged in processes of undergoing and exercising power. On this basis, I argue, it is imperative that people engage in critical reflection about their own agency and the ways in which they have been situated by the development apparatus in order to work toward change. While this aim is laudable, it is no easy task, and better understanding the factors that enable or constrain these forms of reflection and action is a project which must remain central to *rethinking development*.

REFERENCES

Abdi, A., Puplampu, K., & Dei, G. (eds.) (2006). *African education and globalization: Critical perspectives*. Lanham, MD: Lexington Books.

Abdi, A., & Kapoor, D. (eds.) (2008). *Global perspectives on adult education*. New York: Palgrave Macmillan.

Dirlik, A. (2004). Spectres of the third world: Global modernity and the end of the three worlds. *Third World Quarterly, 25*(1), 131-148.

Escobar, A. (1995). *Encountering development: The making and unmaking of the Third World*. Princeton, NJ: Princeton University Press.

Fanon, F. (1963). *The wretched of the earth*. New York: Grove.

Guha, R. (1997). *Dominance without hegemony: History and power in colonial India*. Cambridge, MA: Harvard University Press.

Kapoor, D. (ed.) (2009). *Education, decolonisation and development: Perspectives from Asia, Africa and the Americas*. Rotterdam: Sense Publishers.

Kapoor, D. & Shizha, E. (eds.) (2010). *Indigenous knowledge and learning in Asia/Pacific and Africa: Perspectives on development, education and culture*. New York: Palgrave Macmillan.

Mayo, P. (ed.) (2010). *Gramsci and educational thought*. Oxford: Wiley-Blackwell.

McMichael, P. (2007). *Development and social change: A global perspective* (4th ed). London: Pine Forge Press.

McMichael, P. (ed.) (2009). *Contesting development: Critical struggles for social change.* New York: Routledge.

Mignolo, W. (2000). *Local histories/global designs: Coloniality, subaltern knowledge and border thinking.* Princeton, NJ: Princeton University Press.

Mignolo, W. (2007). Coloniality of power and de-colonial thinking. *Cultural Studies, 21*(2-3), 155-167.

Mudimbe, V. (1988). *The invention of Africa: Gnosis, philosophy and the order of knowledge.* Bloomingtion & Indianapolis: Indiana University Press.

Nandy, A. (1983). *The intimate enemy: Loss and recovery of self under colonialism.* New Delhi: Oxford University Press.

Nandy, A. (1987). *Traditions, tyranny and utopias: Essays in the politics of awareness.* New Delhi: Oxford University Press.

Spring, J. (2009). *Globaliation of education: An introduction.* New York: Routledge.

A. POLICY/THEORETICAL PERSPECTIVES

THE NEO-LIBERAL AGENDA AND THE IMF/WORLD BANK STRUCTURAL ADJUSTMENT PROGRAMS WITH REFERENCE TO AFRICA

Gloria Emeagwali, Professor of History and African Studies, Central Connecticut State University, New Britain, Connecticut

INTRODUCTION

The basic argument in this chapter is that the IMF programs of the 1980s and 1990s were the product of Wall Street and its associates and that the *Structural Adjustment Programs* (SAPs) generated by these interest groups, with no bailouts or stimulus packages, were an extreme form of monetarism, belt tightening economics and austerity, based on drastic cuts in public spending. The SAPs implied the rapid repayment of loans to creditors, with little regard for the suffering and inconvenience caused by the programs. They also led to forced deregulation, the coercive imposition on African governments of policies dictated by Wall Street. I point out that the end result was disastrous for growth and the well being of millions of people. In the final segment of the chapter, I revisit some of the past and present criticisms related to Africa's encounter with the IMF and the World Bank.

WALL STREET AND THE *STRUCTURAL ADJUSTMENT PROGRAMS* (SAPS)

Structural Adjustment Programs were conceived in the early years of the Reagan administration, 1981-82 (Prashad, 2003). The SAPs had some common ideological assumptions, implicit and explicit aims and general *conditionalities.* The imposed conditions included the forced devaluation of the domestic currency, privatization of the ownership of industries, liberalization of trade, and the removal of subsidies on health, education and social services, in general. Expectedly, the last requirement often led to declines in school attendance, sometimes along the lines of gender, and so, too, increased mortality because of the removal of subsidies on health. Prenatal and postnatal care was among the casualties of the IMF *conditionalities.* The liberalization of trade included full exposure to market forces of the domestic industries, whether fledgling or not. Debt repayment was central to the core requirement of the SAPs, and implied the transfer of over 50% of the domestic budget to the creditors, in debt repayment, in some cases (Emeagwali, 1995). I shall revisit some of these *conditionalities* in due course.

D. Kapoor (ed.), Critical Perspectives on Neoliberal Globalization, Development and Education in Africa and Asia, 3–13.

Three major agencies are significant in explaining the various *conditionalities* and the debt repayment expectations that these programs embodied in the 1980s and early 1990s, namely, the US Treasury, the US Public Action Committees or PACs, consisting of corporate donors for election campaigns, and, equally important, the US State Department (Smith, 1988). The Public Action Committees mushroomed between 1974 and the early 1990s. Some constituted the major donors to US presidential campaigns, with Exxon Mobil, BP, Bechtel, Boeing, the now defunct Enron, and Citigroup, at the top of the list of donors (Huffington, 2003). The PACs essentially put the US President in power, through heavy campaign donations, and provided a direct link between Corporate America, Wall Street and the US State Department. Among the PAC activists were former members of the US Congress, former White House officials, legislative staff aides and generally speaking, members of the old boys' network, in support of their mission. They engaged in mass marketing, radio call in shows, op-ed articles, targeted mailings and a host of other activities (Johnson & Kwak, 2010). The SAPs, and the high rate of debt repayment that they demanded, benefitted many companies. Some of these were major creditors and players on Wall Street and they used the PACs to lobby on their behalf.

Neo-conservative interest groups such as the American Enterprise Institute, the Hoover Institute, the Project for a New American Century, the Jewish Institute for the Support of Israel (JINSA) and the Hudson Institute were also influential in policy making in the US in this period. The rise of the neo-conservatives, during the Reagan - Bush administration 1980 to 1989, would have a major impact on the formulation of the SAPs. Among them were Richard Perle, Paul Wolfowitz, Eugene Rostow and Dick Cheney. Paul Volcker, Chairman of the Federal Reserve, and one time Treasury Secretary, during the Reagan administration, was also a major policy maker in the period between 1979 and 1987. Volcker's hike in interest rates from 5% to 20% was a major factor in the rapid increase in Africa's debt. Anne Krueger, Managing Director of the IMF in the mid 1990s was also closely associated with the Reagan administration and the Hoover Institute in the 1980s. The easy flow of bureaucrats and functionaries to and from the IMF, the World Bank and allied institutions should be noted. Simon Johnson and James Kwak provide an illuminating discussion on 'the Wall Street-Washington Corridor' in general (Johnson & Kwak, 2010). As the big banks got bigger, so, too, they could aim at administration jobs in Washington. The South African Stan Fischer moved from being Deputy Managing Director of the IMF to Citigroup. Rubin moved from Goldman Sachs to the post of Treasury Secretary. The Secretary of State in the Reagan administration became the president of Bechtel. Cheney, a former CEO of Haliburton became vice president during the Bush administration. The IMF and the World Bank during the 1980s and 1990s were widely seen as proxies of the US Government as a result of the constant interchange of staff, to and from the agencies described (Bello, 2003). The Secretary of the U.S Treasury became the chair of the National Advisory Council, which supervised the IMF and the World Bank along with the Secretaries of State and Commerce, the Chairs of the Export Import Bank and the Board of Governors of the US Federal Reserve system. It should be noted that Harry White and Hans Morgenthau, founding fathers of the IMF and World Bank were of the US Treasury Department in 1944 (Korten, 1999). The US government held veto power in the IMF, having 85% of the vote needed to pass major IMF decisions, through the phenomenon of weighted voting. Nigeria along with 21 countries collectively had 3.22% of the vote in the World Bank (Hudson, 2003). Another source of power for the US State Department came from the huge bureaucracy. Twenty five percent of the upper managerial work force in the World Bank in the 1980s and 1990s consisted of US citizens. US foreign policy emanated from a network of agencies which also included the Defense and State Departments, the CIA, the National Security Advisor, USIA, the Peace Corps and the US Development Agency, the Commerce Department and the Agriculture Department. Georgetown, where the State Department resided, and Virginia, the seat of Defense and National Security were of central significance for policy making. Interest groups such as the Council on Foreign Relations, the Trilateral Commission and the Bilderberg were also crucial in terms of the transnational elite, some of whose members were heads of state and policy makers of the coalition of Western states that met intermittently in the context of the Group of Seven (G7) or the Group of Eight (G8).

UNDERLYING GOALS AND THEORETICAL FOUNDATIONS OF THE STRUCTURAL ADJUSTMENT PROGRAMS (SAPS)

One may detect several underlying goals of the IMF and the World Bank. Firstly, it would seem that the SAPs were designed to implement US foreign policy as dictated by Wall Street and Corporate America, through the Public Action Committees and the Treasury Department. Secondly, it was aimed at the transfer of steady capital flows to U.S Western companies through debt repayment and debt servicing, at all cost, even in the light of the 70% decline in Africa's economic growth between 1980 and 2000 (Bello, 2003). This in effect meant a transfer of assets through privatization schemes in particular. Thirdly the SAPs were aimed at socialization of the debt through subsidy removal so that the burden of repayment fell on entire African populations, particularly on women and children and the most vulnerable (Emeagwali, 1995). This meant that creditors, money lending agencies and corporate executives would be rescued. Fourthly, it would seem that some of the overzealous neo-conservatives were now in search of 'nation states without borders' and sought to create a pan-global elite of financiers and investors, answerable to none. Fifthly, it would seem that one of the aims of neo-con activism was the integration of African economies into the global economy, to facilitate high rates of profit, in exchange for cheap wages and cheap resources, at minimal rates of remuneration and compensation. Sixthly, one may see the SAPs as directly related to US deficit financing (Hudson, 2003). According to Hudson, the World Bank and the IMF would become facilitators of compulsory lending to the United States Treasury by way of Central Banks around the world. Moreover, countries in Africa and elsewhere were trapped within a web of control, which Hyatt characterized as 'a Marshall Plan in reverse' with the countries of the Global South subsidizing the North (Hyatt, 2007). The US emerged in the 1940s as a major creditor nation. At the 1944 Bretton Woods conference in New Hampshire, the US dollar was adopted as the world's reserve currency. Prices in international trade were set in dollars. Nixon's 1971 abandonment of gold standard convertibility, and his suspension of the agreement to redeem dollars in gold, was ominous (Korten, 2001). By the 1990s the US had become the world largest debtor, with 70% of its debt financed by China, Japan and a few other countries. In 2003 it was $2.4 trillion dollars in debt (Bello, 2005). Foreign resources were being taken in exchange for US Treasury IOUs (Hudson, 2003).

Underlying the IMF/World Bank SAPs of the 1980s and early 1990s were some basic assumptions, some of which can be traced to Adam Smith's highly influential economic treatise, namely, *An Inquiry into the Nature and Causes of the Wealth of Nations,* first published in 1776 (Smith, 2009). Self-interest, non-interventionism by the state, and confidence in the price mechanism would be among Smith's basic assumptions. Smithian theory also implied the sanctity of private property and a belief that inequality was necessary for growth to take place. Some of these assumptions would become crucial for supporters of the free market model and laissez–faire policies. Joseph Stiglitz recently pointed out that Kenneth Arrow and Gerard Debreu, using a model designed by Leon Walras, a French mathematician and economist, tried to demonstrate one of the essential arguments of Smith, namely, that markets were essentially efficient (Stiglitz, 2010). By so doing they would provide additional theoretical basis for supporters of the market model, and by implication, for the IMF, which basically operated on the assumption that markets by themselves 'lead to efficient outcomes' (Stiglitz, 2010). The IMF/World Bank *Structural Adjustment Program* of the 1980s and 90s were indeed variants of the market model. As earlier discussed, among their core propositions were the assumptions that privatization was a necessary process for development, and that embryonic infant industries could coexist with free trade. Massive devaluations of domestic currency were seen as necessary for long-term gain, in a depressed economy, and the removal of subsidies from health, education and social services was seen as a necessary prerequisite for self-reliance and self-sustained growth. A fundamental assumption of the IMF was that adjustment should take place by suppressing demand rather than stimulating supply. Belt tightening and deflation would be among the immediate expectations (Stiglitz, 2002). Increased unemployment, declining consumption, soaring poverty and rising inequality inevitably followed (Bello, 2005).

Supposedly the SAPs aimed at re-establishing equilibrium by means of stabilization and adjustment phases to rectify what was deemed as irrational and inefficient policy. Governments were expected to devalue their currencies, remove price controls, and deregulate prices, whilst parastatals were to be sold to the highest bidder. All restrictions on imports were also to be removed, and so, too, protectionist legislation previously designed to keep fledgling industries afloat. The contractionary, appetite-suppressing, anti-inflationary monetarism embodied in the SAPs, left no room for Keynesian supply side economics. There were to be no bailouts or stimulus packages. The implication for governance and autonomy was even more sinister. Not only could foreign investors buy up the country's assets at bargain prices, but the political elite, whether civilian or military were actually reduced to being functionaries and agents of the IMF and the World Bank, with minimal political power. This created an extreme form of dependence and subordination. Vestiges of autonomy were undermined, hence our metaphorical reference to 'bonds' and 'bondage'. Given the high rate of interest associated with debt repayment in the 1980s and 1990s, it is not unreasonable to invoke the concept of debt slavery and peonage when discussing the general outcome of IMF and World Bank impositions.

A great percentage of the debt incurred included monies borrowed by tyrants and dictators, without due process, and as argued by several scholars, were for that reason unjustly and illegally acquired. The *conditionalities,* invariably gave rise to undemocratic and dictatorial governance in terms of a vicious cycle of dictatorship, a factor which did not deter the US State Department or the US Treasury. It took a dictator to implement the draconian *conditionalities* because democratic governments implementing these policies might have been voted out of power unceremoniously. We can argue that dictatorship and authoritarianism were inevitably the bedfellows and allies of the IMF and the World Bank, whether by design or accidentally, and that their support of democratic elections was contradictory. Michael Woodiwiss argues that the IMF and World Bank acted as 'gangster loan sharks' not only in Indonesia and the Philippines but also in Mobutu's Congo. Human rights abuses, corruption and the transfer of ill-gotten monies to private accounts in Western financial institutions by these autocrats, did not deter the lending activities of the financial institutions (Woodiwiss, 2005). Bello suggests, however, that eventually, by the late 1990s, the US backed away from some of the dictators because of their inability to fully impose the neo-liberal policies, given the strong resistance movements that emerged in some of the regions.

Perkins (2004), in *Confessions of an Economic Hit Man*, goes a step further and points out that dictators were courted and encouraged by these financial agencies, to increase the indebtedness of countries, rather deliberately. Although his major examples were from Panama, Ecuador, and Venezuela, the modus operandi of the Economic Hit Men (EHM) would be applicable to African countries in general. The underlying philosophy of the EHM was that 'global empire was a pathway to increased profits' and by implication the goals of the EHMs and the IMF/World Bank system were one and the same. As an EHM the job of Perkins was to convince Third World countries to accept massive loans, and to guarantee that Halliburton, Bechtel and other such companies controlled the massive projects. Some may argue that the IMF and World Bank encouraged this kind of cycle of indebtedness and debt repayment.

GLOBALIZATION AND THE SAPS

Globalization in the 1980s and 1990s was characterized by the relocation of industries to selected sweatshops in low wage zones, to enhance profits. It was also associated with the dispersal of financial markets and the rapid flow of speculative capital across borders. The progressive incorporation of economies around the world into a new globalized, neo-liberal world order became one of the major goals of the supporters of globalization. A single global market with non-existent and weakened nation states was of direct benefit to the so-called 'electronic herd' of banks, pension funds, insurance companies, and other representatives of the Western world.

The founding fathers of the IMF and the World Bank may not have had globalization in mind, in 1944. At that point in time, the prime concern was restructuring the battered European economies, following the devastation wreaked by the Second World War. The IMF had the fiscal responsibility of assisting such economies and the role of the World Bank was essentially to help in infrastructure development. By the 1980s, however, the mission of these institutions substantially changed, given the ascendancy during the Reagan administration of some of the interest groups earlier identified. Some scholars have referred to the globalization process as a process of recolonization by corporate interests, directly aimed at enabling corporations to make high rates of profit in exchange for low wages.

Jim Garrison, president of the State of the World Forum triumphantly noted that globalization and the IMF/World Bank institutions went hand in hand. In his words:

> No nation on earth has been able to resist the compelling magnetism of globalization. Few have been able to escape the 'structural adjustments; and 'conditionality's of the World Bank and the International Monetary Fund, or the arbitrations of the World Trade Organization, those international financial institutions that, however inadequate, still determine what economic globalization means, what the rules are, and who is rewarded for submission and punished for infractions. (as cited in Perkins, 2004, p. 170)

Steven Hiatt agreed with this point of view, emphasizing in his discussion of 'global empire and the web of control' that one of the major aims of the IMF and the World Bank was the international reinforcement of the neo-liberal model and laissez-faire (Hyatt, 2007). Even so, the 1997 Asian crisis was a severe blow to the IMF and helped to undermine the legitimacy of that institution, in the eyes of many around the world. The 2008 global financial meltdown also challenged the credibility of the IMF in particular. Critics point out that not only was the IMF incapable of detecting the signs of financial instability, mismanagement and irrational behavior, on its doorstep, but that the full fledged imposition of its characteristically monetarist *conditionalities,* would have wreaked havoc on the U.S economy, leading perhaps to a collapse of the global financial system as we know it. The imposition of IMF *conditionalities* would have led to the immediate and total shut-down of all social programs and benefits, including unemployment benefits, social security payments, and subsidized school meals, subsidies to farmers in the mid-West, housing and transportation subsidies, and programs such as Medicare. The US dollar would have been drastically devalued beyond its present worth, leading to hyperinflation, given its high level of imports from China and other countries, and its present status as an import dependent economy. Had the IMF imposed on the U.S economy the extreme shock therapy that it prescribed for African countries in the 1980s and 1990s, secessionism and the breakdown of law and order could have ensued. Military instability may not have ensued, given the almost mysterious checks and balances put in place to check such a phenomenon.

AFRICA'S ENCOUNTER WITH THE IMF/WORLD BANK SAPS REVISITED

Over the last three decades, numerous studies have been done on the effects of IMF/World Bank structural adjustment programs on African economies. Invariably these studies fall into various categories. Supporters of monetarism and orthodox economics, some who were at one time or another associated with either the IMF or World Bank, invariably endorsed the draconian policies of the twin institutions. For them, the imposition of the SAPs was necessary and inevitable, and debt repayment to creditors, a moral imperative. They saw nothing wrong with the virtual takeover of Central Banks by these lenders. They ignored the fact that between 1998 and 1999, one billion dollars left Africa in the form of debt repayment. They were oblivious to the reality that Africa experienced a 70% decline in economic growth since the inception of the SAPs (Bello, 2005) and that a process of deindustrialization was put in place by the programs in some regions. They ignored the fact that a weakening of productive capability meant that African countries fell more deeply into bondage. If only Adam Smith's self-adjusting market system were allowed to operate freely without hindrance, the crisis would not have occurred, they argued. These analysts also ignored the reality that the SAPs gravely exacerbated intra-ethnic relations, and indirectly helped to fuel some of the armed conflicts around the continent.

Ihonvbere (2006) points out that when in 1981 the IMF forced the government of Somalia to liberalize the economy, privatize public services, devalue the currency and cut back in public sector spending, it actually laid the foundation for ruin and disaster. Somalia's currency was devalued by 460% between 1987 and 1989. The cost of food and transportation skyrocketed. In keeping with IMF prescriptions, numerous workers were laid off, thus swelling the ranks of the unemployed. The urban population grew restless, the Barre regime became increasingly repressive, and most ominous, for the future of Somalia, was the increasing perception among the Somali clans that the pain of reform fell unevenly on one clan as opposed to another. The IMF program exacerbated intra-clan conflict. Remarkably, Somalia, in that moment of economic crisis, transferred 47.4% of its export earnings to its debtors, according to Ihonvbere.

In the case of South Africa the lending practice of the IMF was no less questionable. The apartheid regime received a loan of $2 billion dollars in the 1980s, not long after the Soweto uprising and the assassination of Steve Biko, in 1976 and 1977, respectively. Its secret loan of $750 million dollars, in 1993, to the transitional government, included standard *conditionalities* and, according to Patrick Bond, requested the retention of apartheid- era financial bureaucrats in the

9

Finance Ministry (Bond, 2001). The adoption of the Growth, Employment and Redistribution Strategy (GEAR) in 1996, by the Mandela-Mbeki regime, was a major concession to IMF structural adjustment policy, since GEAR implied a cut back on social programs and the general implementation of stringent, fiscal, monetarist policies (Bond, 2001). It also implied the privatization of ESKOM, TELCOM and DENET, South African public enterprises associated with electricity supply, communication and aviation, respectively, a move heavily criticized by the Congress of South African Trade Unions (COSATU). GEAR essentially contradicted the earlier Reconstruction and Development Program (RDP), which embodied the more people, centered approach of the Freedom Charter, voted in by 3000 delegates of the African National Congress, in Kliptown, South Africa, in 1955. RDP was ideologically opposed to IMF monetarism. Naomi Klein suggests that South Africa's democracy was born in chains. Not only were Chris Stals and Derek Keys of the apartheid era retained but the Central Bank was made an autonomous unit, and monetarist policies, such as GEAR won the day (Klein, 2007).

In the case of Nigeria, the defining moment was the Babangida counter-coup of 1985, sometimes dubbed 'the IMF coup'. Fluctuating interest rates, corruption and poor economic planning, were at the root of the debt crisis in Nigeria, by the early 1980s. We should also note some of the inherited abnormalities from the era of colonial occupation (Okafor, 2006). The 1983 coup makers, Generals Buhari and Idiagbon seemed determined to rectify the situation by creative policies. Counter trade with Brazil and other economies in the South was envisaged (Okafor, 2008). The Buhari-Idiagbon team seemed determined not to do business with the IMF. General Ibrahim Babangida reversed this trend, with the 1995 counter-coup. Despite numerous student protests and riots against the adoption of IMF programs, the new regime rapidly adopted such policies. Under the weight of IMF *conditionalities* the Nigerian economy was soon sapped (Okome, 1998). The removal of subsidies on health and education took its toll on wide segments of the population. The Babangida regime remained adamant and was clearly intent on striking more deals with the IMF. Decree no. 36 of 1986 brought into play a foreign exchange market called SFEM and ushered in the devaluation of the domestic currency, the naira. Privatization of parastatals and trade liberalization ensued. Numerous studies have documented the impact of these policies, among which were the deterioration of health care, education and social services.

Liberal scholars were less prone to support the draconian policies of the IMF. Using some of the techniques of mainstream economics, they would identify some of the ill effects of the programs on individual segments of the economy. They pointed out, for example, that once the various sectors of African economies were disaggregated into formal and informal sectors, foreign owned and locally owned, and paid and unpaid segments, the differential effects of the various policies, in the 1980s and 1990s, would be better understood. They conceded that women were highly affected by cuts in health, education and other social services, in their capacity as home managers and mothers and that in countries where female entrepreneurs played a major role in the local fast food and small scale food processing sectors, the shrinking purchasing power of their clientele had detrimental effects on their income. The deflationary, monetarist, IMF approach to the crisis would be seen as an unnecessary bout of state interventionism. They anticipated major recessions, given the absence of stimulus programs and the fact that, additionally, capital would be sucked out of the economy because of debt repayment obligations.

Joseph Stiglitz' criticism of the IMF and the World Bank has been priceless. His seminal work *Globalization and its Discontents* (Stiglitz, 2002) was a major gift to liberal critics of the IMF. His detailed discussion of IMF activities in Ethiopia and Kenya exposed some of the questionable assumptions of the Fund. He pointed out in his lucid analysis that the IMF and the United States objected to Ethiopia's early loan repayment to an American bank, a policy that made sense given the high interest rate on the loan. That the Ethiopian government had done so without the approval of the IMF was one of the reasons for IMF objection. They also wanted Ethiopia to break up its largest bank. Johnson and Kwak have demonstrated that six banking oligarchies, Bank of America, JPMorgan Chase, Citigroup, Wells Fargo, Goldman Sachs and Morgan Stanley control 60% of the gross domestic product of the United States, to the tune of trillions of dollars, banks which have now become 'too big to fail' and their functionaries apparently 'too big to jail.' In the 1990s these US banks were already huge, having benefitted from the junk bond king Michael Milken, in the 1970s, and mortgage securitization in the 1990s. The United States led the world in mergers in the 1990s, and from the start of 1993 to the end of 1997, there were 2,492 of these, worth over 200 billion dollars (Korten, 1999). The Ethiopian bank in question was no larger than a small provincial American bank, and even then, in the 1990s, was not comparable with even the smallest subsidiary of one of the megabanks cited. Stiglitz found this request to break up the bank unreasonable. The IMF also wanted Ethiopia to 'open its financial markets to Western competition.' The Ethiopians were also required to liberalize their financial market, to enable international market forces to determine interest rates. One should note, here, that tinkering with interest rates has been the major activity of the US Chairman of the Federal Reserve, from Greenspan to Bernanke. Presumably, keeping these interest rates artificially low was done with the approval of the IMF, the Secretary of the Treasury and the various forces in the corridors of power in Washington. The IMF demand that Ethiopia should allow global market forces to determine its interest rates, even if this meant increased cost of fertilizers and agricultural inputs for Ethiopian farmers, was indeed misguided.

The monetarists, the original supporters of the SAPs, are yet to recover from this fundamental blow to their intellectual edifice, from Stiglitz, the 2001 winner of the Nobel Prize for Economics who they erroneously thought was one of their own, given his service as chief economist and senior vice president of the World Bank 1997 to 2000. The final blow would come in 2010 with his devastating critique of mainstream economics and 'market fundamentalism'.

Meanwhile, another former insider, John Perkins (2004), cited earlier in this chapter, revealed a tell-all, autobiographical confession from his years as an

Economic Hit Man. Given the fact that the main activity of Economic Hit Men was to get countries in debt, and cheat them out of trillions of dollars for 'loan sharks', his confessions would go beyond the wildest dreams of radical critics, some of whom, prior to this well documented treatise, were accused of being conspiracy theorists. Three years later, in *The Secret History of the American Empire*, Perkins would expose more insider information, including the prophetic words to Perkins of George Rich a veteran American engineer and operative: "And if you ever intend to have children, and want them to live prosperous lives, you damn well better make sure that we control the African continent" (Perkins, 2007, p. 192). George Rich did not work with the IMF or the World Bank, but he would reveal a mindset that functionaries often displayed, according to some scholars.

Studies of the IMF/World Bank Structural Adjustment Programs have been enriched by the works of Walden Bello, Greg Palast, Noam Chomsky, David Korten, Jerry Mander, David Blum, and a host of radical analysts whose insights have provided us with a clearer understanding of the New World Order ushered in by the Reagan-Bush administration in the 1980s.

The recent financial meltdown of 2008 may lead to new retrospective studies on that era of IMF/World Bank intervention, particularly since many of the theoretical underpinnings of mainstream economics are largely being re-examined, given the world wide revelation of market imperfections (Roubini, 2010). Even so, detailed micro- studies by researchers such as Hanson, Ihonvbere, Zack-Williams, Okome, and others, continue to be indispensable in our understanding of the various forms of bondage and subordination that the SAPs were associated with in the 1980s and 1990s in terms of economic subjugation and dependence, and various forms of indirect and direct coercion.

CONCLUSION

In this chapter, I have explored some of the theoretical underpinnings of the IMF *Structural Adjustment Program*s as well as the intersection of US election campaigns, banking and finance, and IMF policy making and implementation. Our emphasis has been largely on the IMF although the World Bank would share some of the underlying features. I reflected briefly on some of the IMF policies in Ethiopia, Somalia, South Africa and Nigeria, in the course of discussion. I also compared the approaches of monetarists, liberals and radicals, expanding on an approach that was introduced in an earlier work (Emeagwali, 1995). I conclude that the global financial meltdown initiated in 2008, would continue to expose many of the irrationalities of the IMF interventions of the 1980s and 1990s.

REFERENCES

Bello,W. (2003). *Deglobalization: Ideas for a new world economy*. London: Zed Books.
Bello, W. (2005). *Dilemmas of domination: The unmaking of the American empire*. New York: Metropolitan Books.
Bond, P. (2001) *Against global apartheid – South Africa meets the World Bank, IMF and International Finance*. Cape Town: University of Cape Town Press.

Emeagwali, G. T. (ed.) (1995). *Women pay the price*. Trenton, NJ: Africa World Press.

Hudson, M. (2003). *Super-imperialism: The origin and fundamentals of U.S. world dominance*. London: Pluto.

Huffington. A. (2003). *Pigs at the trough*. New York: Crown Publishers.

Hyatt, S. (2007). *A game as old as empire*. San Francisco: Berrett- Koehler.

Ihonvbere, J. (2006). The World Bank and IMF in Somalia. In G. T. Emeagwali & W. Brown Foster (eds.), *The African experience: Past, present and future*. New York: Whittier.

Johnson, S. & Kwak, J. (2010). *13 Bankers, The Wall Street takeover and the next financial meltdown*. New York: Pantheon Books.

Klein, N. (2007). *The shock doctrine: The rise of disaster capitalism*. New York: Picador.

Korten, D. (1999). *The post-corporate world*. Hartford: Kumarian Press.

Korten, D. (2001). *When corporations rule the world*. Hartford: Kumarian Press.

Okafor, V. (ed.) (2008). *Nigeria's stumbling democracy and its implications for Africa's democratic movement*. Westport, CT: Praeger.

Okafor, V. (2006). *A roadmap for understanding African politics*. New York: Routledge.

Okome, M. (1998). *A sapped democracy: The political economy of the structural adjustment program and the political transition in Nigeria (1983-1993)*. Lanham, MD: University Press of America.

Perkins, J. (2004). *Confessions of an economic hit man*. San Francisco: Berrett-Koehler Publishers.

Perking, J. (2007). *The secret history of the American empire*. New York: Plume.

Prashad, V. (2003). *Keeping up with the Dow Joneses*. Cambridge: South End Press.

Roubini, N. (2010). *Crisis economics: A crash course in the future of finance*. New York: Penguin.

Smith, H. (1988). *The power game. How Washington works*. New York: Random House.

Smith, A. (2009). *An inquiry into the nature and causes of the wealth of nations*. New York: Classic House Books.

Stiglitz, J. (2002). *Globalization and its discontents*. London: Penguin.

Stiglitz, J. (2010). *Freefall – America, free markets and the sinking of the world economy*. New York: N.W. Norton and Co.

Woodiwiss, M. (2005). *Gangster capitalism. The United States and the global rise of organized crime*. New York: Carroll and Graf Publishers.

NEOLIBERAL GLOBALISATION, SCIENCE EDUCATION AND AFRICAN INDIGENOUS KNOWLEDGES

Edward Shizha, Assistant Professor,
Wilfred Laurier University, Canada

INTRODUCTION

The imposition of neoliberal globalisation and Eurocentric science education in Southern Africa raises questions on how African people develop their African humanity and sociability. Neoliberal globalisation has been imposed on African educational philosophies to determine curriculum developments and implementation, especially in science and technology. Neoliberal globalisation and indigenous knowledges are in a state of contestation. Indigenous knowledges have become colonial captives within science education that ignores indigenous philosophies as peripheral to contemporary society. If neoliberal globalisation marginalises indigenous African knowledges/sciences, how can African students and people reclaim indigenous sciences to act upon their natural world? Indigenous knowledges are known for their resilience and ability to describe, explain, predict and negotiate nature. Can African indigenous philosophies and ways of knowing survive the onslaught of neo-colonialism and globalisation?

In this chapter, I define African indigenous science as culturally-specific knowledge that belongs to the original peoples of Africa that is based on their philosophies. The knowledge incorporates their social and natural wellbeing, their cosmos and their spiritual world. It includes plant biology, the ecological system, manufacturing, agriculture, food processing, civil engineering, animal husbandry, medical practices, transportation, mining, and communication (Snively & Corsilglia, 2001). Indigenous science catalogues contextual everyday activities, objects and events and interprets how the local environment works through a particular cultural perspective to interpret and understand social and natural phenomena. In addition, rational observation of natural events, classification, and problem solving are woven into all aspects of indigenous cultures. It is a science that should be alive in contemporary African schools because it is a living science that mirrors the peoples' lived experiences. Students exposed to this knowledge are capable of making sense of their lives and develop a cultural identity that is symmetrical to their social and cultural communities, and acknowledges their existence. Non-indigenous people ostensibly criticize African science as lacking rationality and relevance to contemporary technical life. They argue that 'western'

D. Kapoor (ed.), Critical Perspectives on Neoliberal Globalization, Development and Education in Africa and Asia, 15–31.
© 2011 *Sense Publishers. All rights reserved.*

science epitomises advanced contemporary societies and is an epistemology for a fact-transmission oriented pedagogy.

This chapter argues that indigenous knowledges and sciences contribute to global knowledge and help in identity formations of African indigenous learners. It also discusses how African students can become knowledgeable in both African indigenous knowledges and Western dominant scientific knowledge through critical pedagogies and a pedagogy of place. A hybridisation of sciences provides students with critical philosophies in developing scientific knowledge, skills and attitudes, if the social contexts of science education are emphasised.

LITERATURE REVIEW

Curriculum Policy and Science Education

An important intellectual challenge posed by globalisation is how Enlightenment science interacts with traditional non-Western worldviews. The battle by indigenous communities to achieve empowerment and self-determination through the preservation, protection and revitalisation of their cultures eroded by colonisation, Western culture, and more recently by globalisation has experienced a renaissance as indigenous communities have recognised the importance of documenting and sharing their cultural heritage. Recent events and studies indicate that indigenous knowledge has been recognised as a valuable science that deserves recognition in the school science curriculum. The formal education that indigenous African students receive does not merely serve the purpose of transmitting formal lessons and bestowing credentials, but also develops social and cultural identities. Nevertheless identities built on cultural learning are under threat from neoliberal constructs of scientific knowledge. Neoliberal globalisation creates artificial wants, both material and symbolic, often leading to individualism and the destruction of communities, ecology, and cultures.

A scrutiny of science curriculum innovations implemented in most African countries indicates a Western bias in the content and practice that alienates African students. The effects of science education on students' identity formations are largely determined by the science curriculum in place, in this case, Western. Innovations introduced after independence did not focus on the culture and the place of learners in science learning raising critical questions about whether innovations were introduced to please foreign donors or to bring about substantive changes in education. Expectations were that after independence African governments would decolonize their science curricula by integrating socio-cultural perspectives.

While curriculum changes were deemed necessary to refocus knowledge and pedagogy on African perspectives, research indicates that most curriculum changes were promoted by outsiders, mainly Western governments and donors. Some changes were 'copy cats' of Western curricula. In Francophone Africa, curricula were borrowed from France and implemented with little or no local input (Holsinger & Cowell, 2000). In South Africa, the origins of an outcomes-based curriculum known as Curriculum 2005 can be traced to competency based debates in Australia, New Zealand, Scotland, Canada and the United States of America (Cross, Mungadi & Rouhani, 2002). Cultural philosophers have criticised African governments for imposing Western perspectives and cultural imperialism (Kallaway, Kruss, Donn & Fataar, 1997) on science without addressing the cultural cognitions of students, and input from indigenous peoples. In Rwanda, a Canadian 'specialist' was invited to harmonise the primary and secondary science curriculum but the final document excluded Rwandese cultural knowledge, skills and attitudes (Jaya & Treagust, 2002).

International organisations have also influenced curriculum change in Africa. After independence, many African countries adopted the UNESCO biology project, the African Education Programme, and the adaptations of the PSSC physics (Holsinger & Cowell, 2000). In countries like Sierra Leon and Egypt, the architect of neoliberalism, the World Bank, forced the introduction of vocational education and science education reforms which did not take into consideration indigenous knowledges and sciences in their models (Hassan, 1997). Even Tanzania, which is usually credited with implementing Education for Self Reliance, a home grown primary education curriculum, borrowed its *Inquiry Science* curriculum from the USA and Britain (O-saki, 2007). Curriculum materials for primary school science courses (PSSC) came from the USA, while the Nuffield Science Project for secondary schools was from Britain. The same curriculum was used in Kenya and Uganda (O-saki, 2007). Where donors have had interest in certain areas of the curriculum, they have managed to influence government to institute curriculum reforms.

Current educational reforms in Africa emphasise inquiry based instruction and laboratory science which are not contextualised and have no relevance to indigenous people and their everyday activities (Shumba, 1999). The perception that science knowledge can be "transferred" to education systems in Africa should be revised in order to design self-regulated contextual and situational learning processes that promote students' identities. Empirical or positivist science isolates African students, whereas context-based indigenous epistemology makes sense to both teachers and learners who can identify with the science content (Shizha, 2008a), while fusing indigenous perspectives provides a paradigm shift in support of African indigenous people's aspirations and their holistic life experiences.

A Brief on Indigenous African Knowledge and Science

There are many ways of conceptualising and defining indigenous knowledge since meanings and terminologies are quite varied and based on cultural, social, political and ideological definitions (Shizha, 2008a). All forms of knowledge are grounded in culture and cultural identities. Culture is multi-faceted; it may function as a tool used by dominant groups to oppress and undermine the less powerful, or it may be a resource that people can draw upon to give energy to their lives and identities, or it may be a vital feature of ongoing social interaction (Schissel & Wotherspoon, 2003). Cultures are not abstract phenomena that exist independently of people, but

17

rather are living, dynamic entities that interact with and take shape in daily social circumstances. African indigenous knowledges are embedded in the daily circumstances and experiences of diverse African people in their local communities. Regarding the interface between cultural identity and indigenous knowledge, Catherine Odora Hoppers (2005) observes that it

> is the template shaping values, behaviour and consciousness within a human society from generation to generation. 'Cultural rights' means the right to preserve and enjoy one's cultural identity and development. … Within this template, the notion of indigenous knowledge systems (IKS) has been defined as the sum total of the knowledge and skills which people in a particular geographical area possess. (p. 2)

Watson-Verran and Turnbull (1995) observe that although knowledge systems differ in epistemologies, methodologies, logics, cognitive structures, or socioeconomic contexts, they all share a characteristic of localness. Indigenous science is a body of knowledge and skills local to a culture, and enables communities to survive. Each epistemology represents an indigenous science for a given culture. Western science is indigenous to the West as African indigenous science is indigenous to Africa. Much of African IKS remain tacit, sacred and embedded in practices, relationships and rituals, often transferred orally between generations. Lack of documentation and clear ownership makes it easy to ignore African IKS in favour of Western knowledge systems, which Shizha (2008b) and others refer to as the 'coloniality of power', enhanced by a globalised politics, economics and culture. Western science in African educational institutions is embedded in coloniality of power. There is an unequal hierarchical placement and acknowledgment of Western science and African indigenous science. Indeed, students are required to master a highly positioned Western empirical laboratory science while being discouraged from broadening their lowly positioned cultural knowledge (Shizha, 2006, 2008a). The colonisation of African knowledge spaces in African educational institutions is highly problematic. African narratives have been marginalised and deemed superficial and irrelevant when in actual fact they are the bedrock of African people's existentiality and identity. The canon in the current science discourse represents the grand narrative that privileges Western-European philosophy. In contrast to mainstream scientific practices, Odora-Hoppers (2000) is convinced that the strategy in Western scholarship is to give a negative cognitive and ontological status to everything African while valorising everything Western culminating in a monopolistic and conformist strategy.

The Essence of Science Education and the Global/Neoliberal Influence

The challenges from globalisation rekindle colonial memories that reify Eurocentric cultural values and predispositions that are considered as scientific or empirical for the official curriculum in Africa (Shizha, 2008b). According to the South African National Science Education Standards:

Science is a way of knowing that is characterised by empirical criteria, logical argument, and sceptical review. Students should develop an understanding of what science is, what science is not, what science can and cannot do, and how science contributes to culture. (South Africa, 1997).

While the South African National Science Education Standards mention science contributing to culture, it is not specific about which culture. What we know is that school science reinforces and reproduces Eurocentric or Western cultural capital, and conversely views indigenous science as "mythical and mystical" despite its applicability to indigenous people's health systems, agricultural production, agro forestry, and biodiversity (Shizha, 2009). In academic circles, science is taught in "simulated experimental teaching" (Ma & Chen, 2009, p. 89) that is predominantly influenced by Western meanings that emphasise empirical evidence on which to build theories (Shizha, 2008b, 2009). In African schools, science is defined from a Western perspective as "the acquisition of systematised knowledge in any sphere of life by methods that are based upon objectively verifiable sense experience" (Makhurane, 2000, p. 64). Western science disregards the people's science or everyday life experiences and focuses on replicable observation, description, prediction, and experimentation related to the physical world (Shizha, 2008a). Although indigenous science also utilises observations, descriptions and predictions, it does not indulge in replicability. Events are natural and situational.

A critical contributing factor that impacts the dynamics in science knowledge construction is globalisation (Esland, 1996). Knowledge production cannot be divorced from the cultural perspectives and the seemingly pervasive interaction of global influences. Because education is a cultural process, it brings endemic local tensions into the larger global arena. The influence of globalisation on science education and education in general cannot be ignored. Globalisation, in its neoliberal sense, refers to a series of economic, cultural and political changes typically viewed as increasing interdependence, integration, and interaction between people and organisations throughout the world (Reynolds & Griffith, 2002). At the level of education, this interdependence includes sharing knowledge and the cross-fertilisation of ideas that are relevant for the scientific and economic development of nations. Cross-fertilisation, or the hybridisation of knowledge, takes into account the differences in socio-cultural needs of local people (Shizha, 2008b). This entails making indigenous knowledges and the so-called 'positive' knowledge part of the scientific knowledge created by the people, especially educators who have the privilege to construct, legitimate and validate knowledge.

School science based on science laboratories, theorisation and positive evidence does not "allow for cultural differences" and "science for all" (Brady, 1997, p. 414). Instead, science education leads to educational disappointments as African students struggle with abstractions that require memorisation rather than applicability in everyday life experiences. Euro-American science, in the form of 'global knowledge', is rooted in "the violence of abstraction" (Baber, 2002, p.

19

747). In contrast, African indigenous science is practical; everyday life is more about learning how to do things rather than passively receiving knowledge. From a traditional African knowledge perspective, learning is a continuous process conducted as an exercise to promote collective consciousness and the continuity of the community.

Science Education and Cultural Dissonance in Africa

In African classrooms, educators may have to address complex challenges in terms of how 'official science' disrupts everyday life experiences and intercultural realities. As change agents, teachers require rethinking strategies to construct opportunities and spaces to recognise and build on learners' knowledge and experiences (Odora-Hoppers, 2001) and ensure that learners are able to position themselves into the democratic learning processes (Prakash & Esteva, 1998). As Schostak (2000) argues, there are no grand narratives concerning what is 'good for all'. Standardisation, to create the curriculum as dictated by neoliberal policies, is patently absurd in diverse contexts of cultural creativity. Standardisation of subject matter, pedagogy and high-stakes testing are perceived as solutions to the 'crisis' of the failure of African schools to create competent workers. Through the application of capitalist ideology, schools are expected to churn out school leavers with the 'correct' work attitudes and skills for the capitalist system; hence schools are engaged in behavioural and ideological remodelling and management of learners. Standardisation of curriculum tends to imply that schools exist "in a vacuum hermetically sealed off from the outside" (Brighouse & Woods, 1999, p. 99). Such a curriculum is more alienating than invitational as it seeks primarily to satisfy the powerful and privileged instead of converging with the needs of learners in their respective personal and social contexts (Odora-Hoppers, 2001).

The culture of a social group includes its distinctive commitment to certain values (Muwanga-Zake, 2009) that are coherent, profound and systemic to the extent that discrepancy in school achievement could be the manifestation of discontinuity between culture at home and the expectations at school. Semali (1999) deplores the rarity of interface between the school and African indigenous sciences in many post-colonial schools. Formal schooling and formal science, a creation of colonisation in Africa, dictate that students follow a prescribed standardised curriculum (Shizha, 2008a). Standardisation means that teachers focus on the subject matter prescribed and predetermined by the State and book publishers. Cultural practices and preferences in terms of individual and intra-individual cultural variation are ignored resulting in the cultural caricaturing of some social groups (Lahire, 2008). The transfer of individual knowledge from the learners' everyday life experience to school science lessons is not always valued and encouraged. In the process, African ways of learning and their associated sciences are not recognised, and often deliberately so by teachers (see Shizha, 2007).

Colonially educated teachers create a cultural dissonance between the learners' acquired life experiences and the abstractions of Euro-American science. Neocolonial education driven by neoliberalism and the credentialisation of learning for market-place certification invalidates African sciences to the extent that they are regarded as 'backward' and 'retrogressive.' Julius Nyerere (1968), the first president of Tanzania, once lamented the lack of consistency between school and learners' indigenous cultures when he stated:

> At present our pupils learn to despise even their own parents because they are old-fashioned and ignorant; there is nothing in our existing educational system which suggests to the pupil that he [she] can learn important things about farming from his [her] elders. The result is that he [she] absorbs beliefs about witchcraft before he [she] goes to school; but does not learn the properties of local grasses; he [she] absorbs taboos from his family but does not learn the methods of making nutritious traditional foods. And from school, he [she] acquires knowledge unrelated to agricultural life. He [she] gets the worst of both systems! (p. 278)

Nyerere recognised the need to integrate school knowledge and home knowledge to make learning relevant to African students in order to disrupt the cultural dissonance that existed in the delivery of the formal curriculum.

Cultural dissonance   Cultural dissonance in this chapter refers to the disturbing inconsistency between African students' cultures and the science curriculum that is taught in African schools. Globalisation has negative effects on cultural congruity as it dislocates and disrupts cultural experiences of African students by introducing external reality that has little practical implication for community survival and progress. Students who are culturally rich and competent in cultural science are regarded as "foolish" because of the negative perceptions regarding indigenous African sciences. According to Heine and Lehman (1997), dissonance destroys self-affirmation that is required to maintain a holistic image of self-integrity. Self-affirmation bolsters a person's perception of their integrity, adequacy and confidence (Schmeichel & Vohs, 2009). The influx of diverse cultural meanings perpetuated through globalisation tends to cause confusion with respect to self-identities.

In African schools, students' self-affirmation is disrupted by the teaching of science that disengages the students from image-maintaining processes. Shizha's (2008b) study on incorporating indigenous knowledges in science learning in Zimbabwe found that students were silenced by the strangeness of what they were taught and were totally disengaged from the learning process. In Kenya, Cleghorn and Rollnick (2002) observed that students who were taught in their language and applied their cultural knowledge in science lessons were active learners. Dissonance between 'formal science' and 'informal science' creates a boundary between "cultural legitimacy" and "cultural illegitimacy" (Lahire, 2008, p. 166). Cultural legitimacy is not purely arbitrary. Rather, it depends in large measure on the specific properties of cultural activities, namely whether they are individual or collective, organised or unconfined, formal or informal, tight or loose, contemplative or participative (Lahire, 2008). Positive science is accorded cultural legitimacy by elites to create socio-historical conditions that produce homogeneous cultural profiles. In turn, it creates cultural dissonances that disregard the contextual diversities that enhance the social functions of culture in interpretations of science.

Dissonance can be eliminated by motivating students to choose alternative learning styles and knowledges to what Western science regards as "truth" and "rational". Spreading the alternatives, as Heine and Lehman (1997) suggest, builds a positive image among students and gives them positive personality feedback that promotes cognitive development and learning competences. Marginalisation of African indigenous sciences alienates students and threatens their confidence and self-affirmation. Spreading alternative learning styles induces high performance motivation and, in that vein, Makuwira (2008) describes the characteristics of pedagogies, which represent indigenous philosophies as holistic, kinaesthetic, cooperative, contextual and person-oriented. These learning attributes should be taken into account in any teaching and learning program designed to enhance students' self-affirmation and self-perceptions to promote superior performance. Makuwira's categorisation can be implemented in science curriculum that is student- and community-centred; a process that utilises social learning through community projects. This model develops a mind and intellect that builds on the holistic and integrated approach that emphasises and strengthens students' imaginations and cooperative learning. There is a keen awareness that knowledge production is socially derived and evaluation in the context of this approach is not associated with objective tests but rather with measuring attitudes and social consciousness (Emeagwali, 2003).

When viewed from the neoliberal perspective, one sees a great divide between expectations of neoliberalism, which promote individualism and competition, and the person-oriented approach linked to indigenous learning strategies. Positive science encourages homogeneity and cultural dissonance in learning settings. Dissonance is in the form of foreign language, assessment, learning style and the irrelevance of science activities, which together have a negative impact on students' perceptions and cognitions of science. African students are likely to struggle to establish meaningful knowledge and learning remains an impenetrable domain. The cause of cultural dissonance could be linked to elite African teachers who shun indigenous African science and, according to Muwanga-Zake (2009), have assimilated into Western intellectual bondage without concern about growing African IKS. This conclusion has led Raseroka (2005) to assert:

> African communities generally have a diminished appreciation of IKS. Imperialism successfully implanted the perception that IKS is worthless or shameful because it did not fit into the colonial education system, its scientific notions and/or the missionary worldview (e.g. perception of all traditional healing practices as witchcraft resulting in some cases to criminalisation of the practice of this form of healing; the demonisation of belief in the ancestral spirit world). (p. 6)

Innovations in African Indigenous Science

Innovations in African indigenous science are required to achieve sustainable growth and technological development. To make advances in scientific development, African scholars and scientists should avoid the absolutisation of any knowledge system and the perception that Western philosophies, which are intolerant to other traditions of knowing, are the best (Ntuli, 1999). Africa was not a *tabula rasa* before colonisation and Western cultural systems were irrelevant in determining the value of Africa's ideas, beliefs and general way of life (Ntuli, 1999). Africa had its own knowledge, ideas and scientific constructs. Because indigenous science and research is largely community based, a major investment in the enterprise is the well being, health and survival of the most valuable resource of all, the people. The knowledge outcomes serve the people and their important resource – the land which is their Mother, and source of identity.

The colossal architectural Great Pyramids of Egypt and the stone structures of the Great Zimbabwe in Zimbabwe are good examples that reflect the mathematical and scientific principles that were used in African technologies. It is therefore crucial that Africa builds on its valuable cultural capital and avoid all that is deskilling or disempowering and disastrous to African development, advancement and sustainability. In contemporary Africa, certain indigenous scientific methods have persevered. Fishing techniques used in East Africa that preserve and conserve fish for future breeding, post-harvest pest control systems found in most of Africa, and methods of food preservation and processing are based on African indigenous ways of knowing.

Concerning health and wellness, the use of different herbs and plants to manage disease among the Maasai in Kenya and Tanzania; the *hoodia* plants used by the Sani people of Southern Africa; the discovery of the healing properties of the African willow (South Africa) and *iboga* (Gabon and Cameroon), botanicals which are revolutionising the Western medical establishment in terms of cancer treatment, dietary care and anti-addictive therapy, respectively (Emeagwali, 2003) highlight the importance of African indigenous science. This knowledge needs to be preserved and promoted among our youth and this can be done through the school. Rather than promoting a Western science that negates African indigenous ecology and excludes other peoples' traditions of knowing, an inclusive science system should be deliberately and vigorously sought and implemented in the education system of the continent (Maila & Loubser, 2003).

The value of indigenous sciences was highlighted by Carlson, Foula, Chinnock et al., (2001) who acknowledged the collaboration of Shaman Pharmaceuticals in South San Francisco with fifty-eight traditional doctors from some provinces and communities in Guinea, West Africa, between 1994 and 1998. In the collaborative venture 145 plant species were identified as useful for the treatment of type 2 *diabetes mellitus*. Guinea's traditional healers' botanical knowledge and medicines were highly acknowledged and the healers' contributions recognised by Shaman Pharmaceuticals. Guinea can apply this known indigenous science in its schools to promote indigenous knowledge. Indigenous botanical knowledge is a vital source

23

of science knowledge that science education in African schools should make use of in addition to Western science. Traditional African medicinal practices and success stories are only part of the wider knowledge base on which indigenous sciences are constructed. An analysis of indigenous sciences should include, for example, discussions on medicine, mathematics, food processing, metallurgy and building technology.

School science in Africa should focus on documenting and analysing the above scientific applications, some of which had gone underground because of colonialism (Shizha, 2006). One way to reengage African indigenous science in education is through integrating African indigenous philosophies and other perspectives. Indigenous sciences have been very innovative and useful in the cultural context in which they were constructed and applied. Regrettably, much of the conventional positivist and phenomenological literature is silent about the contested nature of knowledge production (Semali, 1999). There is also silence and paucity of literature on the development of scientific knowledge in Africa.

Western science has been shielded from other sciences by arguments that focus on purported lack of evidence and impairment of objectivity. African science has evidence based results as acknowledged by Shaman Pharmaceuticals, and the popularisation of *hoodia* by Western pharmaceutical scientists. Regardless, Western scientists use biased political and ideological overtures and financial power to delegitimize non-western sciences. Indigenous science is deemed relatively less transferable than conventional science. However, more and more of indigenous medicinal remedies are being seen on pharmaceutical shelves in Western cities.

The Interface

Africans cannot avoid becoming part of the global village. However, they should not forget that they, too, have something to offer from their cultures and knowledges (de Beer & Whitlock, 2009). In contemporary Africa, science is a fusion of Western and indigenous. Stewart-Harawira (2005) observes that

> despite having been devalued, marginalised, disenfranchised and frequently submerged throughout the history of Western imperialism, traditional indigenous knowledge forms have a profound contribution to make towards an alternative ontology for a just global order. (p. 32)

There are intersections between mainstream science and indigenous science, and at the core of mainstream science is the desire to negotiate nature through sequential processes such as hypothesis formulation, experiment and prediction (Shizha, 2006), while indigenous science is a holistic experience covering the cultural, social, political, economic, spiritual and the ecological. Whereas in Western science the process of discovery and the outcomes are generally predictable and repeatable, and the general thrust is to explain regularity (Emeagwali, 2003), indigenous sciences are situational and contextual.

Gergen (2001) argues that knowledge (whether indigenous or Western) is spawned within a particular segment of society based on power and class. Aronowitz and Giroux (1985) endorse this view when they argue that schools play a particularly important role in legitimising and producing dominant cultural capital through the hierarchically arranged bodies of school knowledge. In Africa, hegemonic Western knowledge continues to be given high status in the school curriculum while disadvantaging indigenous African learners who might have attained indigenous cultural capital. Integrating African perspectives in science education brings learners closer to their cultural identities and experiences leading to a science that is learner friendly and meaningful. Many teachers are hesitant to incorporate IK in the classroom out of fear of 'infecting' classroom teaching with 'pseudoscience' (de Beer & Whitlock, 2009). Neoliberal policies and ideologies that support globalisation tend to reproduce such teacher-perspectives.

In some countries, such as South Africa, Ghana and Kenya, there is enthusiasm to incorporate Indigenous Knowledge Systems in education. In South Africa, environmental education provides a vehicle to incorporate Indigenous Knowledge Systems into the school curriculum (O'Donoghue, Masuku, Janse van Rensburg & Ward, 1999). In 1987, the World Commission on Environment and Development affirmed that society had a lot to learn from traditional skills and knowledge to manage complex ecological systems (Masuku-van Damme, 1997). It is refreshing to note that the South African government has adopted a broad and holistic policy framework for implementing this international resolution (South Africa, 1997). Consequently, indigenous communities and all South Africans are encouraged and called upon to value traditional knowledge and innovations. Furthermore, the National Research Foundation has made Indigenous Knowledge one of its focal areas in collaboration with the Department of Arts, Culture, Science and Technology (South Africa, 1996). While on paper South Africa might appear committed to implementing indigenous ecological policies, we still wait to see how the government will infuse the same into science school curricula.

Educators need to revisit education curricula and align them to African needs. A progressive and robust approach to the transformation of education is critical to the process of emancipating indigenous knowledges. Educators, in a collaborative way, may have to strategically rethink the curriculum challenges in terms of how scientific and technological knowledge will be constructed. A blended or hybridised curriculum that incorporates Western and African indigenous sciences is the way forward. Scientists in South Africa are testing indigenous plants that have potential for healing illnesses like malaria, tuberculosis, and diabetes and for use as immune modulators for liver transplant patients (Horn, 2005). In Zimbabwe, Mapara (2009) reports that

> Among the Shona people, when one was suffering from malaria, they used plants like *chiparurangoma* (borreria dibrachiata) as a form of treatment. It was administered orally and one was usually healed of the ailment within twenty-four hours. The Shona also used the shrub called *muvengahonye* (canthium huillense) to treat and heal wounds that had become septic on both

human beings and livestock. Other plants like *chikohwa/gavakava* (aloe) were and continue to be used to heal people who are suffering from stomach ailments. (p. 146)

Science topics could include ecological sustainability, which requires "a patient and systematic effort to restore and preserve traditional knowledge of the land and its functions ... this is, knowledge of specific places and their peculiar traits of soils, microclimate, wildlife, and vegetation, as well as the history and the cultural practices that work in each particular setting" (Orr, 1992, p. 32). This type of knowledge is vital in most African communities. As an example, the Maasai pastoralists of northern Tanzania and southern Kenya know where to find water, and green shrubs that can be fed to young calves, even during long periods of drought. Likewise, in Ethiopia, often regarded as inevitably dependent on Western aid, the threat of famine can be overcome by local expertise. As Worede (in Seabrook 1993) explains:

> There is a wild plant that grows on the Somali border, under the driest conditions, less than 200 mm of rain a year ... There are other crops; things people have known where to find in distress times. They go to the mountains and pick them and survive somehow. But if you destroy the natural environment of such plants, you lose these resources, and your monocultures won't save you. (p. 13)

By including indigenous knowledge in the curriculum, the particular social identity of the student is acknowledged. By acknowledging students' particular cultures, science programs can turn learning into a more positive experience for students who are resistant to studying the Westernised science curriculum (de Beer & Whitlock, 2009).

The work of indigenous healers is well documented in Africa. Amutabi (2008) observes that in Kenya, little has been written about indigenous medicine and the health practices of alternative healers, but this did not stop the government from incorporating indigenous medical systems into Kenya's health system and succeed in its mission of providing medical services to the majority of the people. A study by Njoroge and Bussmann (cited in Wane, 2010) demonstrates how the Kikuyu administer herbs to cure malaria. *Caesalpinia volkensii, Strychnos henningsii, Ajuga remota, Waarbugia ugandensis,* and *Olea europaea* were identified as anti-malarial herbal remedies found in the majority of the medicines obtained from roots, trees and shrubs. This indigenous science is relevant for school science and should be part of science education in African schools. What kind of knowledge do natural healers have and how different is it from the knowledge taught and researched in Western universities? This question has a determining influence on the way indigenous African knowledge is perceived in the Western countries, and also on how Western knowledge is used in Africa. Thus it is important to understand how indigenous Africans relate to a globalised science.

According to Carter (2004), science learners in developing countries may develop a hybridisation of perspectives and multiple identities that include interactive knowledge and epistemologies from both Western science and traditional ecological knowledge. What is currently missing, in most African science classes, is a system of teaching and learning that can combine the two. African children are either kept in their home environments, missing out on the 'modern' aspects of education, or (increasingly) forced into full-time formal schooling, missing out on the 'traditional'. The latter often furthers the neo-colonial mentality by building aspirations of urban life and encouraging young people to believe that they have no future in rural communities.

Critical Pedagogy of Place and the Interface

The entrenchment in the curriculum of AIK is a challenge for 21st century policy makers and educators (Emeagwali, 2003) that could lead to a consolidation of self-sustaining networks of local researchers, democratically engaged in research that is compatible with community values, aspirations and goals. Place or location is important in the fusion of indigenous and Western sciences. A synthesis of the two sciences can be achieved through a critical pedagogy of place that promotes local sciences and negotiates the globalisation of science. As a theoretical framework, critical pedagogy of place synthesises two educational traditions, 'critical pedagogy' and 'place-based education' and has been proposed as a suitable perspective from which to investigate the connections among ecosystems, culture, and education.

Critical pedagogy challenges the global and neoliberal "assumptions that education should mainly support individualistic and nationalistic competition in the global economy and that educational competition of winners and losers is in the best interest of public life in a diverse society" (Gruenewald, 2003, p. 3). Rather than teaching and assessing student understanding of an abstract, decontextualised science, a critical pedagogy of place "encompasses an explicit understanding of relationships and processes, an embodied knowledge of community relationships and the ecology of place, an awareness of the layered nature of the interdependencies of life-sustaining processes" (Bowers, 2001, p. 152). To date, comprehensive attention to indigenous African science knowledge, its origins, construction, teaching and learning has remained more artefact than fact as reflected in neoliberal prescriptions.

The fact that science teaching and schooling in general is conducted in English, a 'global' language, or any other foreign language, makes the discussion on implementing indigenous sciences in African schools sound like cosmetic romanticisation. The official language in most sub-Saharan countries is an imported European language and education policies that have excluded the use of indigenous languages beyond early primary school. The educational liabilities of using an imported language include poor performance, school drop-out rates, inappropriate and culturally irrelevant materials, and exclusion from participation in national decision making (see Bamgbose, 2000; Bunyi, 1999). Africans have an enriching culture, a history, a way of thinking and doing things that are different from neoliberal global knowledge prescriptions. African philosophies are linked to the places we inhabit and our locations in society. We communicate, interact, socialise and conceptualise issues from a holistic African perspective. We do not operate in a linear pattern of thinking, and should therefore not be captives of globalism and neoliberal thinking that compartmentalise experiences. It is this African culture and way of doing things that should be integrated into the science curriculum. Therefore, academic institutions should apply a pedagogy of place to bring life to science lessons in their classrooms, a science that phenomenologically relates to the lived experiences of African learners.

CONCLUSION

So much is being written and proposed on the viability of indigenous knowledge in Africa and other regions where indigenous people live but the question is: In the face of persistent global and market forces, can indigenous knowledges survive and integrate with science education in Africa? This chapter reveals the viability of African indigenous sciences in indigenous communities. Indigenous science is a continuous holistic everyday experience and it is important in the communities in which it is used. For African students, science education that negates their lived experiences perpetuates and reinforces colonial and neocolonial mentalities that disenfranchise them in a world where multicultural or intercultural knowledge is the basis of most educational projects. Academics must embrace the indigenous intellectual traditions so as not to freeze indigenous people in historic stasis. Needless to say, I am not calling for educational contexts that are not progressively responding to the needs of a changing world, but for a hybrid of cultures that responds to the needs of African children in an African school. Africans do not need 'global' or neoliberal policies to dictate the knowledge that African learners should embrace. It must be accepted that Africans can speak intelligently about issues confronting their communities.

What I have argued for in this chapter is for the need to create a less isolating science system, one that infuses indigenous paradigms to create inclusive spaces of schooling. Indeed, it is this type of education that can achieve two important, pre-credential items for the child: the desire and the need to be recognised, and the empowerment that is partially instigated by that recognition. The fact that Africa experienced colonisation and is a member of the global community, makes the argument for integration of positive science and African indigenous science compelling. School science becomes more meaningful if students have voice and see its relevance and experience it outside of school. Teachers and students should contribute to anti-racist, anti-oppressive educational experiences and diverse perspectives from multiple social locations. Therefore, African students should experience a hybridity of positive science and indigenous science, with the latter accounting for a larger proportion of their cognitive experiences. As van Wyk (2002) argues, the reality is that in an expanding globalised world, learners can easily become alienated from what is taught in science, as well as the way it is taught if they are denied their cultural knowledge in science education. If neoliberal demands for standardisation are applied to science, the curriculum generally tends to imply that schools exist "in a vacuum hermetically sealed off from the outside" (Brighouse & Woods, 1999, p. 99). The assumption that Africa was empty of science and rational knowledge until Europeans arrived is based on a narrow perception of knowledge as a universal resource (Shizha, 2006). Much research in recent years has addressed the contribution of indigenous knowledge to development initiatives in developing countries, thus, proving the important role that indigenous knowledge plays in science education. Only recently have African nations begun to make their way towards establishing genuinely autonomous education systems incorporating elements of indigenous culture. Africa can succeed in implementing indigenous sciences if academics in African schools act proactively and show interest in indigenous research that can facilitate indigenous peoples' struggles against the ravages of colonialism; neoliberalism and globalisation (cf. Shizha, 2010).

REFERENCES

Amutabi, M. N. (2008). Recuperating traditional pharmacology and healing among the Abaluyia of Western Kenya. In F. Toyin & H. M. Matthew (eds.), *Health knowledge and belief system in Africa*. Durham, Carolina: Academic Press.

Aronowitz, S., & Giroux, H. A. (1985). *Education under siege: The conservative, liberal and radical debate over schooling*. London: Routledge & Kegan.

Bamgbose, A. (2000). *Language and exclusion*. Munster: LIT Verlag.

Baber, Z. (2002). Orientalism, occidentalism, nativism: The culturalist quest for indigenous science and knowledge. *The European Legacy, 7*(6), 747-758.

Bowers, C. A. (2001). *Educating for eco-justice and community*. London: University of Georgia Press.

Brady, W. (1997). Indigenous Australian Education and Globalisation. *International Review of Education, 43*(5/6), 413-422.

Brighouse, T. & Woods, D. (1999). *How to improve your school*. London: Routledge.

Bunyi, G. (1999). Rethinking the place of African indigenous languages in African education. *International Journal of Educational Development, 19*(4/5), 337-350.

Carlson, T. J., Foula, B. M., Chinnock, J. A., et al. (2001). Case study on medicinal plant research in Guinea: Prior informed consent, focused benefit sharing, and compliance with the convention on biological diversity. *Economic Botany, 55*(4), 478-491.

Carter, L. (2004). Thinking differently about cultural diversity: Using a postcolonial theory to (re)read science education. *Science Education, 88*(6), 819-836.

Cleghorn, A., & Rollnick, M. (2002). The role of English in individual and societal development: A view from African classrooms. Special issue on language and development. *TESOL Quarterly, 36*(3), 347-372.

Cross, M., Mungadi, M., & Rouhani, S. (2002). From policy to practice: Curriculum reform in South African education. *Comparative Education, 38*(2), 171-187.

de Beer, J., & Whitlock, E. (2009). Indigenous knowledge in the life sciences classroom: Put on your de Bono Hats! *American Biology Teacher, 71*(4), 209-216.

Emeagwali, G. (2003). African indigenous knowledge systems (AIK): Implications for the curriculum. In T. Falola (ed.), *Ghana in Africa and the world: Essays in honor of Adu Boahen*. Trenton, NJ: Africa World Press. Retrieved from, http://www.africahistory.net/AIK.htm

Esland, G. (1996). Education, training and nation-state capitalism. In J. Avis, M. Bloomer, G. Esland, D. Gleeson, & P. Hodkinson (eds.), *Knowledge and nationhood*. London: Redwood Books.

Gergen, K. J. (2001). *Social construction in context*. London: Sage.

Gruenewald, D. A. (2003). The best of both worlds: A critical pedagogy of place. *Educational Researcher, 32*(4), 3-12.

Hassan, F. (1997). Science education in Egypt and other Arab countries in Africa and West Asia. *Frontiers: The Interdisciplinary Journal of Study Abroad, III*. Retrieved from http://www.frontiers journal.com/issues/ vol3/vol3-11_Hassan.htm

Heine, S. J., & Lehman, D. R. (1997). Culture, dissonance, and self-affirmation. *Personality and Social Psychology Bulletin, 23*(4), 389-400.

Holsinger, D. B., & Cowell, R. N. (2000). *Positioning secondary school education in developing countries: Expansion and curriculum*. UNESCO: IIEP Publications.

Jaya, E., & Treagust, D. F. (2002). *Science education reform and the impact on the school environment in transitional societies*. Paper presented at the Annual Conference of the Australian Association for Research in Education, Brisbane, Australia, December 1-4.

Kallaway, P., Kruss, G., Donn, G., & Fataar, A. (1997). Introduction. In P. Kallaway, G. Kruss, G. Donn, & A. Fataar (eds.), *Education after apartheid: South African education in transition*. Cape Town: UCT Press.

Lahire, B. (2008). The individual and the mixing of genres: Cultural dissonance and self-distinction. Poetics: Models of omnivorous cultural consumption. *New Directions in Research, 36*(2), 166-188.

Ma, T., & Chen, W. (2009). The application of simulated experimental teaching in international trade course. *International Education Studies, 2*(1), 89-90.

Maila, M. W., & Loubser, C. P. (2005). Emancipatory indigenous knowledge systems: Implications for environmental education in South Africa. *South African Journal of Education, 23*(4), 276-280.

Makhurane, P. (2000). Science and technology in Zimbabwe in the millennium. *Zimbabwe Journal of Educational Research, 12*(3), 62-79.

Makuwira, J. (2008). Towards pedagogies of mathematics achievement: An analysis of learning advisers' approaches to the tutoring of mathematics in an indigenous tertiary entry program. *The Australian Journal of Indigenous Education, 38*, 48-55.

Mapara, J. (2009). Indigenous knowledge systems in Zimbabwe: Juxtaposing postcolonial theory. *The Journal of Pan African Studies, 3*(1), 139-155.

Masuku-van Damme, L. (1997). Indigenous knowledge within environmental education processes. *EnviroInfo*, 26-28.

Muwanga-Zake, J. W. F. (2009). Building bridges across knowledge systems: Ubuntu and participative research paradigms in bantu communities. *Discourse: Studies in the Cultural Politics of Education, 30*(3), 413-426.

Ntuli, P. (1999). The missing link between culture and education: Are we still chasing gods that are not our own? In M. W. Makgoba (ed.), *African renaissance*. Cape Town: Mafube-Tafelberg.

Nyerere, J. K. (1968). Education for Self-reliance. In J. K. Nyerere (ed.), *Freedom and socialism: Uhuru na Ujamaa*. Dar es Salaam: Oxford University Press.

O'Donoghue, R., Masuku, L., Janse van Rensburg, E., & Ward, M. (1999). Indigenous knowledge in/as environmental education processes. *EEASA Monograph*, No. 3. Howick: Share-Net.

Odora-Hoppers, C. (2000). *Indigenous knowledge systems and the transformation of academic institutions in South Africa*. Pretoria: HSRC.

Odora-Hoppers, C. (2001). *Indigenous knowledge and the integration of knowledge systems: Towards a conceptual and methodological framework*. Pretoria: HSRC.

Odora-Hoppers, C. (2005). *Culture, indigenous knowledge and development: the role of the university*. Occasional Paper, No. 5. Johannesburg: CEPD.

Orr, D. (1994). *Earth in mind*. Washington, DC: Island Press.

O-saki, K. M. (2007). Science and mathematics teacher preparation in Tanzania: Lessons from teacher improvement projects in Tanzania 1965-2006. *NUE Journal of International Educational Cooperation, 2*, 51-64.

Prakash, M. S., and Esteva, G. (1998). *Escaping education: Living as learning within grassroots cultures*. New York: Peter Lang Publishing.

Reynolds, C., & Griffith, A. (2002). *Equity and globalisation in education*. Temeron Press: Calgary.

Schmeichel, B. J., & Vohs, K. (2009). Self-affirmation and self-control: Affirming core values counteracts ego depletion. *Journal of Personality and Social Psychology, 96*(4), 770-782.

Schostak, J. F. (2000). Developing under developing circumstances: The personal and social development of students and the process of schooling. In J. Elliott & H. Altrichter (eds.), *Images of educational change*. Philadelphia: Open University Press.

Seabrook, J. (1993). *Pioneers of change: Experiments in creating a humane society*. London: Zed Books.

Semali, L. (1999). Community as a classroom: Dilemmas of valuing African indigenous literacy in education. *International Review of Education, 45*(3/4), 305-319.

Shizha, E. (2006). Legitimizing indigenous knowledge in Zimbabwe: A theoretical analysis of postcolonial school knowledge and its colonial legacy. *Journal of Contemporary Issues in Education, 1*(1), 20-35.

Shizha, E. (2007). Analysis of problems encountered in incorporating indigenous knowledge in science teaching by primary school teachers in Zimbabwe. *Alberta Journal of Educational Research, 53*(3), 302-319.

Shizha, E. (2008a). Indigenous? What indigenous knowledge? Beliefs and attitudes of rural primary school teachers towards indigenous knowledge in the science curriculum in Zimbabwe. *The Australian Journal of Indigenous Education, 37*, 80-90.

Shizha, E. (2008b). Globalisation and indigenous knowledge: An African postcolonial theoretical analysis. In A. A. Abdi & S. Guo (eds.), *Education and social development: Global issues and analysis*. Rotterdam, the Netherlands: Sense Publishers.

Shizha, E. (2009). Chara chimwe hachitswanyi inda: Indigenizing science education in Zimbabwe. In D. Kapoor & S. Jordan (eds.), *Education, participatory action research, and social change*. New York: Palgrave Macmillan.

Shizha, E. (2010). Rethinking and reconstituting indigenous knowledge and voices in the academy in Zimbabwe: A decolonisation process. In D. Kapoor & E. Shizha (eds.), *Indigenous knowledge and learning in Asia/Pacific and Africa: Perspectives on development, education, and culture*. New York: Palgrave Macmillan.

Shumba, O. (1999). Relationship between secondary science teachers' orientation to traditional culture and beliefs concerning science instructional ideology. *Journal of Research in Science Teaching, 36*(3), 333-355.

Snively, G., & Corsiglia, J. (2001). Discovering indigenous science: Implications for science education. *Science Education, 85*, 6-34.

South Africa (1996). *Constitution of the Republic of South Africa, Act 108 of 1996*. Pretoria: Government Printer.

South Africa (1997). *White paper on the conservation and sustainable use of South Africa's biological diversity*. Pretoria: Government Printer.

Stewart-Harawira, M. (2005). *The new imperial order: Indigenous responses to globalisation*. London: Zed Books.

van Wyk, J. A. (2002). Indigenous knowledge systems: Implications for natural science and technology teaching and learning. *South African Journal of Education, 22*(4), 305-312.

Wane, N. (2010). Traditional healing practices: Conversations with herbalists in Kenya. In D. Kapoor & E. Shizha (eds.), *Indigenous knowledge and learning in Asia/Pacific and Africa: Perspectives on development, education, and culture*. New York: Palgrave Macmillan.

Watson-Verran, H., & Turnbull, D. (1995). Science and other indigenous knowledge systems. In S. Jasanoff, G. Markle, J. Petersen & T. Pinch (eds.), *Handbook of science and technology studies*. Thousand Oaks, CA: Sage.

Wotherspoon, T., & Schissel, B. (2003). *The legacy of school for Aboriginal people: Education, oppression, and emancipation*. Don Mills, ON: Oxford University Press.

31

LEARNING IN STRUGGLE, SHARING KNOWLEDGE: BUILDING RESISTANCE TO BILATERAL FTAS

Aziz Choudry, Assistant Professor, Department of Integrated Studies in Education, McGill University, Canada

INTRODUCTION

For the WTO resistance, it is easier to gather people across countries to mobilize together. But with FTAs, we are struggling on our own. (Participant, Fighting FTAs International Strategy workshop, July 2006, Bangkok)

During the 1990s, the rising opposition to free trade and investment agreements came to be known in many quarters as the "anti-globalization" or "global justice" movement. In Canada, the USA and Mexico, opposition to the North American Free Trade Agreement (NAFTA) and the bilateral free trade and investment deals preceding them were initiated by Indigenous Peoples, women's movements, trade unions, students and peasant/family farmers. In the Asia-Pacific region, a range of social movements and non-governmental organizations (NGOs) mobilized against the Asia-Pacific Economic Cooperation (APEC) forum, which some had felt had the potential to become a free trade and investment agreement – although APEC often seemed far more hype than substance (Choudry, 2008, 2010; Kelsey, 1999). Globally, during the Uruguay Round of negotiations on the General Agreement on Tariffs and Trade (GATT), which set up the WTO in January 1995, many activists, social movements, trade unions and NGOs turned their attention to contest and oppose this multilateral institution and the negative social, ecological, political and economic impacts of its agreements. Meanwhile, the scope and depth of commitments under NAFTA, which covered a range of areas (notably its controversial investment chapter) which were not included in World Trade Organization (WTO) agreements, set the stage as a model for a new wave of bilateral free trade agreements with equally or more expansive scope.

While indeed there had been numerous campaigns against free trade and GATT in many countries, particularly in the Third World, the 1999 mobilizations in Seattle and the failure of the Seattle WTO Ministerial meeting to launch a so-called Millennium Round of negotiations was viewed by many in the global North as the birth of the anti-globalization movement. A number of networks of both direct action-oriented groups and people's movements such as Peoples' Global Action (PGA) (Wood, 2005), the international small and peasant farmers' movement network La Via Campesina (Desmarais, 2007), and the NGO-dominated Our

D. Kapoor (ed.), Critical Perspectives on Neoliberal Globalization, Development and Education in Africa and Asia, 33–50.

World is Not for Sale network arose during the 1990s or the start of this century to coordinate and network international[1] opposition to the WTO. The claims of newness surrounding 'globalization' and 'anti-globalization' obfuscated the fact that in many contexts, particularly in the Third World, there had been long and ongoing resistance to neoliberalism in its different manifestations spanning several decades (Choudry, 2008; Flusty, 2004).

Considerable research (e.g., Bandy & Smith, 2005; Day, 2005; Goodman, 2002; McNally, 2002; Polet and CETRI, 2004; Starr, 2000) has gone into examining popular struggles against capitalist globalization, including campaigns against the World Bank, the International Monetary Fund (IMF), the WTO and the Free Trade Area of the Americas (FTAA). Yet relatively little attention has been paid to newer movements against bilateral free trade and investment agreements (FTAs). This chapter critically discusses the spread of FTAs in the wake of the breakdown of multilateral (WTO) and regional (e.g., FTAA) negotiations, and the rise in social movement activism against these agreements. In doing so, it illustrates the importance of building upon, learning from, and sharing knowledge produced incrementally in social struggles against global capitalism. Drawing on examples from Latin America, Asia and the Pacific, I dispel the assumption that bilateral free trade and investment agreements are less of a threat than multilateral agreements. I will argue that in spite of a multitude of such movements and mobilizations against these agreements, particularly (though not exclusively) in the Third World, the transnational NGO/activist networks that have actively contested the WTO and FTAA have largely failed to connect such struggles with each other, and are largely inconsequential in relation to anti-FTA activism. There has been a disconnect between major mobilizations against FTAs and established NGO networks on globalization, which have generally been slow to react or seriously address the bilateral deals. On the contrary, some of these NGOs have issued triumphalist statements responding to the state of WTO talks which have suggested that neoliberalism is on the defensive, which completely ignore the commitments being made in bilateral free trade negotiations (e.g., IATP, 2008; Menotti, 2008). However, as I outline, connections are slowly being made between movement activists fighting FTAs, and an important feature of such linkages is the production and sharing of knowledge arising from social movements themselves.

First, rather than grounding my analysis in dominant strands of social movement theory or policy discussions put forward by professionalized NGOs, this chapter is informed by my engagement in activism, education and research in struggles against bilateral FTAs, which evolved from work in Aotearoa/New Zealand with activist groups GATT Watchdog and the Aotearoa/New Zealand APEC Monitoring Group opposition to GATT/WTO, APEC, the failed OECD Multilateral Agreement on Investment. In situating my analysis in this way, I concur with Flacks (2004) and Bevington and Dixon's (2005) critiques of the shortcomings of much social movement theory as being driven by attempts to define and refine theoretical concepts which are likely to be "irrelevant or obvious to organizers" (Flacks, 2004, p. 147), and the latter's call for the recognition of existing movement-generated theory and dynamic reciprocal engagement by theorists and movement activists in formulating, producing, refining and applying research. (See also Choudry and Kapoor, 2010, on knowledge production and learning in social movements). In his work on knowledge and learning in social activism, Holst (2002) uses the term "pedagogy of mobilization" to describe

> the learning inherent in the building and maintaining of a social movement and its organizations. Through participation in a social movement, people learn numerous skills and ways of thinking analytically and strategically as they struggle to understand their movement in motion ... Moreover, as coalitions are formed people's understanding of the interconnectedness of relations within a social totality become increasingly sophisticated. (pp. 87-88)

Second, drawing upon my involvement with campaigns and collaborative initiatives against bilateral FTAs in Aotearoa/New Zealand and internationally, this chapter will also outline specific challenges for education, knowledge production/sharing and mobilization campaigns against bilateral free trade and investment agreements by comparison to activism targeting more established global agreements and institutions such as the WTO, the World Bank and the IMF.

Mobilizations against FTAs have taken place in many countries, yet the relatively well-known transnational NGO/activist networks which have formed around the WTO such as Our World Is Not For Sale, and regional networks such as the Hemispheric Social Alliance (in the Americas) have not played any significant role in these. Indeed, there appears to be a knowledge, strategic, and action disconnect between these networks and recent/current struggles against FTAs. The trajectory of transnational networks contesting free trade that has accompanied mobilizations against the WTO operates on a different track from the locally grounded struggles against FTAs, which have sometimes seemed quite isolated from each other. In spite of commonalities of these agreements, and the fact that activists in, for example, Thailand and Colombia have been simultaneously campaigning against deals with the US, there has been little opportunity to learn from each other's struggles. Given the fact that the US essentially modifies its deals from a template, and yet the specifics of these deals are shrouded in secrecy during negotiations, analysis of the texts of other already concluded FTAs has been important in order to generate critical analysis of the exact nature of the disciplines in current FTA negotiations. Because of their very nature, bilateral deals pose some specific challenges for educating, sharing knowledge and mobilizing transnational networks and alliances against capitalist globalization.

GLOBAL CAPITALISM, GLOBAL WAR: CHALLENGES FOR MOVEMENTS

Today, the capitalist crises and strategies of previous decades continue, alongside new aspects, or rather, newer versions of older forms of imperialist aggression. Boron (2005) suggests that we are experiencing "the old practice of conquest and plunder [is] repeated for the umpteenth time by the same old actors wearing new costumes and showing some technical innovations" (p. 12). Regional and global free trade and investment initiatives have made slow progress because of internal divisions among governments and overbearing demands of imperialist powers in WTO, APEC, and FTAA negotiations. APEC continues in a fairly low-profile fashion, largely as a talk shop for economic and security concerns, and partly as a launch pad for new bilateral free trade and investment negotiations (APEC, 2002).

The September 11, 2001 attacks on the World Trade Centre and the Pentagon, and the subsequent 'war on terror' have been used to justify renewed militarization and war, as well as various forms of domestic state intervention in the US economy. Meanwhile, repressive domestic national security and immigration legislation is being ratcheted up in many countries, North and South (Boron, 2005; Mathew, 2005; Petras & Veltmeyer, 2003; Thobani, 2007; Tujan, Gaughran & Mollett, 2004). This has had worldwide consequences for the political space in which NGOs and 'anti-globalization' movements exist. The momentum behind major mobilizations against meetings of the World Bank/IMF, G8, WTO, the Summit of the Americas,[2] the World Economic Forum and other conferences of economic and political elites, mainly in the North, that carried from Seattle into late 2001 faltered somewhat after 9/11. Nonetheless, such mobilizations – and the cycle of 'alternative' NGO/civil society summits have continued, often on a smaller scale, as have questions as to how connected these mobilizations were with mass social movements or everyday resistance against capitalist exploitation, and just how representative they were of the most marginalized voices of the societies for whom they sometimes claimed to speak (Hewson, 2005; Martinez, 2000; Prashad, 2003). In the North, much of the momentum and focus directed against the institutions (and their cyclical meetings) most closely identified with the promotion and maintenance of capitalist globalization has been channelled into anti-war movements (Solnit, 2004; Wood, 2004).

Immediately after 9/11, a number of free trade's strongest proponents, notably former US Trade Representative (now World Bank President) Robert Zoellick, drew dubious connections between opposition to neoliberalism and 'terrorism', and insisted that further trade and investment liberalization (by the USA's trading partners, at least) was the most effective way to fight 'terror'. "[M]any people will struggle to understand why terrorists hate the ideas America has championed around the world," Zoellick (2001) said. "It is inevitable that people will wonder if there are intellectual connections with others who have turned to violence to attack international finance, globalization and the United States." For Petras and Veltmeyer (2003), after 9/11, the divisions between NGOs and labour unions calling for moderate reform of the system, and anti-capitalists or anti-imperialists seeking radical changes "seriously deepened, creating a fundamental rift within the [antiglobalization movement], with an increasing intolerance for radical change and confrontationalist politics" (p. 228). Some NGOs urged others to abandon direct action tactics and more confrontational positions. Debates within networks in North America and Europe regarding 'diversity of tactics' and the parameters of direct action in mobilizations continued, but often with an air of caution and self-censorship after 9/11 (McNally, 2002, Kinsman, 2006; Petras & Veltmeyer, 2003).

In June 2010, this dynamic once again played out in relation to the major mobilizations and state crackdown around the Toronto G-20 protests.

GEOPOLITICS, TERROR AND TRADE

While attempts to link commitments to further advance economic liberalization under the WTO with support for the "war on terror" failed to translate into tangible results in that arena since 2001, the bilateral FTA strategies, in particular, those of the US and EU, have clearly been as geopolitically driven as they have been motivated by narrow economic concerns. The US has been using FTAs with Middle Eastern countries to undermine social and political opposition to Israel, and wants to merge these agreements into a regional Middle East Free Trade Area (MEFTA). The EU is pursuing its own regional agreement through FTAs with North African and Middle Eastern governments. The US FTA with Morocco was supposed to signal Washington's support for "open, optimistic and tolerant Islamic societies" (USTR, 2004). The EU's current FTAs based on the 2006 'Global Europe' vision insists that parties (e.g., India, Korea and ASEAN) sign a Political Cooperation Agreement before an FTA. Energy security is emerging as an important element in the FTA strategies of countries like Japan, China, the EU and the USA, with separate chapters of FTAs between Japan and Indonesia and Japan and Brunei guaranteeing the Japanese government a supply of gas and oil, for example. The world's most powerful governments are competing to sign bilateral deals with the same countries in order to serve their distinct geopolitical and military agendas. FTAs often have little to do with trade and much to do with securing spheres of political influence and control. Access to 'natural resources' such as oil, gas, agrofuels, minerals and biodiversity can be seen as significant in terms of both economic aspects as well as their geopolitical implications.

As Sidney Weintraub (2003), of the Centre for Strategic and International Studies in Washington, D.C., puts it:

> The sense that is now being conveyed around the world is that US policy is to sign free trade agreements with other countries only if they are prepared to adhere to US foreign policy positions. An FTA, in other words, is not necessarily an agreement in which all parties benefit from trade expansion, but rather a favor to be bestowed based on support of US foreign policy."
> There are few signs that the Obama Administration is taking a substantively different direction on trade policy. The latest global economic crisis has led many people to question the claimed benefits of free market capitalism, even as world leaders gathered at the 2010 G-20 Summit in Toronto on the theme of "recovery and new beginnings.

BILATERAL FTAS: FROM THE WTO'S POOR COUSINS, TO TOOL OF CHOICE

Initially seen as a default for slow-moving WTO negotiations, observers and activists came to see the bilateral free trade and investment strategy as being a preferred option. Former EU trade commissioner and current Director-General of the WTO, Pascal Lamy said of EU trade policy: "We always use bilateral FTAs to move negotiations beyond WTO standards. By definition, a bilateral trade agreement is 'WTO plus'. Whether it's about investment, intellectual property rights, tariff structure or trade instrument, in each bilateral FTA we have the 'WTO plus' provision" (Jakarta Post, 2004). Transnational capital has always forum-shopped to get what it wants in terms of international regulatory frameworks enforcing protection of investment and property rights. Through these deals, it is possible to isolate and divide governments outside of a forum where they could on some level bond together to resist demands of Northern governments within the WTO. Bilateral deals conveniently had far lower profiles than WTO negotiations and so came under the radar of many activists and popular mobilizations against capitalist globalization.

Another factor is the imbalance/asymmetry between governments such as the US and EU that have a small army of trade negotiators at their disposal, and smaller countries in the Third World who may have less than a handful of officials dealing simultaneously with multilateral, regional and bilateral negotiations. The FTA process is often more of an imposition by a larger power than a real 'negotiation'. Like WTO agreements, and given their lower profile, perhaps even more so, they are negotiated in virtual secrecy, with negotiating texts routinely unavailable for public scrutiny in either country until it is much too late – or, it some cases, not even available for a significant period of time after the agreement has taken effect. Smaller countries face negotiations fatigue when overstretched and under-resourced officials have to deal with agreements with multiple countries, bilaterally, regionally and multilaterally.

Bilateral agreements typically allow for deeper and faster levels of liberalization and deregulation than could be achieved in the WTO, ('WTO-plus' provisions) and specific measures and policies could be targeted. FTAs often break new ground. As governments commit to standards of liberalization that go further than the WTO through FTAs, this has implications for negotiating positions in multilateral trade talks should WTO talks get more momentum: countries will not be able to stand up to demands from Northern governments for WTO expansion when they have already signed onto WTO-plus commitments bilaterally. Bilaterally, it is sometimes easier to set precedents on a range of issues which can then at some point be multilateralized. For example, when the US negotiates a bilateral agreement with a WTO developing member country, the most-favored nation principle of the WTO – whereby any privilege granted to one WTO member has to apply to all others – assures the EU that it gains the benefit of the standards that the US obtains. For all practical purposes then, these WTO-plus standards may become the "new minimum standards from which any future WTO trade round will have to proceed" (Drahos, undated). There is thus a built-in snowball and ratchet effect of FTAs that allows for the bottom-up development of new international rules and standards.

The US has comprehensive bilateral free trade and investment agreements with several countries, including Vietnam, Singapore, Chile and Jordan, Australia,

Bahrain, as well as the Central American Free Trade Agreement (CAFTA-DR) – a fusion of several bilateral FTAs into a sub regional FTA. FTAs with South Korea, Colombia and Peru have been signed but await ratification by the US administration (and in Korea's case, by Seoul). Washington is pursuing FTAs with Thailand and Malaysia while also moving ahead with a number of Bilateral Investment Treaties with Pakistan, China and India, and Trade and Investment Framework Agreements with countries such as Mozambique that are precursors to full FTA negotiations.

Meanwhile, the EU, through its "Economic Partnership Agreements" with 77 former European colonies in Africa, Caribbean and Pacific countries, is pushing these nations to further liberalize their agriculture and open up their services and other sectors to European companies for investment and takeover. Australia and New Zealand are also regional players in the Asia-Pacific, through a free trade deal with Pacific Island nations, the Pacific Agreement on Closer Economic Relations (PACER) which is triggered by the entering into effect of the EU-Pacific EPA, and both Wellington and Canberra have concluded, or are currently in talks towards, free trade and investment agreements with other countries.

Japan has become an active bilateral player and recently concluded "economic partnership agreements" with the Philippines, Indonesia and Thailand. Canada has also concluded several bilateral free trade agreements with Israel, Chile, Costa Rica, Jordan and Colombia and is negotiating on several other fronts as well, with current negotiations with the EU attracting some critical attention in 2010. Emerging powers like China, India and Brazil are becoming more and more active in pursuing bilateral free trade deals with smaller Asian neighbours and outside the region. Other FTAs between "developing" countries in different regions, such as between Asian governments and Latin American governments are also growing.

With the seventh WTO Ministerial in late 2009 failing once again to kick-start negotiations at the multilateral level came continued statements and reassertions by a number of governments that they would be taking the bilateral route for trade and investment liberalization.

FTAS: NEW THREATS FOR PEOPLE, NEW OPPORTUNITIES FOR
CORPORATE CAPITAL

Compliance with WTO agreements has been hard for many countries, but bilateral deals with WTO-plus provisions are even tougher. Through FTAs and bilateral investment treaties (BITs), EU and US trade negotiators push governments into going further and faster in adopting what are essentially corporate wish lists on areas such as intellectual property (further endangering access to treatment to millions of people living with HIV/AIDS and other life-threatening diseases, undermining traditional agriculture by imposing agribusiness monopoly rights on areas such as seeds, and expanding patent protection over all life forms), financial liberalization, and issues (e.g., government procurement and investment) which have been kept out of WTO negotiations or severely limited in their scope due to Third World governments' opposition to industrialized government demands.

US agribusiness and pharmaceutical corporations are both the scripters and cheerleaders of TRIPs-plus provisions. For example, Monsanto urged US trade negotiators to seek an end to Thailand's moratorium on large-scale field trials of genetically-modified crops either "in a parallel fashion with the FTA negotiations or directly within the context of the negotiations. Monsanto (2004) said that

> in the current context of free trade … it is imperative that the US work with Thailand to eliminate the current barriers to biotechnology-improved crops and establish a science-based regulatory system – including field trials of new crops – consistent with their international trade obligations in order to bring the benefits of these products to market in Thailand and to further promote consistent access to American agricultural technologies and products.

Former Thai Prime Minister Thaksin Shinawatra announced his intention to reverse Thailand's moratorium on GM field trials (which came into effect after pressure from farmers and consumer groups in April 2001). While he and his Cabinet were forced to uphold the moratorium after Thai farmers, Buddhist organizations, consumers and anti-GMO activists protested, US and Monsanto officials – who seek to make Thailand its regional base for GM Roundup-Ready corn and Bt corn – continue to have the moratorium in their sights in the context of on-again, off-again FTA talks.

The Secretariat of the US-Thailand FTA Business Coalition comprises the US-ASEAN Business Council, representing US corporations with interests in ASEAN, and National Association of Manufacturers (NAM), the USA's largest industrial trade lobby group. NAM boasts: "Our voice is not compromised by non-industry interests" (NAM website, undated). Business lobbies view unions, NGOs, communities as 'special interests', which should be subordinated to the interests of the corporate sector in relation to trade and economic policymaking processes.[3] BusinessEurope (formerly the Union of Industrial and Employers' Federations of Europe – UNICE) states:

> Given the increasingly important role of services in EU exports, all future FTAs must ensure comprehensive liberalization of key sectors including financial services, telecommunications, professional and business services and express delivery services…The EU has a comparative advantage across the board in services and needs to ensure that this advantage is pressed home in future FTAs. (UNICE, 2006)

MOVEMENTS AGAINST FTAS

Investment Threats and People's Resistance

FTAs and BITs contain broad definitions of 'investment' which throw the door wide open for disgruntled corporations based in one signatory country to take a case against the other signatory government to a binding disputes tribunal. Thus far, these have often related to conflicts after the privatization of state-owned enterprises and public utilities such as water, but could extend to include almost anything.

Argentina and Bolivia have already been sued under obscure BITs. Canadian investment analyst Luke Eric Peterson (2001) says: "It seems the high-profile disputes under the NAFTA appear to have inspired many litigators to dust off the NAFTA's more obscure predecessors." A number of innocuous-seeming bilateral investment agreements which few had even heard had been signed included clauses allowing for private investors to initiate binding dispute arbitration against governments. Such disputes are fought out behind closed doors in arbitration proceedings at the World Bank's International Centre for the Settlement of Investment Disputes (ICSID).

Azurix, a former subsidiary of Enron won a bid to run the privatized water and sewage system for 2.5 million people in parts of Buenos Aires province, Argentina, in May 1999. Bahia Blanca residents complained that their water smelt bad and looked brown, while regulators considered sanctions against Azurix for very low water pressure. After the water supply was found to be contaminated, health authorities warned people not to drink or bathe in the water. The local regulating agency forced the company to deliver free bottled water to all those affected, not to charge for a period when the water was of poor quality, and also fined Azurix for breach of contract. In October 2001, Azurix stated that it would withdraw from the contract, complaining that the province would not let it charge rates according to the tariff specified in the contract and would not deliver infrastructure. The province rejected the termination notice. Then, under a 1991 US-Argentina bilateral investment treaty, Azurix sued Argentina's bankrupt government for US $550 million. Azurix said that the authorities' actions amount to interference with its investment. In July 2006, ICSID awarded Azurix $165 million against Argentina.

The popular struggle against the privatized water system of Bolivia's third largest city, Cochabamba, is a symbol of the fight back against neoliberalism and privatization. This followed Aguas del Tunari (an affiliate of US water corporation Bechtel) sharply increasing prices. But after the privatization was reversed, the water system handed back to the public and it was forced to leave Bolivia, Aguas del Tunari/Bechtel lodged a "request for arbitration" against Bolivia at ICSID. It sought $50 million, claiming as "expropriated investment" the millions of dollars in potential profits it had hoped to make. (For the same amount, 125,000 Bolivian families without access to water could be connected.) The company turned to a 1992 BIT between Holland and Bolivia. While it was establishing its operations in Cochabamba, Bechtel was filing papers to shift its subsidiary's corporate registration to Holland from the Cayman Islands. After international protests and pressure, at the end of 2005, Bechtel abandoned its claim against Bolivia.

Challenges to Resistance Movements against FTAs

Despite the fact that these bilateral deals are being signed and implemented in many countries, the focus of many international NGO and trade union networks critical of free trade often seems to remain on the multilateral talks that have failed to advance very much. There has been some belated focus on EPAs being signed between the EU and African, Caribbean and Pacific countries among European and Australasian NGOs but relatively few connections have been made with local grassroots struggles against these agreements. It has been difficult to coordinate national-level opposition to EU EPAs, and much of the international campaign work on this has been driven by Northern-based NGOs which have had varying levels of connection with social movements in the countries affected. Conceptually, this weakness can partly be attributed to these organizations' overemphasis on the WTO, and a failure to take a clear stance against neoliberal capitalism, with a spectrum of platforms calling for anything between mild reform to complete rejection, coupled with funding and institutional focus on these institutions which were traditional targets of mobilizations.

While many of the stronger campaigns against FTAs build upon and draw from mobilization against the WTO, FTAA, other neoliberal reforms at international and domestic levels, the lower profile of these deals has allowed negotiations to take place well under the radar of many activist movements and organizations. Notwithstanding the fact that some of the largest and most militant mobilizations against capitalist globalization in recent years have been anti-FTA protests, for example in Korea, where street protests against the recently concluded FTA with the US numbered in the tens of thousands regularly and sometimes more in Seoul, in CAFTA countries (200,000 demonstrated in San Jose, Costa Rica on 26 February 2007 against CAFTA), mobilizing transnationally or internationally against these agreements has not had the same momentum or focus as anti-World Bank or WTO demos. The question is often asked about how to maximize leverage/opposition against these agreements by cooperating with activists in the other country, but there has been very little sustained joint activism in this regard.

In at least two cases, in Ecuador (Guttierez) and Thailand (Thaksin Shinawatra), anti-FTA movements and sentiments have contributed to the overthrow of governments. Subsequently, after popular pressure led to the cancellation of Occidental Petroleum's oil extraction contract in Ecuador, the proposed FTA with the US was effectively scuttled. The geopolitical aspects of these deals, such as the US-Korea FTA, become mobilization targets in themselves. In Korea, opposition was also related to older struggles (and the knowledge/conceptual resources which they generated) against US domination and military bases. By comparison with multilateral talks, such aspects have been in clearer focus in bilateral FTA struggles because of the close attention paid to other aspects of foreign affairs linkages with the other signatory government.

In many ways resistance to the Chile-Korea FTA set the stage for an even larger phase of mobilization against Korea's FTA with the US. Korea-Chile FTA negotiations began in 1998 and a deal was eventually concluded in 2003. Although the agreement was quite comprehensive (including services, investment and other areas), it was its agriculture provisions – and particularly the implications for Korea's domestic fruit growers – that were the focus of opposition in Korea. The FTA reduced tariffs on South Korean manufactured products in return for reduced barriers to Chile's agricultural exports. This FTA was opposed by farmers outside of the National Assembly (NA) in Seoul. Farmers occupied a bridge over the Han river and conducted daily rallies in front of the NA. They conducted a relay sit-in strike in front of the NA and spoke to the public about their concerns. During their campaign, farmers used thousands of trucks to block highways and tunnels to hold up traffic in protest, and also let pigs loose inside the National Assembly. Some farmers chained themselves to pillars, while the farmers' movement also wrote to MPs and occupied the offices of some legislators to pressure them to oppose the agreement. Protests were frequently met with police violence, but helped to delay the ratification of the deal several times. While over 50% of Korea's lawmakers promised that they would oppose the FTA, they ratified the agreement. From this experience, the Korean Peasant League (KPL) drew two lessons for future FTA fights: firstly, a struggle by small farmers alone (10% of Korea's population) would not lead to victory. The majority of the population were made to believe that sacrifice of the farmers was a necessary evil to achieve economic growth. Secondly, one cannot rely solely on parliamentarians – despite all the mobilizations, the government ratified the deal anyway. So KPL learnt that it is vital to build a mass struggle with other sectors to defeat current and future FTAs. According to Korea's Ministry of Agriculture and Forestry, in a report less than a year after the Korea-Chile FTA took effect, 12, 644 peach, kiwi and grape farms across Korea shut down because of the adverse effects of the FTA on domestic fruit growers. Korean farmers, unsurprisingly, were at the forefront of struggles against an FTA with US.

Even before the fight against the Chile and US FTAs, Korean social movements had mobilized against the imposition of neoliberal reforms since the 1980s, whether imposed by Seoul, or, after the 1997-1998 economic crisis, by the IMF. The Korean fight back against the US-Korea FTA (still to be ratified by US Congress at the time of writing) has been a major multi-sectoral struggle, illustrating the importance of strong national movements in the context of cross/binational networks against a deal. While there is a strong movement in Korea, there is far less social movement activism in the US. There were some joint actions and statements by Korean and US unions against the FTA, and Korean protest expeditions to the USA during negotiating rounds, but little sustained focus in the US. Similarly a small symbolic protest action in Brussels was held against the EU-Korea FTA, and an Australian Council of Trade Unions and AFL-CIO joint media statement critical of the Australia-US FTA was issued, but was more or less a one-off action.

Just as there is a great diversity in positions, ideologies, perspectives and tactics among opposition movements against the WTO, so too, we can find among opposition to bilateral FTAs those who call for reform of these agreements (largely major trade union bureaucracies and Northern NGOs) and those who reject these agreements altogether. Arguably, in many cases there has been an overemphasis on the individual institutions such as the Bretton Woods trio. NGO technical policy analyses of these agreements, institutions and processes are often detached from political economy/geopolitical factors, and lack a systemic critique of capitalism and imperialism which understand ALL of these institutions, agreements and processes – global regional, sub regional, bilateral, national and sub national (i.e., state/province/municipal level) as demanding oppositional responses.

Compartmentalized approaches to addressing capitalist globalization which do not confront the systemic nature of capitalism can only be of limited effectiveness. For many NGO campaigns, this compartmentalization occurs around issues (e.g., agriculture, services), sectors (women, workers, farmers, Indigenous Peoples) and institutions and agreements (WTO, FTAA, etc.) without a broader underlying framework of analysis necessarily informing action against global capitalism per se. This tends towards a rather fragmented analysis. Certainly, in some anti-FTA struggles, particular aspects of these agreements attract more attention than others, such as intellectual property provisions of the US-Thailand agreement, and the toxic waste dumping provisions of the Japan-Philippines Economic Partnership Agreement, but many of the most vibrant and sustained anti-FTA mobilizations have seen broad fronts of opposition grow through an understanding of the comprehensive threats posed by these agreements. For example, movements of people living with HIV/AIDS in Thailand found common cause and forged alliances with farmers because of the intellectual property chapter in the proposed US-Thai FTA. Meanwhile, the Korean government's removal of the film quota (to promote Korean films) as part of FTA negotiations, and commitments to further liberalize Korean agriculture brought film actors, directors and producers together with farmers and trade unionists in the streets against the US-Korea FTA.

On the other hand, in Northern campaigns on FTAs, such as in Canada, there is relatively little mobilization or awareness, and positions of NGOs and trade unions have focused on rather narrow platforms such as the Canadian Autoworkers Union focus against the proposed Canada-Korea FTA because of threats to the Ontario auto assembly sector and Canadian labour/NGO framings of the Canada-Colombia FTA agreement around human rights situation in Colombia. Such conceptualizations of these agreements obscure broader and deeper instruments of neoliberalism which impact the lives of peoples in both signatory countries.

BILATERALS.ORG AND FIGHTING FTAS PROJECTS

Given the challenges to organizing cross-nationally on bilateral free trade and investment agreements, a major concern among some opponents of FTAs has been how to facilitate the sharing of knowledge, research, analysis and experience with each other around struggles against FTAs. In September 2004, a number of organizations[4] initiated a collaborative website to support peoples' struggles against bilateral free trade and investment agreements http://www.bilaterals.org. Behind the establishment of the website was a concern that in the celebration of the stalling of the WTO and FTAA negotiations, there was little focus on the bilateral free trade and investment agreements actually being signed.

bilaterals.org is an open-publishing site where people fighting bilateral trade and investment agreements exchange information and analysis and build cooperation. Those campaigning against bilateral deals had found it hard to link up with others around the world to share analysis and develop broader and complementary strategies. By early 2008, the site was attracting around 200, 000 hits a month. It has been used to leak draft negotiating texts which have otherwise not been made public, such as a draft IPR chapter of the US-Thailand FTA (The Nation, 2006). It is also a forum for activists to directly alert others about developments in their struggles, not least during intense periods of mobilization and state repression in Korea and Costa Rica in 2007 and 2008, more recent mass mobilizations in Peru against proposed FTAs with the EU and the USA, and a wave of anti-FTA protests in India in 2009-2010.

People's movements to stop FTAs are often isolated from each other, a direct reflection of the 'divide and conquer' strategy that bilateralism thrives on. A number of anti-FTA movements have made it a priority to break the isolation and link with others fighting such agreements in order to share analysis and learning's from each other's struggles. The Thai anti-FTA movement has been quite proactive in this respect, organizing several events which have brought activists from different countries together to strategize on FTAs (similar collaboration has also taken place in Latin America among movements fighting bilateral deals). FTA Watch, a Thai coalition, invited bilaterals.org, GRAIN and the Bangkok office of Médecins Sans Frontières to help co-organize a global strategy meeting of anti-FTA movements. Dubbed 'Fighting FTAs', the three-day workshop was held at the end of July 2006 in Bangkok. It brought together around 60 social movement activists from 20 countries of Africa, the Americas and the Asia-Pacific region to share experiences in grassroots struggles against FTAs and to build international strategies and cooperation. For many participants, it was the first time they had been able to physically sit down with other movement activists fighting FTAs and discuss strategy and experiences. In February 2008, GRAIN, bilaterals.org and BIOTHAI (Biodiversity Action Thailand) produced a collaborative publication and launched a multimedia website called "Fighting FTAs: the growing resistance to bilateral free trade and investment agreements" which provides both a global overview of the spread of FTAs and maps the growing resistance and learning's from people's experiences of fighting FTAs. This resource was merged into a relaunched and redesigned bilaterals.org website in 2009.

GROWING ATTENTION TO THE SPREAD OF BILATERAL FTAS

There are further signs that a number of significant international movement networks are taking the threat of bilateral free trade and investment agreements seriously. A critique of the Japan-Philippines Economic Partnership Agreement issued by the Asian Peasant Coalition on 26 November 2006 denounced the Philippines' first bilateral free trade pact as "a very onerous deal … worse than the impositions by the WTO itself", and called upon the Philippine government to scrap it. Predicting that Filipino farmers would be hardest hit by the deal, the statement predicted that JPEPA would "further sink the Philippines into being a beggar state." Starting in October 2006, militant Filipino farmers, led by the Kilusang Magbubukid ng Pilipinas (KMP), launched several protest actions at the

Japanese embassy. Members of the APC have joined Filipino farmers in protest actions against JPEPA.

La Via Campesina has also made a number of statements explicitly opposing bilateral FTAs. A number of its member organizations, particularly in Central America, Korea and Africa are engaged in struggles against (mainly) US and EU-driven FTAs. For example, in a statement issued from a meeting in Dijon, France, on January 13 2008, entitled "No to Free-Trade Agreements, Yes to Food Sovereignty and People's Rights!" Via Campesina members from Asia, Europe, Africa and Latin America stated that

> all bilateral and bi-regional free-trade agreements, be they called "Tratados de libre-comercio" (TLC), "Free-trade agreements" (FTA) or "Economic Partnership Agreements" (EPAs), are of the same nature. They lead to the plundering of natural resources and only serve transnational companies at the expense of all the world's peoples and environment. These are not partnership agreements but Economic Plundering Agreements.

The organizations demanded "that governments not sign or withdraw from these agreements". In a statement by the Asian regional conference on "Informalization of Work Through Free Trade Agreements: Eroding Labour Rights", organized by the Committee for Asian Women, in Bangkok in June 2008 delegates declared:

> We strongly urge sovereign governments to resist the pressure from international corporations and international financial institutions to sign onto FTAs on dubious promises of growth, development and poverty reduction. We demand a moratorium on existing trade agreements and reject any new unequal bilateral and regional trade agreements, particularly in view of climate change and rising energy prices, which are incompatible with international transport of goods.

CONCLUSION

The responses of movements to bilateral FTAs in the post-9/11 climate illustrate a growing disconnect between anti-neoliberal activism in the North and South. As McNally, (2002), Petras and Veltmeyer (2003, 2005), Boron (2005), Desmarais (2007) and bilaterals.org, BIOTHAI and GRAIN (2008) illustrate, people's struggles against neoliberalism, particularly peasant movements, Indigenous Peoples, and militant trade unionists in Latin America and Asia, have continued to vigorously challenge states and transnational capital, notwithstanding increasing militarization and the use of anti-terror legislation against activists and communities of resistance. Major popular struggles in several countries throughout Asia, Africa and Latin America continue against bilateral free trade and investment agreements (bilaterals.org, BIOTHAI and GRAIN, 2008). With few exceptions, (often lobbying campaigns by NGOs such as those on EPAs in Europe, for example, Dür and De Bièvre, 2007) there has been very little activism addressing these agreements in the North. In many Northern activist networks, campaign focuses around the connections between war and links to questions of political economy and neoliberal capitalism have often been limited to articulating US oil interests in the Middle East with the invasion of Iraq. Yet for many on the frontlines against FTAs in Colombia, for example, South Korea or the Philippines, and in the daily struggles of Indigenous Peoples and immigrant communities in the North, these links are often identified and articulated in a far more relevant and sophisticated manner (bilaterals.org, BIOTHAI and GRAIN, 2008; Choudry, 2009, 2010; Mathew, 2005; McNally, 2002; Petras & Veltmeyer, 2003).

Even critically engaged scholars in the North tend to normalize, centre, and universalize their analyses of the modalities of activism in the North against the major summits. As McNally (2002) and Katsiaficas (2002) contend, within 'anti-globalization' networks, a disproportionate focus and awareness about the modalities of mobilizations and activism in North America and Europe lends itself to overlooking what are often far more complex, mass-based and sustained forms of resistance to capitalism and colonialism in the Third World, including new fronts of struggle against bilateral free trade and investment agreements. Since most of these mobilizations have taken place in Asia and Latin America, and with little sustained major mobilization against such deals in Northern countries, these struggles have also escaped attention in both activist and broader public circles, and in scholarship.

Bilateral agreements represent an intensification of capitalist globalization. The comprehensiveness of many FTAs has engendered the building of common fronts of struggle at national levels in many countries. Internationally, however, there is a tendency of NGO campaigns to become compartmentalized around individual institutions, and 'issues' (agriculture, human rights intellectual property rights, labour, women, etc.) and to put forward a rather standard formulation or platform of opposition to be mounted against the WTO, IMF/World Bank with relatively little focus placed on FTAs although these impose more immediate threats. There remains a reticence to reconceptualize 'globalization' to include threats detached from global institutions such as the WTO, World Bank and IMF, and to see dangers inherent in what appear to be smaller deals. The question still remains regarding how to conceptualize capitalist globalization as being equally driven by a web of smaller agreements and to find ways to target this process in a concerted manner.

In understanding the significance of many of these anti-FTA movements, the question of their success may hinge on whether they can build long-term alliances against neoliberalism rather than stopping a FTA, and to sustain a critique of capitalist globalization in whatever form it may take – and as we can see with NAFTA, the fight is not over when the deal is signed. The extent to which academic interest is piqued by these movements in ways similar to the extensive focus on anti-WTO activism, remains to be seen.

CHAPTER 3

NOTES

1   See http://www.ourworldisnotforsale.org
2   Initiated in 1994, the Summit of the Americas has met a number of times to lay the groundwork for a (stalled) US-led proposal for a free trade and investment agreement covering all the nations in the Americas except for Cuba – knows as the Free Trade Area of the Americas.
3   To cite one more example of the corporate machinery behind FTAs, FedEx, General Electric Company, New York Life, Time Warner and Unocal are US-Thailand FTA Business Coalition corporate chairs. Steering Committee members include: AIG, Cargill, Caterpillar, Citigroup, Corn Refiners Association, CSI, Dow Chemical, Ford, National Pork Producers Council, PhRMA, PricewaterhouseCoopers, SIA, UPS and the US Chamber of Commerce.
4   The initiators included the Asia-Pacific Research Network, GATT Watchdog (New Zealand), Global Justice Ecology Project (USA), GRAIN, IBON Foundation (Philippines), XminY Solidariteitsfond (Netherlands).

REFERENCES

APEC (2002, 27 October). APEC economic leaders declaration. Los Cabos, Mexico. Retrieved from http://www.apec.org/apec/leaders_declarations/2002.html
Bevington, D. & Dixon, C. (2005). Movement-relevant theory: Rethinking social movement scholarship and activism. *Social Movement Studies, 4*(3), 185-208.
bilaterals.org, BIOTHAI and GRAIN (eds.) (2008). *Fighting FTAs: The growing resistance to bilateral free trade and investment agreements.* London: bilaterals.org, BIOTHAI and GRAIN.
Choudry, A. (2008). *NGOs, social movements and anti-APEC activism: A study in knowledge, power and struggle.* Unpublished Doctoral dissertation, Concordia University, Montreal, Canada.
Choudry, A. (2009). Challenging colonial amnesia in social justice activism. In D. Kapoor (ed.), *Education, decolonization and development: Perspectives from Asia, Africa and the Americas.* Rotterdam: Sense.
Choudry, A. & D. Kapoor (eds.) (2010). *Learning from the ground up: Global perspectives on social movements and knowledge production.* New York: Palgrave Macmillan.
Choudry, A. (2010). Global justice? Contesting NGOization: Knowledge politics and containment in antiglobalization networks. In A. Choudry & D. Kapoor (eds.), *Learning from the ground up: Global perspectives on social movements and knowledge production.* New York: Palgrave Macmillan.
Committee for Asian Women (2008). Declaration. Asian regional conference on *Informalization of work through free trade agreements: Eroding labour rights.* Bangkok, Thailand, June 19-20. Retrieved from http://www.cawinfo.org/Article354.html?POSTNUKESID=cdc8ad0517854af3b3ae7627f067750a
Day, R. J. F. (2005). *Gramsci is dead: Anarchist currents in the newest social movements.* London: Pluto Press.
Desmarais, A. A. (2007). *La via campesina: Globalization and the power of peasants.* Halifax: Fernwood.
Drahos, P. (undated). The new bilateralism in intellectual property. Retrieved from http://www.maketradefair.com/assets/english/bilateralism.pdf.
Dür, A. & De Bièvre, D. (2007). Inclusion without influence? NGOs in European trade policy. *Journal of Public Policy, 27*(1), 79-101.
Fighting FTAs. (2006, September). Summary Report. *Fighting FTAs: An international strategy workshop.* Bangkok, Thailand. Retrieved from www.grain.org/i/fta-bilaterals-2006-en.pdf.

Flacks, R. (2004). Knowledge for what? Thoughts on the state of social movement studies. In J. Goodwin & J. Jasper (eds.), *Rethinking social movements: Structure, culture, and emotion.* Lanham, MD: Rowman and Littlefield.

Flusty, S. (2004). *De-coca-colonization: Making the globe from the inside out.* New York: Routledge.

Goodman, J. (ed.) (2002). *Protest and globalization: Prospects for transnational solidarity.* Sydney: Pluto.

Hewson, P. (2005). 'It's the politics, stupid'. How neoliberal politicians, NGOs and rock stars hijacked the global justice movement at Gleneagles ... and how we let them. In D. Harvie, K. Milburn, B. Trott, and D. Watts (eds.), *Shut them down! The G8, Gleneagles 2005 and the movement of movements.* Leeds: Dissent! and New York: Autonomedia.

Holst, J.D. (2002). *Social movements, civil society and radical adult education.* Westport, CT: Bergin and Garvey.

Institute for Agriculture and Trade Policy (IATP) (2008, 29 July). Trade talks collapse, new direction needed. Press release. Retrieved from http://www.tradeobservatory.org/library.cfm?refID=103455.

Jakarta Post (2004, 9 September). 'Singapore issues' part of EU's trade agenda: Lamy. Retrieved from http://old.thejakartapost.com/yesterdaydetail.asp?fileid=20040909.N01.

Katsiaficas, G. (2002). Seattle was not the beginning. In E. Yuen, G. Katsiaficas & D. Burton Rose (eds.), *The battle of Seattle: The new challenge to capitalist globalization.* New York: Soft Skull Press.

Kelsey, J. (1999). *Reclaiming the future: New Zealand and the global economy.* Wellington: Bridget Williams Books.

Kinsman, G. (2006). Mapping social relations of struggle: Activism, ethnography, social organization. In C. Frampton, G. Kinsman, A. Thompson & K. Tilleczek (eds.), *Sociology for changing the world: Social movements/social research.* Black Point, NS: Fernwood.

La Via Campesina. (2008, 13 January). No to free trade agreements, yes to food sovereignty and people's rights! Statement. Retrieved from http://www.viacampesina.org/en/index.php?option= com_content&view=article&id=475:no-to-free-frade-agreements-yes-to-food-sovereignty-and-peoples-rights&catid=38:stop-free-trade-agreements&Itemid=61.

Martinez, E. (2000). Where was the color in Seattle? In K. Danaher & R. Burbach (eds.), *Globalize this! The battle against the World Trade Organization and corporate rule.* Monroe, ME: Common Courage Press.

Mathew, B. (2005). *Taxi! Cabs and capitalism in New York City.* New York: New Press.

McNally, D. (2002). *Another world is possible: Globalization and anti-capitalism.* Winnipeg: Arbeiter Ring.

Menotti, V. (2008, 30 July). Derailing Doha and the pathway to a new paradigm: How WTO's collapse clears the way to solve today's food, fuel, and financial crises. International Forum on Globalization. Retrieved from www.ifg.org/programs/derailing_doha-vmenotti-30july08.pdf.

Monsanto (2004, 8 April). Written comments concerning the US-Thailand FTA submitted by Monsanto to the Office of the US Trade Representative. Retrieved from http://www.us-asean.org/us-thai-fta/ Monsanto_Comments.pdf.

The Nation (2006, 8 February). 'Secret' FTA details on the Net. *The Nation*, Bangkok. Retrieved from http://www.bilaterals.org/article.php3?id_article=3760.

NAM Website (undated). NAM at a glance. Retrieved from www.nam.org/s_nam/doc1.asp?CID=53 &DID=224181.

Peterson, L.E. (2001, May). Investment litigation, bit by bIT, bridges between trade and sustainable development. Bulletin 5, No. 4.

Petras, J & Veltmeyer, H. (2003). *System in crisis: The dynamics of free market capitalism.* Black Point, NS: Fernwood.

Polet, F. & CETRI (2004). *Globalizing resistance: The state of struggle.* London: Pluto.

Prashad, V. (2003). *Keeping up with the Dow Joneses: Debt, prison, workfare.* Cambridge, MA: South End.

Solnit, D. (ed.) (2004). *Globalize liberation: How to uproot the system and build a better world.* San Francisco: City Lights.

Starr, A. (2000). *Naming the enemy: Anti-corporate movements confront globalization.* London: Zed Books.

Thobani, S. (2007). *Exalted subjects: Studies in the making of race and nation in Canada.* Toronto: University of Toronto Press.

Tujan, A., Gaughran, A., & Mollett, H. (2004). Development and the 'global war on terror'. *Race and Class, 46*(1), 53-74.

UNICE (2006, 7 December). UNICE strategy on an EU approach to free trade agreements. Brussels. Retrieved from http://bilaterals.org/spip.php? article7265.

US Trade Representative (2004, 15 June). United States and Morocco sign historic free trade agreement. Press release. Retrieved from http://www.ustr.gov/Document_Library/Press_Releases/2004/June/ United_States_Morocco_Sign_Historic_Free_Trade_Agreement.html.

Weintraub, S. (2003, 3 September). The politics of US trade policy. Retrieved from http://news.bbc.co.uk/2/hi/business/3169649.stm.

Wood, L. (2004). Organizing against the occupation – US and Canadian anti-war activists speak out. *Social Movement Studies, 3*(2), 241-257.

Wood, L, (2005). Bridging the chasms: The case of peoples' global action. In J. Bandy & J. Smith (eds.), *Coalitions across borders: Transnational protest and the neoliberal order.* Lanham, MD: Rowman and Littlefield.

Zoellick, R, (2001, 24 September). American trade leadership: What is at stake? Speech to International Institute of Economics, Washington D.C. Retrieved from www.peterson institute.org/publications/ papers/zoellick 1001.pdf.

ON LEARNING HOW TO LIBERATE THE COMMON: SUBALTERN BIOPOLITICS IN THE ENDGAME OF NEOLIBERALISM[1]

Sourayan Mookerjea, Associate Professor,
University of Alberta, Canada

INTRODUCTION

Two figures of political agency are today unavoidable points of departure for critical scholarship and leftist political engagement with global inequality and injustice: the multitude and the subaltern. This essay plots an encounter between these two characters. I begin with a critical engagement with Hardt and Negri's (2000, 2004, 2009) the figure of the multitude, examining its relationship to their concepts of biopolitical production and of the common. The second section then takes up the figure of the subaltern, first in the work of the subaltern studies collective in India and then subsequently by others. The third section takes us to a software technology park in the suburbs of Kolkata, India called Sector Five (or more officially, Rajarhat New Town), in order to locate both figures of multitude and subaltern at a specific site of production and its politics. Based on field research I carried out with my colleague Dr. Gail Faurschou in 2006 and 2010, this section of the essay presents a case study. I examine the international and local division of labour through which middle class software professionals and information technology enabled service clerks are articulated to a transnational ruling class, on the one hand, and a large, informalized, marginal subsistence sector of petty manufacturing and services on the other. The focus here is on a description of the complex structure of exploitation on which Kolkata's articulation with the world economy rests via Sector Five and on the conjunctural processes through which these arrangements were put into place. The final part of this essay tries to draw lessons from this case study. I return here to the issues raised in the first two sections and argue that multitude and subaltern, as mediatory figures, pose a narrative form problem without generic solution. Rather, for the experimental social movement learning processes the Left today needs to undergo, the encounter of multitude and subaltern demands a kind of storytelling and cultural production where each character mediates the other as its symptomatic imposter or problematic allegorical double.

D. Kapoor (ed.), Critical Perspectives on Neoliberal Globalization, Development and Education in Africa and Asia, 51–68.

GLOBALIZATION AND BIOPOLITICAL PRODUCTION

Drawing a more rigorous distinction between Foucault's concepts of biopower and biopolitics, Hardt and Negri argue that a new mode of "biopolitical" production is now in "hegemonic" ascendency. At the very outset, Hardt and Negri's formulation of this epochal transformation in capitalist production presents formidable difficulties: What can it mean to describe the articulation of new modes of production with all others as a relationship of "hegemony"? What can it mean to say that "[e]conomic production is going through a period of transition in which increasingly the results of capitalist production are social relations and forms of life. Capitalist production, in other words, is becoming biopolitical" (Hardt & Negri, 2009, p. 131)? But, of course, in one way or another, the results of capitalist production, like any other mode of production, must be social relations and forms of life, as always, and virtually by definition. The historically new emergence therefore needs to be found somewhere else, in contemporary processes re-making the forms of social life. To this end, Hardt and Negri specify three characteristic features of the epochal change through their analysis of technical and organic composition of capital.

Production is now said to be increasingly "anthropogenetic"; in which the "production of forms of life is becoming the basis of added value"; in which "putting to work human faculties, competences, and knowledges – those acquired on the job but, more important, those accumulated outside work interacting with automated and computerized productive systems – is directly productive of value" (Hardt & Negri, 2009, p. 133). But the production of services in the world economy encompasses a vast range of different kinds of production, under very different circumstances and arrangements. We will look closely at one location of such articulations below.

The second feature of the emergent mode of production Hardt and Negri point toward they call the feminization of work. Their account of this, however, is very symptomatic and makes clear that a northbound monocentric perspective is being normalized theoretically: "Part-time and informal employment, irregular hours, and multiple jobs – aspects that have long been typical of labor in the subordinated parts of the world – are now becoming generalized even in the dominant countries" (Hardt & Negri, 2009, p. 133). Conditions of production 'that have long been typical of labor' in most of the world become characteristics of a major trend, an index of the new, only when they appear in 'the dominant countries'. We will return to unfold the implications of this logic later. Indeed, we will see that the process of informalization in the periphery may be considered in some cases to be a condition of possibility of the informationalization of production.

The third feature Hardt and Negri cite as characteristic of the biopoliticization of production involves "new patterns of migration and processes of social and racial mixture" (Hardt & Negri, 2009, p. 134). Here, the difficulties are manifold, even though Hardt and Negri have revised their position in the face of criticism.[2] They now acknowledge the political significance of the full spectrum of labour migration rather than the privilege *Empire* (2000) had given before to the south to north flows. Nevertheless, patterns of migration and processes of social and 'racial mixture' are long-standing processes of historical capitalism. Instead of merely denying their novelty for that reason, however, what might be a more productive reading of this argument would be to insist that the newly emergent, has its own slow-motion temporality of occurrence. I will return to this issue as well.

For Hardt and Negri, these crises of rule attending service, precarity and migration constitute both objective and subjective "transcendental" historical conditions of possibility for a political project of the making of the multitude. There are two main steps to their argument here. The first involves their innovative intervention in contemporary discussions of privatization and commodification that understand them to entail new enclosures of the commons. Hardt and Negri connect these critical analyses with the key insight underlying Marx's critique of both political economy and German ideology. This critique draws its political lessons from its demystifying recognition of the social character of all production, whether of goods, services or images and ideas. Marx (1973) draws out the full implications of this insight in his concept of *general intellect* and this serves as Hardt and Negri's point of departure for their elaboration of a concept of the commons that includes but goes beyond the idea of the common bounty of nature. Their concept of the commons, rather, is

> dynamic, involving both the product of labor and the means of future production. This common is not only the earth we share but also the languages we create, the social practices we establish, the modes of sociality that define our relationships... This form of the common does not lend itself to a logic of scarcity as does the first. (Hardt & Negri, 2009, p. 139)

Such a concept of the common "blurs the division between nature and culture" (Hardt & Negri, 2009, p. 139) and, in relation to the crises of rule connected to service, precarity and migration, point the way toward the autonomy of biopoliticized production from capitalist power and class inequality. Insofar as services require the autonomous organization of networks of cooperation, insofar as precarity requires the autonomous management of time, insofar as migration depends on the autonomous negotiation of differences in urban life, the intensified dependence of biopolitical production on the common also intensifies and augments the possibility for biopolitical production to reproduce the common and produce ever new kinds of commons without the mediation of capitalist institutions.

These aspects of production together constitute a common power that various ruling class governmental instruments of command and control are said to be increasingly having a harder time subsuming and exploiting:

> All three of these contradictions point to the fact that capital's strategies and techniques of exploitation and control tend to be fetters on the productivity of biopolitical labor. Capital fails to generate a virtuous cycle of accumulation, which would lead from the existing common through biopolitical production

to a new expanded common that serves in turn as the basis of a new productive process (Hardt & Negri, 2009, p. 149).

The transnational ruling classes cannot ride these contemporary processes with mastery; their very efforts to steer and reign the common powers deepens the crises and makes them more explosive. While capital accumulation depends upon the dominance of biopolitical production, increasingly production does not need Empire. This then is the objective situation of our present, as Hardt and Negri describe it. Let us note in passing the apparent dialectical character of the inversion on which this second step of their argument here turns: it is the very intensified dependence of biopolitical production on the common that is said to amplify and intensify the common's capacity to serve as a platform of liberation. This impression is only deepened by their description of this boomerang effect as a "vertiginous loop" in the production of subjectivity unleashed by biopoliticization: "One might still conceive of economic production as an engagement of the subject with nature, a transformation of the object through labor, but increasingly the "nature" that biopolitical labor transforms is subjectivity itself" (Hardt & Negri, 2009, pp. 172-73). Indeed, it would seem that, against the drift of their own rhetoric throughout the trilogy, their concept of the common now concedes a dialectical formulation: Biopolitical production depends on the common and to this extent it is immanent to Empire. But the common is also what makes biopolitical production creatively excessive to itself so that biopolitical production is already on the road to autonomy from Empire: "Crossing the threshold gives us a first definition of the process of biopolitical exceeding, which overflows the barriers that the tradition of modern political economy built to control labor-power and the production of value" (Hardt & Negri, 2009, p. 317). In the first two books of the trilogy, the slogan had been "there is no outside" to Empire. But now the common is posited crucially as *outside-in* Empire. We will also return to this issue below. For the moment, let us only note that it is because the common is a social world of "historical and ontological overflowing", that biopolitical production entails the production of subjectivity and that "multitude" names nothing else than its own "perpetual becoming other, an uninterrupted process of collective self-transformation" (Hardt & Negri, 2009, p. 173). In this precise sense, the multitude then is a figure of political agency and a political project to be organized, rather than an identity position.

Here, several questions can be raised. The main one I will take up in the discussion below has to do with how we understand the alleged hegemonic ascendency of biopoliticized production. The contemporary world system is made up of many different modes of production articulated with industrial and post-industrial or biopolitical production. How are these modes of production articulated together and what does that tell us about the organization of exploitation and domination on local and world scales? Does it even make sense to conceive of the articulation of one mode of production with others in terms of the concept of hegemony? Does the growth of services always and everywhere promote the autonomous organization of cooperation or is cooperation obtained through assemblages of dependency? Does precarity in fact promote the autonomous management of time or is the timing of practices being organized at some more abstract level? Moreover, does the consecration of the migrant's metropolis as the privileged social space of the common lead the materialist telos toward a dead-end, especially on ecological matters? Questions such as these, however, cannot be answered in general but only in relation to the singularity of local situations. I will return to them in my discussion of the new urban forms that are being constructed for the global and Indian IT industry in Kolkata, West Bengal. But first, let us allow our second figure of agency to step onstage for a turn.

THE SUBALTERN LINE OF FIGHT

In the early work of the Subaltern Studies Collective, the Gramscian category of the subaltern is deployed by way of a critique of elitist historiography, whether colonialist or nationalist. In this first stage of the collective's research practice, the problematic of agency occupies centre stage. The strategic turn to the category of subaltern history seemed to be full of promise as it was made in response to a peasant uprising, the Naxalite movement (1967-76) and the crisis this presented for the organized mass communist movements. The emphasis on insurgent peasant culture, myth and ritual as well as insistence on a domain of politics 'autonomous' from elite leadership indeed broke new ground, as did the new focus on overlooked and marginalized events such as struggles over forest rights, hill tribe revolts, food riots, communal conflicts, and insubordination against landlord domination. The subaltern, in Ranajit Guha's redefinition, referred to a popular configuration of social locations "as a name for the general attribute of subordination in South Asian society whether this is expressed in terms of class, caste, age, gender and office or in any other way" (Guha & Spivak, 1988, p. 35). On the one hand, the problem of subaltern agency then presents itself as a methodological issue: Insofar as an oral culture and a non-literate collectivity leaves behind no documents of their own authorship in the archives, how is their insurrective participation both in the Indian nationalist movement but also beyond it in direct revolts against landlord and colonial domination to be studied? The need to invent a hermeneutic strategy capable of deciphering this absent presence leads to Guha's (1996[1963]) theoretical innovations, drawing on Barthes and Foucault, which finds a way to read various symptoms in the texts of colonial administration and rule for traces of subaltern agency.

The main point we need to note here about Guha's theoretical intervention, however, is the link it establishes between the question of mediation and the problematic agency. Insurrective agency cannot be accessed directly and immediately. Rather, its effectivity and intelligibility must be reconstructed on a distinct register of representations and codes that have their own internal history. Now the problematic of agency presents a further dilemma which the subaltern studies project in its first phase thematizes and tackles through its critique of colonialist and nationalist historiography. This is the dawning recognition, widespread among twentieth century and especially postcolonial historians, that the practice of history writing itself folds back and begins to have effects on the unfolding of history; in the project of nation-building and its characteristic pedagogic methods of domination, for example. For subaltern studies, this was the common point of 'nationalist' collusion between bourgeois and Marxist historiography and this is what gave urgency to the project of retrieving an autonomous domain of subaltern politics able to slip the leash of elite leadership. (No doubt, the fact that the Communist Party of India was able to accommodate itself to the Congress-led postcolonial state and so opt for the parliamentary road in 1950 and that the dissenting splinter Communist Party of India, Marxist repeated the same trauma in 1966 were crucial conditions for the elaboration of these historiographical-theoretical positions). In Dipesh Chakrabarty's (2000) work, this line of critique is developed theoretically into a critique of the discipline itself. What the subaltern studies project then enables us to grasp clearly is that these two facets of the problematic of agency are connected but not reducible to one another. How and why does the past matter in and to the present? Agency *in* the past and agency *of* the past pose linked but not the same narrative problem for historiography and the historical turn in the social sciences. Between them is an incommensurable or heteroclite space demanding the invention of dialectical figures that would allow us to plot a story through the interaction of the two force fields of these two narrative problems.

The subaltern studies project, however, proved to be unequal to the task of confronting the very conditions it had initially established for its historiography. As numerous commentators and critics have observed (Lal, 2003; O'Hanlon, 1988; Ortner, 1995; Sarkar, 1997; Sivaramakrishnan, 1995), the subsequent work of the collective, especially after Ranajit Guha's resignation from his editorial position there, became mired in various reified binary oppositions. Indeed, the major binary oppositions structuring the core concerns of subaltern studies subsequently – subaltern religiosity versus elite secularism, community versus class, myth versus rationalism, the West versus the indigenous – are all derivatives of the hoariest ideological and orientalist binary of them all, that of tradition and modernity. As a result, the slippage from locating a practical space of autonomy from elite political leadership to a quest for the authenticity of traditional consciousness was easily made. The potential of the category of the subaltern to lead to a more concrete determination of class relations as a social multiplicity dissipated instead into another ideal type with even less analytic usefulness. Adrift in the ambivalences and dead-ends of the dominant Anglo-American reading of Foucault, unable to locate the crucial movement in Foucault's thought underscored by Hardt and Negri's terminological distinction between biopower and biopolitics, the critical energies of the collective relaxed in this second stage of its career into an Americanized area-studies cultural nationalism, drawing withering criticism from both feminist and Dalit scholarship (Bannerji et al., 2001; Nanda, 2003).

However, a newer generation of historically oriented social scientists (Bannerjee-Dube, 2007; Da Costa, 2008; Dube, 2004a, 2004b; Ghosh, 2006; Kapoor, 2009a; Mayaram, 2004; Munda & Mullick, 2003; Shah, 2006a, 2006b, 2007) have re-appropriated the figure of subaltern in order to understand the struggles of immiserated forest dwellers, landless cultivators, migrant labourers and theorize the politics of industrialization, urbanization, biopiracy, contract farming, resource extraction to name only a few aspects of contemporary subaltern social movements. For this new third stage of the subaltern problematic, the emphasis is on the one hand on locating subaltern agency in relation to domination and exploitation institutionalized on regional, national and transnational scales. On the other hand, instead of a focus on cultural alterity and primordial or authentic religiosity, there is a return to question of political autonomy, now understood in relation to a worldwide struggle in defence of the commons. Indeed, these new thematics connect the studies of subaltern social movements of the subcontinent to research on contemporary subaltern movements elsewhere (Kapoor, 2009b; Lee, 2005; Mignolo, 2005), on the local impact of neoliberalized political economies and the global significance of the struggles for the common that very often make up their sites of study. In many respects, the theory of the multitude will stand or fall on the question of whether it can yield new perspectives on subaltern politics and subaltern anti-systemic movements. In order to probe such possibilities, I will now turn first to a critical discussion of the information technology industry in Kolkata, West Bengal.

SECTOR FIVE, OR, A SUBALTERN RIGHT TO THE METROPOLIS

While India's 8.8% annual growth rate has been making headline news in the business press world wide, India's information technology industry has shared much of this limelight. While some casual or interested observers like to claim that IT and software exports in particular have served as the main engine of growth, such claims can and have been disputed. Some scholars observe that India's growth rate was on an upward swing well before liberalization policies were introduced (let alone had a chance to take effect) (Basu, 2008; Subramanian, 2008) and that domestic demand, particularly for old-economy industrial production, has been the more significant driver (Basu, 2008). Nonetheless, the size and growth of software exports has been striking, growing 28.7% (compound annual growth rate) in the last five years and totaling 71.7 billion US dollars in 2008-9 alone, comprising now 5.8% of India's GDP (India Brand Equity Foundation [IBEF], 2009). Direct employment in the IT sector has grown by 26% (compound annual growth rate) over the last decade, employing now more than two million Indians. However, not only IT but the entire formally organized sector, public and private, employs at most ten percent of India's population while the rest are located in informal modes of production (Bhaduri & Patkar, 2009).

The IT and ITES (information technology enabled services) industries in India have their roots in a constellation of circumstances. A crucial precondition was the establishment of a network of advanced research and teaching campuses, the famed Indian Institutes of Technology (IIT), by the postcolonial state. Bangalore, the most renowned of Indian IT centers, however, was where the Indian Air Force and the Indian Space Research Organization had located its research and development labs, and was therefore a major center of computational research going back to the

1960s. All of the other major centers of IT in New Delhi (Gurgaon), Mumbai, Pune, Hyderabad and Kolkata are home to either IIT campuses or major Indian universities. Secondly, the Y2 K2 problem was largely addressed by U.S. based industries by importing large numbers of Indian engineers to grind through the algorithms on cheaper contracts. According to industry insiders we interviewed, this set in place the personal networks between Indian engineers in Silicon Valley, corporate America and corporate India that would be crucial to the emergence of IT/ITES startups with access to U.S. markets at one end and Indian labour, capital and political will at the other. Thirdly, the dot-com bust of 2000 suddenly and precipitously dropped the cost of transmitting data through trans-oceanic fiber optic cables. Lobbied by interests sensitive to the opportunities, (the National Association of Software and Services Companies – NASSCOM – was founded in 1988), the central government launched its Software and Technology Parks of India initiative (seeding tax free export processing zones) in 1991, opened a special ministry dedicated to overseeing foreign investment in information technology in 1997, and introduced a new IT/ITES policy in 2003. In intense competition with other states for capital investment, the government of West Bengal soon began reclaiming wetlands, expropriating farmland and developing infrastructure for a new Special Economic Zone, called "Sector Five", on the marshy edges of Kolkata's suburb of Salt Lake in order to locate the IT/ITES firms it was trying to attract. As investment began to flow into the generously subsidized gridwork, plans for the expansion of Sector Five into Rajarhat New Town, encompassing over 3000 hectares of prime agricultural land, were set into motion by dispossessing farmers by stealth and by force.

The main reason by far for the dramatic growth of IT and ITES industries in India is the labor cost saving realized when the work is done in India compared to the U.S. or the E.U. According to the Indian government's own estimates, this cost saving ranges from twenty-five to sixty percent of an invested dollar. So a politically crucial question to ask is where does the saving on the cost of production go? Workers in the north who are losing their jobs to relocation are told that new, better jobs are on the horizon and that it is poor India's turn to have a slice of the pie. Middle class Indians are led to believe that the wealth produced by this industry is trickling down. Our research, along with that of others, however, suggests that wealth is rather trickling up and out (Upadhya & Vasavi, 2006). The policy framework for the industry in fact ensures such a flow, as only formal sector incomes and consumption is taxed but not export sales or profits where the margins are incomparably larger. Nor does the policy framework ensure that any of the expected technology transfer to Indian MNCs will ever become a public resource. While it is the case that India has gained many higher paying jobs as a result of outsourcing, two aspects of the situation offset this gain as well. First of all, ever since India accepted an IMF loan after the oil price hike following the first Gulf War, the Indian government has scaled back social security programs under pressure from the World Bank and redirected public resources to the needs of the corporates (Chandra, 2010; Ray, 2010). In the case of West Bengal in particular, public spending on the development of infrastructure for Sector Five has entailed the reallocation of budgets from other public commitments. Secondly, liberalization has meant the arrival of global brands and consumption patterns, so some of the gains in higher wages are repatriated through nonlocal consumption. But in order to gain a deeper understanding of the structure of exploitation through which the IT/ITES industry is articulated to the world economy, we need to take a closer look at the social relationships on which it depends and which link Sector Five not only to the older urban fabric of Kolkata but beyond that metropolis to rural India as well.

Industry observers classify formal occupations in the IT/ITES sector into three broad categories. First, there are the relatively lower skilled and lower paid jobs in call centers and data entry stations. Secondly there are middle skill level jobs in technical support and back office business processing operations. Thirdly there are relatively higher skilled, higher paying jobs in IT-enabled professional (legal, financial, research) services and in IT software development, product design and engineering firms. There are significant differences in conditions of work and remuneration between these three strata of employment. While attrition is high in call center and data entry operations, employment in top tier jobs are more secure and sometimes offer opportunities to move up into management positions. Top tier employees are also more likely to receive health insurance and pension benefits. Nonetheless, as far as the production process itself is concerned, all of these kinds of service work are examples of what Hardt and Negri call biopolitical production. Not only do they involve information technology and its world spanning networks of cooperation but also the predominance of symbolic operations and affective production. While call centers and back office business process operations usually run rotating shifts "24-7", engineers, designers and other professional service providers regularly take work home with them or find themselves responding to "emergency" work demands on a regular basis. We find here the very production of subjectivity itself said to be the signature of biopoliticization, whether as an Americanized or Anglicized friendly neighbourhood character on a service or sales call, or as corporate team player sucking it up to make the deal for the chief. If there is a multitude in the making in Kolkata, these workers are certainly potential subjects of such a process of becoming, according to the definitions.

But this entire location of biopolitical production depends for its condition of possibility on several other social spaces we now need to consider. Most immediately, there is another vast body of service work without which Sector Five's internally differentiated division of biopolitical virtual labour power could not be mobilized into production at all. These are the cooks, the cleaners, drivers, bearers, security guards, domestic workers, construction workers, carriers, rickshaw and autorickshawallahs, bus drivers, and street vendors who all play their crucial part in the everyday social reproduction of the very space of immaterial service production. Not only is the availability and accessibility of IT/ITES labour power to the globalized production process dependent upon this other branch of the social division of biopolitical labour but, just as crucially, the all-important cost saving the Indian IT worker offers the world economy is a saving drawn from this vast urban sprawl of subsistence wage production and pooled in the biopolitical virtual labour power brought to market in Sector Five, from where it is transferred up and out (Patnaik 2010). The IT workers thus serve as the mediation by which this saving is converted into profit. As such, the exploitation and domination articulating the local division of labour is also re-instrumentalized through them, as we shall see.

One of the main reasons for this cheapness is the precarious situation of this broad array of services. This precarity, in turn, is mainly predicated on a cluster of conjunctural conditions: de-industrialization and informalization, political dis-articulation, and a renewed rural crisis. Let us briefly examine the implications of each of these processes.

At the time of national independence, West Bengal was one of the most highly industrialized states in India, where British managed, colonial era export oriented processing industries predominated, especially in jute and tea (Chakravarty, 2010). Postcolonial India's emphasis on import substitution industrialization resulted in neglect for Bengal's export industries, already floundering from the recession of the 1930s, the disruptions of Second World War and Partition in 1947. Through a period of protracted class conflict throughout the first half of the twentieth century, industrial manufacturing in West Bengal nonetheless emerged politically well organized through several mass trade unions; so much so that the organized labour movement provided crucial support enabling a Left Front to be elected into government in 1977 and to keep winning elections until recently. But the ascendence of the Left to state level governmental power was punished by capital flight and West Bengal lost ground to other states, ending up with a concentration of labour intensive but low productivity, low wage manufacturing units in the national division of industrial labour. Liberalization brought two political changes that have dramatically transformed West Bengal's labour market as the CPI-M, the leading party of the Left Front, then embraced neoliberalism with relish and has assiduously worked to create a favourable investment climate for national and multinational corporations. One of the main tasks in this, of course, was the government's attack on organized labour. Here we come face to face with a couple of remarkable contradictions, for the attack was relentless, and yet West Bengal had and still has one of the most pro-labour codes on the books. In so far the CPI-M's popular front alliances in particular, and Left Front hegemony more generally, depended on a militantly pro-labour and militantly pro-poor public political platform, the cultivation of a favourable investment climate was a delicate matter. Here the very arrangement that had been instrumental to consolidating labour's power proved to be its undoing. This was the subordination of the main trade union organization, Congress of Indian Trade Unions (CITU) to the CPI-M. Deepita Chakravarty's (2010) study of trade unions in West Bengal provides key insight into these changes out of which the informal sector expanded prodigiously. For it were CITU's close ties with the CPI-M that ensured collaboration so that permanent workers' positions were replaced by contract/casual positions through lockouts and attrition. CITU continued to bargain adamantly for wage increases for its core permanent constituency but collaborated with the government in refusing to organize the growing ranks of casual and contract workers. As workers continued to be locked out by firms, they eventually returned casualized or joined the main trend moving into (mostly subsistence) informal manufacturing and service sectors (Chakravarty, 2010).

This flow from formal industrial manufacturing into informal manufacturing and services is being joined by another flow from agriculture, as rural West Bengal has also slid into crisis over the last two decades. Along with labour militancy of the 1960s and 70s, another political force that initially brought the Left Front to power was an armed peasant revolt (the Naxal movement, 1967-76) that has currently reincarnated itself as the Maoist "peoples' war". Eventually brutally suppressed, the Naxals nevertheless were crucially influential in defining the initial character of Left Front hegemony. They ensured a radicalization of the CPI-M, especially with regard to its rural policies, even though the parliamentary party splintered on the question of whether and how to ally itself with the Naxalites. The Left Front won several convincing majorities because of their land reform, social justice and social equality policies. Indeed the extent of the Left Front's land reform program and panchayati raj initiatives (decentralized rural participatory democracy) have been unprecedented in India. In the late 1960s, a spontaneous subaltern uprising, supported by left United Front parties, distributed 500,000 acres of 'benami' land to landless cultivators in rural West Bengal (Dasgupta, 1984). The Left Front came to power riding this tide of revolt and among its key initiatives of agrarian reform was "operation barga" where share tenants were registered in order to break the exploitative relation between landlords and sharecroppers. Secondly, the new government re-distributed surplus land beyond a negotiated ceiling to the landless which also reduced agrarian inequality somewhat without dismantling landlord power any further (Bhattacharyya & Bhattacharyya, 2007). Moreover, the Left Front imposed a minimum wage rate for agricultural labourers. These agrarian reforms were implemented through the local self-government institution of panchyati raj. Not without their own contradictions, limitations and problems, land reform and panchayati raj did transform rural West Bengal, so that researchers and other observers could claim by the late 1980s that the Left Front government had achieved impressive agricultural growth and significant poverty alleviation in the countryside. (Chattopadhyay, 2005; Khasnabis, 2008).

However, these improvements began to rollback once liberalization policies began to take effect, as Maumita and Sudipta Bhattacharyya's (2007) study of West Bengal's "agrarian impasse" shows. As the public food distribution system, an institution designed to avert famine and endemic hunger, was dismantled under orders from the World Bank, and as food, fertilizer and credit subsidies were withdrawn and the market opened to agricultural imports, agricultural producers faced rising costs of production and declining prices for their produce simultaneously (Bhattacharyya & Bhattacharyya, 2007). The resulting shock has been especially devastating for landless agricultural labourers as rural employment began to shrink. This unfolding crisis has then resulted in a flow of migrant labour from the countryside to metropolitan Kolkata where they too seek a place in the informal service economy. This indeed was the biography of most of the women construction workers we interviewed building Sector Five's IT parks and executive condominiums. (Several of the younger drivers and security guards we interviewed, on the other hand, told us their fathers had lost their jobs in manufacturing many years ago). Joining this steady flow of migrants are not only those from the countryside of adjacent states of Assam, Bihar, Orrissa, but also from a vast and densely populated rural belt stretching as far north as Nepal and Bhutan and east into Bangladesh who are being displaced from agriculture for similar reasons. All these migrants form a reserve army of service workers in the streets and slums of Kolkata who ensure that the broad base of the division of labour remains at the most meagre of subsistence. In Kolkata, then, service, precarity and migration come together, articulating the agrarian to the metropolitan through the "contingent structuring" of these conjunctural processes.

SUBALTERN AND THE MULTITUDE: VANISHING MEDIATORS
OF THE POLITICAL

Kolkata and its environs then may be thought of a vast, predominantly informal, biopolitical service and manufacturing metropolis onto which Sector Five and its satellite townships have been implanted as one node of articulation with the world economy. The sons and daughters of relative privilege who work long, odd and variable hours in state of the art IT campuses are mostly distinguished from the security guards, drivers, clerks, construction workers, cooks and domestic servants who work among them and the small manufacturers and scavengers all around them primarily by their command of English, the quality and extent of their education, as well as their caste and class backgrounds. The IT workers hail from every strata and location of India's middle class which, contrary to the claims of North American journalism, is not a new formation but one with roots that go well back into the nineteenth century. What is new is their global brand consumption, the only thing that catches the eyes of the business press. Also new, in a way, is the *growing* inequality between the small core of the IT sector and the large mass of the labouring urban poor variously serving it. What we find, then, is a clear segmentation in the division of labour of biopolitical production in which both segments are exploited by a transnational capitalist class (in which non-resident Indians figure prominently) but are also articulated by a structure of exploitation between them.

How then are we to now mobilize the categories of class, multitude or subaltern in order to grasp the possibilities here, if any, of social transformation, liberation, or even of some rupturing event of revolutionary becoming? The well-nigh infinite gradations of the stratification of class and status inequality that we find here in Kolkata is but the local appearance of the fine gradations of inequality now characteristic of the world economy. Let us first consider how Hardt and Negri themselves raise the problem of coordinating the two figures: The postcolonial criticism of their theory of the multitude, they say, is that it excludes the subaltern, that their analysis forgets about the subalterns and about the subordinated global south, etc. They understand this criticism to claim that they have failed to be fully dialectical, of grasping the remainder through which the multitude as a concept becomes delimited and intelligible. Hardt and Negri's response to their characterization of this criticism is two-fold. On the one hand, *Multitude* and *Commonwealth* do attempt to bring histories of colonialism and processes of the development of underdevelopment more comprehensively into their analyses of contemporary politics. Indeed, in this regard, their trilogy is a welcome and important advance over many other major positions in political theory today (such as Agamben, in whose work these issues are largely and typically absent, or even Zizek, who reads it all through *Avatar* [2010]). On the other hand, they argue that the concept of the multitude somehow "transposes the exclusive and limiting logic of identity-difference into the open and expansive logic of singularity-commonality" (Hardt & Negri, 2004, p. 225); that it may be the case that there happens to be nodes outside a given network, such exclusions are not necessary and structural. On this ground, they underscore their argument that multitude names a task of political organization that the multitude must be made. Consequently, we are invited to suppose that the theory calls for some project of articulation between subaltern and multitude. Nevertheless, the problem with their theory is not only one of exclusion, but rather one of obscuring or erasing the complex structure of exploitations constituting the very multiplicity of the social on a world scale.

For example, the predominance of service, or actually of the informal sector whether in services or small scale manufacturing, may provoke the self-organization of networks of cooperation without the direct intervention of capital in some situations but this is clearly not the case in the IT industry in Kolkata. To the extent that it is so in the ancillary services such as with drivers and autorickshawallahs, these remain entirely dependent on the IT boom. For example, men and women who had been able to set up street food stalls across from the gates of the campuses preparing meals for the IT workers had organized their own management committee to collectively solve problems like refuse removal, water and produce delivery, and to settle minor disputes. Such self-organization has the potential to raise and press for other political demands. Nonetheless, the stall proprietors and their staff cannot be said to possess even the most rudimentary autonomy from the FDI flows into Sector Five.

Nor can we say that precarity universally enables workers to regain control over their management of time. As is notoriously well known, the work schedule of IT workers are set by their clients in North America or Europe whereas the marginal subsistence nature of much of the supporting services requires ceaseless engagement in production. Domestic workers we interviewed, for example, without exception complained of being at the beck and call of their employers; as did private household drivers, whereas those working for car pool companies reported that they frequently worked through the one day off they are supposed to get.

The lesson to be learned from this case study, then, is that social multiplicity must be understood not as an open series of identity positions on a number line (race, class, sex, gender, one thousand and one ethnicities, etc.) in discourse as most postmodern social theories presume (Hardt & Negri, 2009, p. 167), but rather as a multiplicity of exploitations, crises and contradictions. For social multiplicity is not a matter of the multiplicity of positions but rather of positionality. In this, the multiplicity of exploitation mediates all other political multiplicities insofar as the (international) social division of labour is the very nonsensical objectivity of all histories at their world scale. The division of labour is both a historically given result of subaltern and class struggles of the past as well as the very site of ongoing subaltern class struggles of the present. As such it is, indifferently, a cultural, political, economic, juridical and ideological artefact of such struggles, the very body of their occurrence. No mode of subjectivization can escape being decentered and relativized by it, for there is no transcendent heaven or hell outside of social reproduction. Any specific point or place in the division of labour, after all, crucially depends on other places or points on the division of labour, some very obviously and heavily, but also ultimately on most if not every other point as well. Any singular configuration of movements of production can be set into motion only through their determination by all other movements of production. After all, this is precisely what a division of labour in effect is: The very fact that somebody doing one thing enables someone else to do something else. This is precisely where the main potential for gains in productivity lies – in multiplying the power of cooperation through differentiation. The crucial point to be underscored here, though, is that part and whole of the division of labour cannot be represented or understood separately or discretely. Rather the representational challenge is precisely that of figuring the multiplicity of exploitations that relates part to whole and vice versa.[3]

If the figure of the multitude is to be distinguished, then, from the concept of the people, on the basis of an imposed unity of the latter versus the open network multiplicity of the former as Hardt and Negri insist, then, this distinction can only turn on the very objectivity of the social division of labour as historically and politically constructed and given to all possible subjective becomings. For this body of accumulated human history on a world scale, as a crucial transcendental condition of possibility of the common, can never be completely subjectified itself. The objectivity of histories at their world scale is a dimension of the common but this is why the common exceeds itself. Here, the key argument of postcolonial subalternist critique must be kept clearly in focus. For contemporary eurocentric cultural and political theory mystifies in two ways: Either capitalism is assumed to be eternal, inscribed in human nature; or the break of industrial capitalism is assumed to be a total one that completely transcends its own historical situation. But as a broad range of scholarship in historical sociology, postcolonial studies and the world history movement has demonstrated, this very break creates its own world scale context by bringing all other modes of production into an equally new machinic assemblage as its ground. Thus it is that any relationship of exploitation or domination is never identical to itself but supplemented by some other kind of accumulated violence.

Returning then to Kolkata, we can say that "multitude" and "subaltern" are two distinct ways of totalizing this complex articulation of exploitations and fine stratification of inequality into utopian figures of nonidentical agency. As elsewhere, the left in India faces a cultural, educational and ideological task, as much as an economic, political or organizational one, of constructing some kind of new politics based on new solidarities and new identifications. In such a situation, both multitude and subaltern are utopian figures, in Fredric Jameson's (2005) sense: Each figure naming a narrative form problem for the cultural and aesthetic pedagogy on which all political movements depend. As agents, neither is available without cultural-pedagogical mediation. But as mediating pedagogical characters, they are both alternate ways of telling the story of social and political change, of struggling to defend the common, of plotting a political future. Subaltern and multitude then are two irreconcilable ways of mapping how the conjunctural processes and ongoing struggles unfolding in Kolkata may be organized to lead into a transformative event, how a passive revolution might be turned into active revolution. They are both figures operating at local and global scales simultaneously. But the two figures do not add up to a complementary unity nor do they coincide with each other, nor can we choose between them. Rather, each posits a different chronotope of agency insofar as we read each figure as a vanishing mediator in relation to the other. The two figures pose a narrative form problem without a generic solution. For this very reason, it is in the allegorical mediation of each figure by the other, that we need to search for a new political pedagogy and social movement learning process for the left that is both locally grounded and yet not provincial.

Let us begin by observing that the core experiences and raw materials of the new solidarities to be made still remain unclear but they will nevertheless have something to do with the conjunctural processes we have discussed above. Any programmatic story that one could then try to learn to tell of the multitude's liberation will at some point fall apart, as we have seen above, because an unplaceable figure of the subaltern will eventually turn up as a symptom, a ghost, a geoperspectival aporia with its own local pedagogical lessons, re-articulating the metropolis to its agrarian and forest ecologies.[4] As a mediating figure for the multitude, the subaltern then is a supplementary historiographical figure which forestalls the multitude's reification into unity and its transcendence into northbound epic discourse of a noncontradictory, undifferentiated New Dawn. On the other hand, similarly, any story of the subaltern's liberation will breakdown and grind to a halt before it can slide back into some renewed nationalism, ethnocentrism, communalism, or populism, insofar as the subaltern will keep setting off on a line of flight and keep melting away into the multitude and into insurgencies breaking out across the planetary common. In this regard, the multitude, as a mediation of the subaltern, is a supplementary sociological figure, which forestalls the subaltern's reification into culture, ethnicity, and community by networking subalternity into the common.

As a result, left cultural production and social movement learning today, whether in West Bengal or elsewhere, will have to assume this oscillation between these two figures, this narrative form problem, for its pedagogical aesthetic. If only for the good reason that any figure of agency, if it is not to relax into a facile discursivist platitude about "undoing fixity", needs to face squarely not only the unimaginable weight and glacial duration of our human history; of accumulated violence; of subaltern defeat and dispossession whether from the neolithic revolution or even before; but also the historically unprecedented quantum leap in inequality and in the imbalance of power between the transnational ruling classes and the multitude that has emerged over the neoliberal decades into what Samir Amin (2003) calls global apartheid. Narratives which foreclose the future consequences of both this historical duration and these conjunctural processes, such narratives of transcendence (whether of biopolitical production floating free of all other modes of production that comprise it, or of this or that posthuman or technopoetic overcoming of production itself, or any other fleshless event without conjuncture) will be sites at which the figure of the subaltern will continue to emerge as a symptom of that foreclosure. Badiou writes somewhere that events are never miraculous. The figure of subaltern agency is there to remind us of the long revolution of the past that must take place before the future can arrive; of the geological slowness of the multitude's event as it emerges across the duration of accumulated violence and out of the contradictions of conjunctural processes. The agency of the past is not reducible to agency in the past, but we cannot escape determination by the former without understanding the latter. But this is precisely the wide open space where the prodigious force animating the figure of the multitude by sheer theoretical will becomes most necessary and advantageous to the left's learning processes and cultural-political production today: Equally utopian, the multitude names the event of the subaltern's disappearance through its own autonomous, networked, world-scale struggle for liberation.

NOTES

[1] Support from the Social Sciences and Humanities Research Council of Canada for the field research discussed in this essay is acknowledged by the author with gratitude.
[2] For further discussion of Hardt and Negri's account of migration in *Empire*, see Mookerjea (2007).
[3] For a discussion of these representational issues, see Mookerjea (2001).
[4] For a discussion of geoperspectival aporias (and the Jamesonian idea of narrative form problems) see Mookerjea (2001).

REFERENCES

Amin, S. (2003). *Obsolescent capitalism: Contemporary politics and global disorder*. London: Zed Books.

Basu, K. (2008, February 3). India's dilemmas: The political economy of policymaking in a globalised world. *Economic and Political Weekly, 45*(5), 53-62.

Bhaduri, A. & Patkar, M. (2009, January 3). Industrialisation for the people, by the people, of the people. *Economic and Political Weekly, 44*(1), 10-13.

Bannerji, H., Mojab, S., & Whitehead J. (eds.) (2001). *Of property and propriety: The role of gender and class in imperialism and nationalism*. Toronto: University of Toronto Press.

Bannerjee-Dube, I. (2007). *Religion, law and power: Tales of time in Eastern India, 1860–2000*. London: Anthem Press.

Bhattacharyya, M. & Bhattacharyya, S. (2007, December 29). Agrarian impasse in West Bengal in the liberalisation era. *Economic and Political Weekly, 42*(52) pp. 65-71.

Chakrabarty, D. (2000). *Provincializing Europe: Postcolonial thought and historical difference*. Princeton, NJ: Princeton University Press.

Chakravarty, D. (2010, February 6). Trade unions and business firms: Unorganized manufacuring in West Bengal. *Economic and Political Weekly, 45*(6), 45-52.

Chandra, N. K. (2010, February 20). Inclusive growth in neoliberal India: A facade? *Economic and Political Weekly, 45*(8), 43-56.

Chattopadhyay, A. K. (2005, December 31). Distributive impact of agricultural growth in rural West Bengal. *Economic and Political Weekly, 40*(53), 5601-5610.

Da Costa, D. (2008). Tensions of neo-liberal development: State discourse and dramatic oppositions in West Bengal. *Contributions to Indian Sociology, 41*(3), 287-320.

Dasgupta, B. (1984). Sharecropping in West Bengal: From independence to operation Barga. *Economic and Political Weekly, 19*(26), A85-A96.

Dube, S. (2004a). Terms that bind: Colony, nation, modernity. In S. Dube (ed.), *Postcolonial passages: Contemporary history-writing on India*. New Delhi: Oxford University Press.

Dube, S. (2004b). *Stitches on time: Colonial textures and postcolonial tangles*. Durham, NC: Duke University Press.

Ghosh, K. (2006). Between global flows and local dams: Indigenousness, locality and the transnational sphere in Jharkhand, India. *Cultural Anthropology, 21*, 501–34.

Guha, R. & Spivak, G. (eds.) (1988). *Selected subaltern studies*. Delhi: Oxford University Press.

Guha, R. (1996 [1963]). *A rule of property for Bengal: An essay on the idea of permanent settlement*. Durham, NC: Duke University Press.

Hardt, M. & Negri, A. (2000). *Empire*. Cambridge: Harvard University Press.

Hardt, M. & Negri, A. (2004). *Multitude*. New York: Penguin Press.

Hardt, M. & Negri, A. (2009). *Commonwealth*. Cambridge: Harvard University Press.

Indian Brand Equity Foundation (2009). *Information technology*. IBEF: New Delhi

Jameson, F. (2005). *Archaeologies of the future: The desire called Utopia and other science fictions*. London: Verso.

Kapoor, D. (2009a). Subaltern social movement learning: Adivasis (original dwellers) and the decolonization of space in India. In D. Kapoor (ed.), *Education, decolonization and development: Perspectives from Asia, Africa and the Americas*. Rotterdam: Sense Publishers.

Kapoor, D. (2009b). Participatory action research (par) and People's Participatory Action Research (PAR): Research, politicization and subaltern social movements in India. In D. Kapoor & S. Jordan (eds.), *Education, participatory action research and social change: International perspectives*. New York: Palgrave Macmillan.

Khasnabis, R. (2008, December 27). The economy of West Bengal. *Economic and Political Weekly, 42*(53), 103-115.

Lal, V. (2003). *The history of history: Politics and scholarship in modern India*. Delhi: Oxford University Press.

Lee, C. J. (2005). Subaltern studies and African studies. *History Compass, 3*(162), 1-13.

Marx, K. (1973). *Grundrisse: Foundations of the critique of political economy* [trans. Martin Nicolaus]. London: Penguin.

Mayaram, S. (2004). *Against history, against state: Counterperspectives from the margins*. New Delhi: Permanent Black.

Mignolo, W. (2005). On subalterns and other agencies. *Postcolonial Studies, 8*(4), 381-407.

Mookerjea, S. (2001). Montage in spatial ethnography: Crystalline narration and cultural studies of globalization. *Symploke, 9*(1&2), 114-131.

Mookerjea, S. (2007). Cultural studies with multitudes: Immanence and the multicultural commons. *The Review of Education, Pedagogy and Cultural Studies, 29*, 261-305.

Munda R. D. & Mullick S. B. (eds.) (2003). *The Jharkhand movement: Indigenous peoples' struggle for autonomy in Jharkhand.* Copenhagen: International Work Group for Indigenous Affairs; New Delhi: Uppal Publishing House.

Nanda, M. (2003). *Postmodernism and religious fundamentalism: A scientific rebuttal to Hindu science.* Pondicherry: Navayana.

O'Hanlon, R. (1988). Recovering the subject: subaltern studies and histories of resistance in colonial South Asia. *Modem Asian Studies, 22*(1), 189-224.

Ortner, S. (1995). Resistance and the problem of ethnographic refusal. *Comparative Studies in Society and History, 37*(1), 173-93.

Patnaik, P. (2010, March 6). The diffusion of activities. *Economic and Political Weekly, 45*(10), 40-45.

Ray, S. (2010, April 3). Economic growth and social cost: Need for institutional reforms. *Economic and Political Weekly, 45*(14), 17-20,

Sarkar, S. (1997). *Writing social history.* Oxford University Press: New Delhi.

Sivaramakrishnan, K. (1995). Situating the subaltern: History and anthropology in the subaltern studies project. *Journal of Historical Sociology,* 8(4), 395-429.

Shah, A. (2006a). The labour of love: Seasonal migration from Jharkhand to the Brick Kilns of other states in India. *Contributions to Indian Sociology, 40*, 91-118.

Shah, A. (2006b). Markets of protection: The "terrorist" Maoist movement and the state in Jharkhand, India. *Critique of Anthropology, 26*, 297-314.

Shah, A. (2007). Keeping the state away: Democracy, politics and the state in India's Jharkhand. *Journal of the Royal Anthropological Institute, 13*, 129-145.

Subramanian, A. (2008). *India's turn: Understanding the economic transformation.* New Delhi: Oxford University Press.

Upadhya, C. & Vasavi A. R. (2006). *Work, culture and sociality in the Indian IT industry: A sociological study.* School of Social Sciences, Indian Institute of Science Campus, Bangalore: National Institute of Advanced Studies.

Zizek, S. (2010, March 4). Return of the natives. *New Statesman.* http://www.newstatesman.com/print/201003040015.

NEOLIBERAL GLOBALIZATION, SAFFRON FUNDAMENTALISM[1] AND DALIT POVERTY AND EDUCATIONAL PROSPECTS IN INDIA

Dip Kapoor, Associate Professor, Department of Educational Policy Studies, University of Alberta, Canada

INTRODUCTION

The teacher would ask me to keep a distance from him so that he could not be touched. He would not accept my notebook from my hand – he would ask me to place it on the table after checking it, would throw it on the ground in front of me to pick up. He never hands me the notebook as he does with the others. He has never accepted water from my hand and I have been told not to use the common drinking glass and am always forced to sit in the last row of the class. (Bunty, 11-year-old boy)

During the mid-day meal I was standing first in the queue but the teacher, who was drunk, came and pinched my cheeks, dragged me out of the queue and started beating me saying, "The Chamar wants to become a Brahmin after studying in school, does she now?" (Mamta, 7-year-old girl) (National Campaign for Dalit Human Rights/NCDHR, 2007, pp. 20-29)

NCDHR had to persevere to try and ensure the inclusion of Dalit rights on the agenda for the World Conference against Racism held at Durban (2001) and eventually managed to do so with mixed results (Guru & Chakravarty, 2005). The Indian government's position in international and UN forums has been to assert that caste is not race and therefore caste-discrimination fails to fall within the ambit of racism and racial discrimination. Furthermore, the state points to existing Constitutional and Legislative mechanisms in India as being adequate for the protection of Dalits and often resorts to pointing out that socio-cultural change is a slow process, i.e., there is no need to apply external human rights mechanisms to what is essentially seen to be within a realm of "cultural practice" (UN CERD, 2007, p. 3). According to the UN Committee on the Elimination of Racial Discrimination (UN CERD, 2007), however,

> there is a strong comfort level in both society and the state that crimes against Dalits do not matter, and need not be punished. This attitude of impunity is rooted in social and cultural values and though the Constitution has made a very conscious change, the mindset in society has not changed .... Protecting

D. Kapoor (ed.), Critical Perspectives on Neoliberal Globalization, Development and Education in Africa and Asia, 69–86.

the rights of marginalized and vulnerable persons is probably the most overlooked and disregarded area of human rights in India. (p. 3)

For these reasons perhaps, Dalit movements and campaigns including the International Dalit Solidarity Network, the World Council of Churches Dalit Solidarity Program and the National Campaign for Dalit Human Rights (NCDHR) systematically engage international forums and transnational alliances in a boomerang pattern of activism which puts pressure on the Indian State by activating transnational networks at UN forums and international conferences such as the Global Conference against Racism and Caste-based Discrimination (New Delhi, 2001) and various World Social Forum (e.g., Mumbai World Social Forum) events.

Our own work through the Center for Research and Development Solidarity (CRDS),[2] suggests that casteism in its various garbs, Dalit poverty/inequality and the practice of untouchability are manifest and prevalent in the state of Orissa (Kapoor, 2007a; 2007b). Caste-blind rhetoric that equates the legal ban on untouchability with its disappearance (Deshpande, 2003) and the subsequent relegation of critical caste conversations to the dustbin of history or to the work of an allegedly misguided or obsessive critical minority, is at the very least, naïve if not mischievous and/or simply casteist in a vain attempt to buttress caste-priviledge while simultaneously denying its continued relevance in the perpetuation of caste-hegemony.

Contrary to indulging in a gratuitous sensationalism or engaging in a production of a narrative of suffering as spectacle for commoditization through professional appropriation (Kleinman & Kleinman, 1997) or what other's have referred to as a "trafficking in national identity for international consumption" (Spivak, 1992, p. 803), the impetus for this chapter is derived from the pressing and unfortunate reality, if not the sheer intensity, of caste-based atrocities and injustices in Orissa[3] and the decibel level of the *mute appeals* of persevering victims (e.g., 2007/08 violence perpetrated by saffron groups against Dalit Christians for the most part and Adivasi Christians in Kandhamal, Orissa). Every society and culture has its schisms and attendant oppressions which simultaneously compel critical examination and the need to act to privilege the categories of those being oppressed (Nandy, 1987). Post-structural criticisms of caste/subaltern post-mortems while instructive in terms of the cultural politics of re/presentation by "caste/other outsiders" (etic perspectives), when taken to a political extreme, produce an "analytical standpoint" akin to "a theory-imposed disarticulation of social suffering" (Baxi, 2000, pp. 37-39). Taking a page from Spivak (1992) herself, "in a crisis, no hand is clean" (pp. 781-782) and the onus, then, is on academics (scholar-activists and vice versa) for instance, to make the history and predicaments of the caste-subaltern known.

The changes and gains made during the post-independence period whether they be Constitutional, cultural, educational or political-economic are first and foremost a testimony to the perseverance of a multi-trajectory Dalit politics. Given the Vedic roots of the caste system going back to 1500BC, these changes over a relatively mere sixty three year period of independence from a British colonial experience which valorized caste and deployed it in the interest of colonial rule given the symbiotic political-economic and cultural links between cultural (Hindu/caste) nationalism, imperialism and colonialism (Deshpande, 2003; Guru, 2007; Sarkar, 2005), give continued cause for optimism for Dalits, Indians and radical democrats alike .

This chapter considers the role of deploying (making productive) theory/academic perspective, research and scholarship in a politics of caste expositions and related prospects for a politics of social change that addresses the caste-class nexus of power and inequality in India. It is suggested that such an endeavour could benefit from a macro-scoping of the emergent imbrications and impacts of neoliberal globalization (i.e., the globalization of capitalism and market fundamentalism post 1991 liberalization of the Indian economy) and saffronization (post-Mandal in the 1980s and after the 1992 demolition of the Babri Masjid and the concomitant rise of the party-political Hindu right) and their implications for Dalit poverty, educational prospects and assertion. This in turn (or simultaneously) requires a re-negotiation of theoretical/perspectival discourses that have guided caste scholarship; a re-negotiation that begins to priviledge (or makes more space for) "critical sociological deployments" than has typically been the case to date (Deshpande, 2003).

A *critical-indigenous Gramscian-Marxism* is proposed as an example of one possibility that would continue to help build momentum in this direction. It is suggested here that the conscious deployment of critical sociological perspective(s) is more likely to enable scholarship that seeks to develop a political understanding of caste and to expose caste/ism, while pointing to the realm of possibility for political-economic and socio-cultural change in the interests of a Dalit political and educational agenda. Education and schooling spaces need to be subjected to similar analyses for both, the potential to encourage and produce socio-cultural change while paradoxically (or predictably – as per Gramscian notions of hegemony – see Peter Mayo, 1999, pp. 35-57) also being implicated in the reproduction of caste privilege, untouchability and discrimination against Dalits.

After a brief excursion (as background for those unfamiliar with this territory) into caste constructions and Constitutional provisions, the chapter focuses on the question of critical sociological (theoretical) deployments and Dalit political and educational agendas; a discussion of perspectives that culminates in introducing/ moving towards what is being referred to as a *critical-indigenous Gramscian-Marxism*. The following and final section considers how such a critical sociological deployment might lend itself to an examination and exposition of the imbrications and impacts of neoliberal globalization and saffronization on Dalit poverty, educational prospects and related avenues for socio-political assertion.

CASTE CONSTRUCTIONS AND CONSTITUTIONAL PROVISIONS

Derived from the Latin word *castas*, meaning chaste or unmixed, caste references the mainly segregated social groups of a hierarchical ordering of Indian society according to four *varnas* or broad caste categories, including *Brahmins*, *Kshatriyas*, *Vaishyas* and *Shudras*. Outside these four *varnas* are the casteless (outcast or *avarnas*) 'untouchables' (*achyut*) or Dalits, a term preferred by politically active anti-caste groups. The theological basis of caste is derived from the *Purushasukta* verse from the *Rig Veda* (ancient Hindu scriptures) and the Code of Manu (ethical and legal commandments pertaining to custom, caste and caste-institutional practical prescriptions inspired by the *Vedas*) which states that the *Brahmans* came from His mouth, the *Kshatriyas* from His arms, the *Vaishyas* from His thighs and the *Shudras* from His feet implying vertical hierarchy and corresponding occupational specialization as the *Brahmans* performed religious rituals and were the keepers of sacred knowledge, the *Kshatriyas* were warriors and protectors, the *Vaishyas* farmers and traders, while the *Shudras* performed menial/labor tasks. The 'outcasts' (Dalits) were relegated to performing polluted and polluting tasks such as sewage disposal, tanning of hides and the removal of carrion and refuse. Pollution-purity divides (e.g. refusal to share well-water or cooking utensils or refusing food from the hands of an *achyut)*, caste endogamy, refusal of entry in to places of worship and the denial of freedom of movement (e.g. use of certain village streets/thoroughfares) are some of the visible manifestations of casteism, untouchability and the daily assault on the dignity of persons (see Guru, 2009 for related theoretical/discussions on untouchability and "humiliation"), allegedly sanitized by appeals to the theological justifications for such degradations.

The term Scheduled Caste (SC) was introduced by the British in the 18th century and today's Constitutional Schedules list 1,116 SC groups who together constitute 17% of the Indian population (over 167 million Dalits). Article 46 of the Constitution recognizes that the state is obligated to protect these constitutionally recognized marginalized social groups from all types of exploitation and social injustices and must actively promote with special care the education and economic interests of SCs. Article 14, meanwhile, prohibits discrimination on the grounds of religion, race, caste, sex or place of birth and Article 17 states that the practice of untouchability is abolished and its practice in any form is forbidden. Article 23 prohibits any form of forced labor and this is significant given that over half the Dalit workforce are landless agricultural laborers, while some 66% of bonded laborers are Dalits (Sainath, 1996). Additionally, India ratified the Convention on All forms of Racial Discrimination in 1968, the International Covenant on Civil and Political Rights in 1979 and the Convention of the Elimination of all Forms of Discrimination against Women (CEDAW) in 1993, a significant commitment since Dalit women bear the brunt of caste prejudices and exploitation as "the boundaries and hierarchies of caste are articulated by gender" in contemporary Indian society (Dube, 1996, p. 21). However, state amelioration related to such commitments only applies to Hindu, Buddhist and Sikh Dalits, since the Indian state is yet to recognize Christian and Muslim Dalits as Scheduled Castes (SC) entitled to such protections (Massey, 1998, p. 6). Such communal conceptions of caste based on a sacral view are misguided attempts to withdraw and limit the number of groups entitled to state support and protection, as studies have demonstrated that caste exists and affects the Christian community today, even though castes are rarely a part of the "Christian sacral order", i.e., caste alone determines who a Dalit is and not class or religion as even if a Dalit moves up in social class or changes religion, the social stigma of caste remains (Webster, 2007).

CRITICAL SOCIOLOGICAL DEPLOYMENTS AND DALIT POLITICAL AND EDUCATIONAL AGENDAS

According to French Indologist and anthropologist Louis Dumont, the "caste system is a state of mind, a state of mind which is expressed by the emergence, in various situations, of groups of various orders generally called 'castes'" (Dumont, 1972, p. 71). For Dumont, the "conscious model" is the most important level of reality determining how people are to act or will act in a given situation. The conscious structure of ideas and beliefs act as determinate infrastructure/base in pre-capitalist societies and subsequently, for him, Hindus avail of the benefits of industrialization only in areas which the caste system considers unimportant (Dumont, 1972). Beliefs (caste beliefs) then become the absolute determinants of human behavior. The very origins of the caste system are tracked to the "Hindu mind" which is guided solely by an original caste perspective of sorts and is perpetually bound by it. It follows that if a more just and egalitarian order is to be brought about through, for example, educational attainment and social mobility, the belief in the caste system will first have to be erased from the minds of Indians or relatedly, the constraining logic of the purity/pollution divide can only be exploded when "the purity of the Brahman is itself radically devalued" (Dumont, 1972, p. 92). "The road to their [caste] abolition is likely to lie in caste actions, and only the content of a caste action indicates whether it initiates for or against caste" (Dumont, 1972, p. 270). By claiming the primacy of the ideological level, Dumont's religio-culturological perspective worked towards crystallizing specific cultural traits peculiar to caste minds and "the finessing of ideological details by returning to Hindu texts like Manusmriti... as if caste practices in everyday life are unquestioningly preordained by what Brahmanical texts have had to say" (Gupta, 2000, p. 181). Ideology as primary level of reality and the notion that all social action conforms to it, was hugely influential in sociological and anthropological theorizing/studies on caste, amplifying the belief that caste conditions material reality in its own image and that caste consciousness is delinked from all traces of economics and politics. By receding in to the mind (or Brahmanical texts) to unearth caste inscriptions and in the process simultaneously dehistoricizing caste construction, such scholarship depoliticized the prospects for progressive change in caste structures by indulging in a politically impotent descriptive prognosis of caste and the relatively mute prospects thereof for "caste action" and education for social change. Furthermore, by paying attention to ideological formations alone, Dumontian-Indologists failed to account for the possibility that traditional intelligentsia often seal knowledge from forces contrary to it thereby preserving the illusion that in tradition "thought remains the same" (Mannheim, 1960, p. 6). That is, Dumont is blind to the role of hegemonic possibility in social configurations, not to mention that he dismisses the significance of political-economic interplays as secondary aspects of the caste system and subsumes them within religious values and beliefs emergent from the Brahmanic ideology of purity and pollution: "Just as religion in a way encompasses politics, so politics encompasses economics within itself. The difference is that the politic-economic domain is separated, named in a subordinate position as against religion whilst economics remains undifferentiated within politics" (Dumont, 1988, p. 165).

Predictably, the architects of *Hindutva* (Hindu nationalism) capitalize on such conceptualizations of a social order not founded on a social compact but on an organic growth where "the structure is born, not made" (Sarkar, 2005, p. 71). Asymmetries are then fated to remain so (chaos and anarchy are posited as the alternative) and neither the individual nor the caste group should have educational aspirations to move beyond the predestined and born order which is akin to an organ of interrelated and mutually sustaining parts ("Dumont's Religious-Structuralist Holism", Michael, 2007; Selvam, 2007). This conceptualization/logic precludes the possibility of a critical analysis of caste oppression, poverty, the class character of states or the contradictions within civil society and proposes little in the manner of possibilities for education and social change or indeed, even the need/possibility for change or education for Dalits, i.e., in an interesting inversion of approaches to postcolonial critique and directionality, Dumont does not see caste as an inexplicably unequal system that violates a fundamentally egalitarian human nature and suggests that "the idea of equality, even if it is thought superior, is artificial" (Dumont, 1970, pp. 54-55), a realization that the West has been systematically denying for 300 years given its failure to recognize the legitimate innateness of homo hierarchicus. Dumont goes further in response to his critics when he states that they confuse inequality with exploitation by pointing to "their failure to see that the system assures subsistence to each proportionately to his status" (Dumont, 1988, p. 32) thereby borrowing from the karmic theory of compensation prescribed under Brahmanism which fails to acknowledge that appropriations at the top of the hierarchy are at the expense of those at the bottom (exploitation), not to mention that it is a system pronounced by self-appointed spokespersons (Brahmins) who stand the most to gain from such conceptions. Dumont's conceptions would point to the futility of a pedagogy of the caste-oppressed, let alone a pedagogy of liberation for oppressors (dominant castes) and oppressed (Dalits) alike (Freire, 1970) and if nothing else, helps us "understand" dominant caste attitudes towards Dalit educational aspirations to better themselves and their lot in life or the self-evident convictions of a teacher who said, "What is the point in teaching Dalit children? Let them learn how to beat drums, that is good enough" or another who referred to Dalit's as "kadu-jana" (forest people) incapable of learning with or without being beaten (NCDHR, 2007, p. 25). Such treatment and attitudes are, in turn, partially responsible for poor attendance and higher drop out rates among Dalit children, as high as a 66.6% drop out rates for Dalit-girls at the elementary stage or 50% Dalit-girl dropout rate in rural areas (Nambissan & Sedwal, 2002).

Liberal scholarship, notably the work of M.S.A. Rao (1982) as suggested by Gopal Guru (2007), views the Dalit condition and prospects for change in terms of a sociology of regulation and incremental change founded in notions and concepts of relative deprivation, reference groups and social mobility that may have described/captured the Dalit condition at a particular historical juncture when Indian society was trying to release itself from the feudal ethos. This, however, fails to explain current situations of absolute deprivation (inadequate descriptions of social phenomena) as the total marginalization and annihilation of rural Dalits, the Hinduisation of the Dalit masses (given a resurgent Hindutva nationalism/ politics) and the growing crisis of the Indian welfare state (neoliberal globalization and privatization impacts with deleterious consequences for weaker social segments relying on state ameliorative actions) have together created the conditions for the "total alienation and exclusion and the threat of physical liquidation" of Dalits (Guru, 2007, pp. 153-54). Such liberal conceptions fail to appreciate the extent of marginalization and subsequently underplay the need for more drastic intervention through intensive (given the extent of marginalization) state provisions for livelihood and education and/or radical challenges to caste-structurations of selective deprivation/privileging in education, as when Dalit children are deprived of free school text books when there is an "orchestrated shortage" (NCDHR, 2007, p. 23). More significantly, such an approach

> denies to sociology a critically subversive character [and] denies an emancipatory consciousness to the groups under reference ... it impels Dalit groups to organize their thought and action not in their own authentic terms but in terms of those privileged sections whose hegemonic world view underlines the structures of domination. (Guru, 1988, p. 157)

Additionally, the liberal conception of relative deprivation of Dalits and associated deficit-views of those "relatively deprived" provides a blue print for a meager caste-paternalistic state-reformist welfarism that shrewdly moves to re-distribute resources through welfare mechanisms at a rate of trickle down that is just enough to mitigate the prospect of radical challenges to caste privilege, thereby all-the-while ensuring the place of such privilege. Perhaps it is a case in point when India ranks at the bottom (115th) with Bangladesh when it comes to its dismal 3.6% of GNP education allocation for countries with populations of 100 million or more (Tilak, 2002). Until the VIth plan, barely 0.52% of plan outlay was allocated as Special Central Assistance (SCA) exclusively for addressing the educational needs of Dalits, Tribes and other backward castes. Improvements to 12% by the VIIIth Plan are welcome trends (Nambissan & Sedwal, 2002, p. 76).

The functionalist sociology of M.N. Srinivas (1952), while presenting sociological insight in to Hindu religion and society by placing religious beliefs and practices in their socio-historical context, can be similarly criticized for the same excesses as liberal conceptions of caste and society. Moving from the onto-epistemic position that all society is functionally integrated to ensure social solidarity, Srinivas' work is preoccupied with explaining the spread of Hinduism all over India, primarily by Brahmans and through the concept of Sanskritization,

CHAPTER 5

whereby Hindu beliefs and ritual have been adopted by an ever increasing number
of groups, including Dalits, in a relatively harmonious manner. In an expanded
conception of Sanskritization, Srinivas (1966, p. 6) defines it as a

> process by which a low Hindu caste or tribal or other group changes its
> customs, ritual and ideology and way of life in the direction of a high,
> frequently twice-born caste. Generally such changes are followed by a claim
> to a higher position in the caste hierarchy than that traditionally conceded to
> the claimant by the local community.

As Hardiman notes, "One is made to believe that the goal towards which everyone
is expected to strive is that of Brahmanical purity" (1984, p. 214) or to put it in
Selvam's (2007, p. 186) words,

> though he admits in a later study that economic and political conditions
> should be taken in to consideration, his analysis is based mainly on cultural
> elements and does not provide an insight in to the origin, sustenance and
> hegemony of this specific cultural process that placed a group of castes above
> the rest and made their cultural practices influential.

In fact, Srinivas does not recognize the political function of the Brahmanical rituals
and ideology and though he attempts to combine history, his analysis makes this
cultural process appear as though it takes place outside the realm of ideology,
politics and economy (Hardiman, 1984). Such renditions also fail to explain the
rise in Dalitisation as a counter-force, as a new assertive identity and as part of an
increasing sense of confidence and dignity among the people of lower castes.

Alternatively, Gupta (2000, p. 178) argues for a sociological approach that seeks
to unearth the material and historical roots of the caste system in order to correct
the "widespread impression that caste is somehow a peculiar ideological
construction that the Hindu mind spontaneously conjured" and that the sociology
of caste return to investigating the "social and historical forces responsible for the
rise and transformations of different knowledge and belief systems" (p. 179). By
returning to the material and historical roots of the caste system and the specific
features of India's material history which were responsible for the genesis of the
caste system and its development, Gupta (2000) points to the centrality of Marxism
and Gramscian-Marxism that links ideology with material reality and seeks to
locate ideological articulations and political expressions in relation to concrete
social practices and struggles for dominance within the context of class struggle.
However, he is quick to point out that there are certain Marxist and/or Gramscian
conclusions that would need to be avoided. "It should not be assumed that the
ideology of caste is a creation of Brahmans alone, or that it is thrust on others,
either against their will, or that the lower castes are in the ideological thralldom of
upper castes, to justify economic exploitation" (Gupta, 2000, p. 182). While
Brahmans have played a major role in codifying the caste system, they are not the
sole motivators. Similarly, while upper castes strain to maintain economic
exploitation on caste grounds, this is not blindly accepted by lower castes as had
this been the case, there would have been little evidence of caste mobility in any

76

form. While dominant castes work to hegemonize caste constructions and most castes abide by these norms, it does not mean they intrinsically believe (thick theories of hegemony) in them since lower castes are also kept in line through the use of violence and the threat of force. The role of agency and the place for education and praxis addressing attempted caste-hegemonies is left open, despite the odds of a contest with historically-ossified caste-power, as has been made abundantly clear by Dalit campaigns and movements for access to education/schooling and employment (NCDHR, 2007) and adult education processes within these movements that nurture and magnify counter-hegemonic possibilities (Kapoor, 2009; Omvedt, 2006).

Dominant class analyses of Indian poverty have also generally tended to neglect the consequences and imbrications of caste and the economy. As Gopal Guru and Anuradha Chakravarty (2005) note, Marxist analysis has largely ignored the economic consequences of the caste system and is silent on many fronts, including for example, the links between caste and income distribution. Caste is explained away as the residue of feudal and semi-feudal modes of production (Asiatic modes), which in turn is seen to constrain our ability to understand the economic impact of caste under conditions of capitalism and the globalized market. And as noted by Gupta (2000), Marxist understandings of social relations as superstructure determined by economic base limit an appreciation of the independent impact of social structure (e.g. caste) on the control over the means of production. Furthermore, when it comes to prospects for class solidarity and struggle, the correspondence of class (stemming from occupation/occupational history) and caste can no longer be assumed as numerous studies have documented this among all castes. This problematizes the possibility for activating caste ideology for economic or class war as caste ideology separates classes over and above the fundamental classes of Marxism. If caste divisions do correspond with social class distinctions then such activation might prove useful as an instrument for caste-class social change processes. Similarly, Deshpande (2003) notes the paucity of statistical aggregations, profiles and analysis based on caste categories as Marxist and other statistical compilations point to rural-urban divides and/or religous/communal divides in poverty and education but the "Dalitization of poverty" and education (Guru and Charavarty, 2005, p. 136) and its disproportionate impacts on the educational access, experience, completion and subsequent employment prospects of Dalits is a relatively recent development in terms of a sociology of poverty, education and inequality that is informed by caste-structuration of Indian society (Govinda, 2002; NCDHR, 2007). Marxist analysis, while quick to pick up on the impacts of the privatization of schooling in urban/rural areas on different classes/social stratifications, has been less forthcoming in terms of identifying similar impacts in terms of caste (Gupta, 2000; Jogdand and Michael, 2006).

Despite the short-comings, such insights can mostly be gleaned from a *critical-indigenous Gramscian-Marxist* scholarship/research agenda that politicizes the historical, political-economic and sociological appreciation (macro-scoping) of the shifting terrain and interests of caste ideology/culture (the exercise of caste-hegemony) and its material ramifications (links to an *indigenized* caste-conscious Marxist political-economy) and related prognosis for social change. That is, *critical-indigenous Gramscian-Marxism* recognizes the fundamental caste-Hindu structuration of Indian society (hence the importance of critical excavations of *saffronization*) and its shaping influences on class dynamics (political-economy) and the related prospects for radical struggle (counter-caste-class hegemonic politics of resistance) squarely aimed at the subversion of caste-structurations of both. The relatively recent entry of the macro-dynamics of neoliberal globalization and its real/potential contribution towards the exacerbation and continued caste-class-structuration of the impoverishment of Dalits (or the Dalitization of poverty) and educational marginalization/inequality also predictably becomes a key focus and defining element of caste-concerned research agendas and macro-scopes. Such *indigenized* critical-sociological deployments are more likely to excavate, expose and suggest directions for change in educational spaces and in relation to how the education of Dalits can lead to a subversion of caste and a renewed political-economic and socio-cultural-religious engagement in the country.

CRITICAL SOCIOLOGICAL PERSPECTIVES, RESEARCH AGENDAS AND
CASTE EXPOSITIONS/DIRECTIONS FOR SOCIAL ACTION:
NEOLIBERAL GLOBALIZATION, SAFFRONIZATION AND DALIT
POVERTY AND EDUCATIONAL PROSPECTS

A *critical-indigenous Gramscian-Marxism* (see Selvam, 2007 for a possible partial-application/example in relation to Brahamanic hegemony and ideology and what I am alluding to here) that is cognizant of the centrality of caste structurations (ideological and political-economic), malleability and agency (as opposed to purely anthropological and religio-culturalogical standpoints or liberal-structural functionalist perspectives that speak *within and from* caste), will encourage scholarship that looks at Dalit-relevant questions and research pertaining to several possible and connected critical caste-expository foci (see Kapoor, 2008a), including (for instance): (a) the Dalitization of poverty (Guru and Chakravarty, 2005) and its implications for Dalit education and vice-versa and (b) the real (emergent) and potential impacts of the socio-political and economic trajectories being unleashed by neoliberal globalization (Guha, 2008; Menon and Nigam, 2007) and saffronization (Desai, 2004; Guru and Chakravarty, 2005; Sarkar, 2005) (as distinct and conjoint social vectors which compound socio-economic and educational marginalizations) with respect to the Dalitization of poverty, inequality and the structuration of dubious educational prospects for Dalits. As Ravi Kumar (2008) notes, "The neoliberal onslaught on education in India has not only commodified education but has created a host of institutions to produce knowledge congenial for the new economy ... and has also manipulated alternative discourses on education within a framework suited to its own ends" (p. 9); i.e., educational policies need to be understood in relation to theoretical/research deployments (encouraged by relations of rule) that connect such policy to the ruling caste-class interests and the enactment of the current politics of domination and hegemony.

The Dalitization of Poverty and Educational Inequality/ Marginalization

The state of poverty and inequality in India would need to be exposed and explained in terms of its caste-basis and its Dalit face. As the revolutionary poet, Narayan Survey says, for Dalits the roti/bhari (round bread) is not only round as the moon but is also just as distant, as they are forced to "consume poisoned bread, a symbol of the domination of human dignity, each time Dalits eat leftover food from the homes of upper castes as a routine course of survival, or are forced to consume wild leaves and the flesh of dead animals in times of drought" (quoted in Guru and Chakravarty, 2005, p. 139). Sixty-six percent of bonded labor in India is Dalit, while 66% of migrant agricultural laborers are Dalit women who earn 17-54 cents/day (Sainath, 1996). Forty-eight percent of Dalits in rural India live below the poverty line (Parikh and Radhakrishna, 2005). Three quarters of rural Dalits are agricultural laborers of whom 70% own less than an acre of land, while 1% have access to irrigation facilities and cultivation can not ensure enough food for even two meals a day (Guru and Chakravarty, 2005). Oommen notes (1984, pp. 46-47) that Dalits as a group continue to be subjected to "cumulative domination" and experience multiple deprivations that stem from "low ritual status, appalling poverty and powerlessness". On the job front, Deshpande (2003, p. 120) and Panini (1996) both note that "caste clustering" and the dominance of upper caste control continues to be true in engineering, medicine, banking journalism and academics. Despite public sector job reservations and affirmative action quotas, in 2001 60.45% of central government jobs held by Dalits were in the category of "sweepers" (NCDHR, 2006, p. 33).

Poverty and inequality shape Dalit prospects in education and the educational experiences themselves. Dalit women's literacy rates are at 27% compared to 38 or higher for other women and in 1994, only 46% of Dalit girls in the 5-14 years age group attended school in rural areas compared to 61% for others (Govinda, 2002). While school attendance rates have been improving, drop out rates for Dalit girls is at 66.6% at the elementary stage (49.9% for the same in rural areas), while 40.5% (rural) and 27% (urban) discontinue school (Nambisan & Sedwal, 2002, p. 83). According to the same study, irregular income, frequent migration in search of work and the death/illness of a breadwinner places Dalit children and their education under pressure as Dalit poverty remains a huge deterrent to Dalit education. Untouchability and caste-discrimination in schools are other mitigating factors as caste-based segregation (due to pollution-purity divides) affect social and physical access to schools (Govinda, 2002) as Dalit children are forced to walk around (as opposed to through) dominant caste villages, teachers refuse to teach Dalit children (just 11% of teachers are scheduled caste) and Dalits are special targets of verbal abuse and physical punishment by teachers and higher caste classmates, not to mention one study's observation that children of the Balmiki caste (scavengers) were made to sit on their own mats outside the school room/at the door (Dreze and Gazdar, 1996; Govinda, 2002; Sainath, 1996). When it comes to Dalit students in higher education, Dalits constitute a mere 8.37% of graduate students and 2.77% at the doctoral and research levels (NCDHR quoting from the University Grant's Commission Annual Report of 1999-2000, 2006, p. 26).

Neoliberal Globalization, Saffronization and Dalit Poverty/Inequality and Educational Prospects

Unlike the emphasis on national production/building under the post-independence Nehruvian scheme where producers addressed the needs of the nation, the contemporary neoliberal policy regime values production for the global market place and foreign exchange earnings, as the patriotic producer gives way to the cosmopolitan consumer. The later is emblematic of a post-patriotic identity built upon the pro-globalist imaginary driven by transnational ideas and institutions or a patriotic pride derived from the ability to partake of global consumption patterns previously enjoyed by an international elite (Deshpande, 2004). The adoption of IMF-World Bank driven liberalization schemes by successive governments since the 1991 fiscal crisis has opened the economy (including education) to foreign investment on corporate terms and has led to:
- The shrinkage of the state/public sector which is the only sector obligated to carry out affirmative action and educational upliftment of Dalits, not to mention provision of food subsidies, health and agricultural supports/services to the poor which have been severely curtailed under IFI driven adjustments leading to poverty, hunger and malnutrition (Patnaik, 2007) (e.g., neoliberal globalization is encouraging a further decline in agricultural share of GDP from 53% in 1960-61 to just 13% in 2002-03, while the workforce in agriculture has declined only marginally and market rates of return have come down, prompting cotton-farmer suicides in the thousands in Andhra Pradesh and at least four other states, as the invidual debt burden climbs – Kumar, 2008) and;
- The acceleration of development dispossession (e.g., TNC mining/dam displacements) in the rural hinterlands or market/economic violence (Kapoor, 2009, 2008b; Rajagopal, 2003) which have a disproportionate impact on marginalized castes/Dalits alike, who are then doubly challenged by virtue of development-led impoverishment and prior conditions of economic exploitation/impoverishment (as development-displaced-persons or what the state euphemistically refers to as DDPs) to seek an education for children in an increasingly privatized/fee paying school system.

Under the neoliberal regime, while higher education has been opened to private capital, the state is now encouraging pubic-private partnerships in secondary education subsequently paving the way for private providers and subsequent divestments by the state as per "the demands of private capital and the larger conglomeration of the ruling elite" (Kumar, 2008, p. 9). The franchising of parts of the education infrastructure to corporate and civil society/voluntary religious bodies (see related discussion on saffronization below) enables the Central Government to "close down it's schools, sell it's assets and to deliberately allow government schools to deteriorate, allowing replacement of same by fee-charging private schools" (Sadgopal, 2006, p. 23). Micro studies on the privatization of schooling (there are now well over 38000 private unassisted schools/PUAs in the country according to the NCERT) suggest that the clientele in these schools is biased towards males and the privileged castes (Govinda, 2002) and that Dalit families sending children to these schools are doing so at considerable cost to the family as PUAs take advantage of the "perception of quality" (Nambissan & Sedwal, 2002, p. 79). Teltumbde's (2006) analysis of higher education prospects and realities for Dalits points to a similar process of reproduction of caste privilege/discrimination as neoliberal globalization and privatization enhances dominant caste control over higher education while actively raising the barriers to entry by Dalits.

The privatization agenda encouraged through neoliberal globalization has also led to the concomitant enhancement of civil society (development NGO) involvements in education in pursuit of Education for All (EFA) and the Millennium Development Goals (MDGs), i.e. education has not only been opened up to private-for-profit investment in education markets (market-led privatizations) but liberalization has also meant an increase in funding/provision by international NGO actors and multilateral agents (voluntary/civil-society led non-profit privatizations) (Govinda, 2002; Jogdand & Michael, 2006; Kumar, 2008) as the neoliberal state is presented with two possible avenues for the abdication of what were considered a state welfarist responsibility for all citizens. While NGO-led education has opened up some opportunities (e.g., NGOs have improved access to basic education for Dalits/poorer segments – see Watkins, 2000), the proliferation of parallel systems of education, state provided and NGO or market-provided, encourages state withdrawal and the likely exacerbation of educational inequalities as the scale of provision is weakened (Watkins, 2000), not to mention that international/donor control over NGOs often ensures that such interventions are dependent on the donor-fad of the day (erratic provisions) and more significantly, can become portals for linguistic imperialism and neocolonial control over the substance (curriculum and methods) of what is taught and learned (Wickens & Sandlin, 2007).

Gramscian/Marxist perspectives also point to the reality and continued possibility that service and charitable NGOs stifle movement struggles (dissent) directly aimed at the class-caste basis of society and related state policy (e.g., caste control over state education) while NGOs are also considered likely agents (educational and material) for the penetration of "small c" capitalism (e.g., micro-credit schemes) (Kamat, 2002; Kapoor, 2009; Petras & Veltmeyer, 2001), which, when taken in the Indian context, is tantamount to assisting with the continued entrenchment of caste control, given the interpolations of caste and economic domination. More importantly, when it comes to dealings with Eurocentric agencies (INGOs and national level NGOs) and western (including the affluent transnational modern-urban classes) "benevolence and charity", this needs to be critical assessed in terms of the "politics of doing good", given Gayatri Spivak's (1992) cautionary observation that "The most frightening thing about imperialism, its long-term toxic effect, what secures it, what cements it, is the benevolent self-representation of the imperialist as savior" (p. 781).

The linkage between neoliberal globalization (marketization of education) and saffron agendas (saffronization of education via market and civil society/religious NGO privatizations) also needs thorough exploration (as has been alluded to already) when, for example, a study in the state of Orissa concludes that:

> with the increasing impetus to privatize education (the neoliberal compulsion), the RSS has been ... actively inaugurating schools [and that the] government of Orissa has neglected to provide functioning, viable and affordable schools, therefore creating an educational vacuum and market for the education offered by Sangh-affiliated schools [which] seek to offer education that teaches hate and intolerance, and self-loathing (for Dalits) and uses education as a tactic in building citizenship that will rally to formulate an authoritarian state in India. (Chatterjee & Desai, 2006, pp. 17-18)

The same report points to the development of a "parallel structure of power to that of the state government" (p. 17) and alludes to foreign funding of RSS and Sangh-affiliated schools made convenient through the globalization of capitalism and the privatization of education and the economy as Indian diaspora top the charts when it comes to non-resident Indian (NRI) remittances ($29.6 billion in 2006) (William Kole, 2007). For instance, the US-based NGO, Campaign to Stop Funding Hate (CSFH), in its report "Foreign Exchange of Hate" (www.stopfundinghate.org) alleges that 83% of funds raised and disbursed by the India Development and Relief Fund (IDRF) between 1994 and 2000, went to Saffron organizations/front organizations aimed at assisting with Hindutva-education, re-conversions and the spread of an anti-minority sentiment. Research reports (see "In Bad Faith? British Charity and Hindu Extremism", 2004) from the UK/London-based secular network, Awaaz-South Asia Watch Ltd., make similar substantiated allegations pertaining to monies raised in relation to major natural disasters such as the 1999 Orissa supercyclone and the Gujarat earthquake of 2001. Such possibilities begin to suggest avenues for research that examine and expose imbrications between neoliberal globalization and saffronization as privatization agendas create 'civil society' spaces for such reproductions and could well be enabling a politics of caste-class-subordinations and the institutionalization of discrimination and inequality.

Such caste-based political-economic analysis of education along with a research agenda that highlights the contributions, gains and possibilities in education and beyond made by Dalit movements/campaign assertions (Guru & Chakravarty, 2005; Jogdand & Michael, 2006; Ray & Katzenstein, 2005) or of Dalit-based political party assertions (e.g., the rise of the BSP and its varied implications – see Guha, 2008; Sarkar, 2002) will make significant contributions towards the further development of Dalit political and educational agendas in India.

When taken together, these related projects will continue to expose the pervasiveness and intensity of caste-discrimination in the contemporary Indian scenario, while pointing to possibilities for change through state policy, institutional mechanisms and anti/caste assertions (in party political and social movement spaces-local, national and transnational), including through the significant avenue of a liberatory education (as opposed to reproductory and caste-domesticating approaches) and schooling (Freire, 1970) for Dalit children waiting to take their place as equal citizens of India.

CONCLUSION

This chapter makes the case for a *critical-indigenous Gramscian-Marxism* inspired caste scholarship and for the general deployment of a critical sociological research agenda committed to expositions (i.e., macro-scopic perspectives pertaining to the Dalitization of poverty/educational marginalization and related imbrications with neoliberal globalization and saffronization agendas in Indian society and political-economy) of casteism/untouchability in the interests of informing a Dalit politics (assertions) and educational agenda. While such a proposition is by no means definitive in any sense when it comes to "militating against the ontological hurt endured by untouchables" (V. Geetha, cited in Guru, 2009, p. 107), it is proffered as a minor contribution to a growing chorus of possibility and to a "celebration of reviled knowledge" (p. 107). Dr. Ambedkar's indictment of Hindu society continues to pose a challenge that deserves an answer and subsequently bears repeating as a stark reminder of the difficult but necessary road ahead, quote, "I stand today absolutely convinced that for the depressed classes there can be no equality among the Hindus because on inequality rest the foundations of Hinduism. We no longer want to be a part of Hindu society" (quoted by T. Pantham in Guru, 2009, p. 186).

NOTES

[1] Refers to the rise of Hindu fundamentalism in contemporary Indian electoral politics and beyond from the early 1980s and related responsibility for the post-Mandal (affirmative action/job reservations) backlash, the demolition of the Babri Masjid (1992) and Godhra communal violence (2002) as key examples of some defining moments of this trend. See Tanika Sarkar (2005); Radhika Desai (2004) for what she refers to as the systematic 'saffronization' of state and civil society; Sumit Sarkar (2002); Menon and Nigam (2007); and Guha (2008).

[2] An Adivasi-Dalit people's organization in South Orissa that supports Adivasi-Dalit social movement struggles (Adivasi-Dalit Ekta Abhijan or ADEA) to secure and push for Constitutional Rights and Safeguards, at least theoretically available to Scheduled Tribes (Adivasis) and Scheduled Castes (Dalits – literally meaning downtrodden or broken peoples, as defined by Dalit leader and Indian Constitutional architect, Dr. B. R. Ambedkar) in the Scheduled Areas to ways of life, water, forest and land.

[3] For instance, see Chatterji and Desai (2006) for a report on communalism in Orissa.

REFERENCES

Chatterji, A. & Desai, M. (2006). *Communalism in Orissa: Report of the Indian People's Tribunal on environment and human rights.* Mumbai: New Age Printing Press.
Baxi, U. (2000). Human rights: Suffering between movements and markets. In R. Cohen & S. Rai (eds.), *Global social movements.* London: Athlone Press.
Desai, R. (2004). Forward march of Hindutva halted. *New Left Review, 30*, Nov-Dec, 49-67.

Deshpande, S. (2004). *Contemporary India: A sociological view*. New Delhi: Penguin.

Dreze, J. & Gazdar, H. (1996). Uttar Pradesh: The burden of inertia. In J. Dreze & A. Sen (eds.), *Indian development*. New Delhi: Oxford University Press.

Dube, L. (1996). Caste and women. In M.N. Srinivas (ed.), *Caste: Its twentieth century avatar*. New Delhi: Penguin.

Dumont, L. (1970). *Religion, politics and history in India*. Paris: Mouton.

Dumont, L. (1972). *Homo hierarchicus*. Delhi: Vikas Publications.

Dumont, L. (1988). *Homo hierarchicus: The caste system and its implications*. New Delhi: Oxford University press.

Freire, P. (1970). *Pedagogy of the oppressed*. New York: Seabury.

Govinda, R. (ed.) (2002). *India education report: A profile of basic education*. New Delhi: Oxford University Press.

Guha, R. (2008). *India after Gandhi: The history of the world's largest democracy*. New York: HarperCollins.

Gupta, D. (2000). *Interrogating caste: Understanding hierarchy and difference in Indian society*. New Delhi: Penguin.

Guru, G. (2007). The Dalit movement in mainstream sociology. In S. Michael (ed.), *Dalits in modern India: Vision and values*. New Delhi: Sage.

Guru, G. (ed.) (2009). *Humiliation: Claims and context*. New Delhi: Oxford University Press.

Guru, G. & Chakravarty, A. (2005). Who are the country's poor? Social movement politics and Dalit poverty. In R. Ray & M. Katzenstein (eds.), *Social movements in India: Poverty, power and politics*. Lanham, Maryland: Rowman & Littlefield.

Hardiman, D. (1984). Adivasi assertion in South Gujrat: The Devi movement of 1922-3. In R. Guha (ed.), *Subaltern studies III: Writings on South Asian history and society*. New Delhi: Oxford University Press.

Jogdand, P. & Michael, S. (2006). *Globalization and social movements: Struggle for a humane society*. New Delhi: Rawat Publications.

Kamat, S. (2002). *Development hegemony: NGOs and the state in India*. New Delhi: Oxford.

Kapoor, D. (2007a). Gendered caste discrimination, human rights education and the enforcement of the Prevention of Atrocities Act in India. *Alberta Journal of Educational Research, 53*(3), 273-286.

Kapoor, D. (2007b). Gendered-caste violations and the cultural politics of voice in rural Orissa, India. *Gender, Place and Culture, 14*(5), 609-616.

Kapoor, D. (2008a). Caste, Dalits and education in contemporary India. In A. Abdi & S. Guo (eds.), *Education and social development: Global issues and analyses*. Rotterdam: Sense Publications.

Kapoor, D. (2008b). Globalization, dispossession and subaltern social movement (SSM) learning in the South. In A. Abdi & D. Kapoor (eds.), *Global perspectives on adult education*. New York: Palgrave Macmillan.

Kapoor, D. (2009). Adivasi (original dwellers) "in the way of" state-corporate development: Development dispossession and learning in social action for land and forests in India. *McGill Journal of Education, 44*(1), 55-78. Retrieved from, mje.mcgill.ca/article/vi#8D6F6F.

Kleinman, A. & Kleinman, J. (1997). The appeal of experience; the dismay of images: Cultural appropriations of suffering in our times. In A. Kleinman, V. Das, & M. Lock (eds.), *Social Suffering*. Berkeley: University of California Press.

Kole, William J. (2009, August 19). Migrant Cash is World Economic Giant. *The Associated Press*. Retrieved http://www.washingtonpost.com/wpdvn/content/article/2007/08/18/AR2007081800636.html.

Kumar, R. (2008). Against the neoliberal assault on education in India: A counternarrative of resistance. *Journal for Critical Education Policy Studies, 6*(1), 1-18.

Mannheim, K. (1960). *Ideology and utopia: An introduction to the sociology of knowledge*. London: Routledge & Kegan Paul.

Massey, J. (1998). *Dalits: Issues and concerns*. Delhi: BR Publishing Corporation.

Mayo, P. (1999). *Gramsci, Freire and adult education*. London: Zed.

Michael, S. (ed.) (2007). *Dalits in modern India: Vision and values.* New Delhi: Sage.

Menon, N. & Nigam, A. (2007). *Power and contestation: India since 1989 (Global history of the present).* London: Zed.

Nambissan, G. & Sedwal, M. (2002). Education for all: The situation of Dalit children in India. In R. Govinda (ed.), *India education report: A profile of basic education.* New Delhi: Oxford University Press.

Nandy, A. (1987). *Traditions, tyranny and utopias: Essays in the politics of awareness.* New Delhi: Oxford University Press.

NCDHR (2007). *Realising Dalit children's right to education.* New Delhi: NCDHR.

Omvedt, G. (2006). Social movements in Western India: Visions for the future. In P. Jogdand & S. Michael (eds.), *Globalization and social movements: Struggle for a humane society.* New Delhi: Rawat Publications.

Oommen, T. (1984). Sources of deprivation and styles of protest: The case of Dalits in India. *Contributions to Indian Sociology, 18*(1), 45-61.

Patnaik, U. (2007). *The republic of hunger and other essays.* New Delhi: Three essays collective.

Petras, J. & Veltmeyer, H. (2001). NGOs in the service of imperialism. In J. Petras & H. Veltmeyer (eds.), *Globalization unmasked: Imperialism in the 21ˢᵗ century.* Halifax, NS: Fernwood.

Panini, M. (1996). The political economy of caste. In M. N. Srinivas (ed.), *Caste: Its twentieth century avatar.* New Delhi: Penguin.

Parikh, K. & Radhakrishna, R. (eds.) (2005). *India development report: 2004-05.* New Delhi: Oxford University Press.

Rajagopal, B. (2003). *International law from below: Development, social movements and Third World resistance.* Cambridge: Cambridge University Press.

Rao, M.S.A, (1982). *Social movements in India* (Vol. 1). New Delhi: Manohar Publications.

Sadgopal, A. (2006). Privatization of education: An agenda of the global market. *Combat Law, 5*(1), 22-27.

Sainath, P. (1996). *Everybody loves a good drought: Stories from India's poorest districts.* New Delhi: Penguin.

Sarkar, S. (2002). *Beyond nationalist frames: Postmodernism, Hindu fundamentalism, History.* Bloomington, Indiana: Indiana University Press.

Sarkar, T. (2005). Problems of social power and the discourses of the Hindu Right. In R. Ray & M. Katzenstein (eds.), *Social movements in India: Poverty, power and politics.* Lanham, Maryland: Rowman & Littlefield.

Selvam, S. (2007). Sociology of India and Hinduism: Towards a method. In S. Michael (ed.), *Dalits in modern India: Vision and values.* New Delhi: Sage.

Spivak, G. (1992). Acting bits/identity talk. *Critical Inquiry, 18*(4), 770-803.

Srinivas, M. N. (1952). *Religion and society among the Coorgs of South India.* Oxford: Clarendon Press.

Srinivas, M. N. (1966). *Social change in modern India.* Bombay: Allied publishers.

Teltumbde, A. (2006). Globalization and education for the Dalits: A perspective for the future. In P. Jogdand & S. Michael (eds.), *Globalization and social movements: Struggle for a humane society.* New Delhi: Rawat Publications.

Tilak, B. (2002). Financing elementary education in India. In R. Govinda (ed.), *India education report: A profile of basic education.* New Delhi: Oxford University Press.

UN CERD (2007). *Shadow report to the UN CERD 2007.* New Delhi: NCDHR.

Watkins, K. (2000). Partnerships for change: States and NGOs in education reform. In K. Watkins (ed.), *The Oxfam education report.* Oxford: Oxfam Publishing.

Webster, J. (2007). Who is a Dalit? In S. Michael (ed.), *Dalits in modern India: Vision and values.* New Delhi: Sage.

CHAPTER 5

Wickens, C. & Sandlin, J. (2007). Literacy for what? Literacy for whom? The politics of literacy education and neocolonialism in UNESCO-World Bank sponsored literacy programs. *Adult Education Quarterly, 57*(4), 275-292.

GENDERED GLOBALIZATION: A RE-EXAMINATION OF THE CHANGING ROLES OF WOMEN IN AFRICA

Sidonia Jessie Alenuma-Nimoh, Assistant Professor Gustavus Adolphus College, Saint Peter, United States

Loramy Christine Gerstbauer, Associate Professor, Political Science and Peace Studies, Gustavus Adolphus College, Saint Peter, United States

INTRODUCTION

Despite the euphoria around globalization, the sad reality is that while it may arguably benefit women, the situation of many of the world's women is deteriorating due to globalization. Globalization, a process whereby owners of capital are enabled to move their capital around the globe more quickly and easily, has resulted in the removal of state controls on trade and investment, the disappearance of tariff barriers and the spread of new information and communications technologies. The opportunities created by this process have opened avenues for development, but in most cases its benefits have not been equitably distributed, thereby impeding efforts to promote the advancement of women, particularly those living in poverty. In this chapter, we begin by discussing the gendered nature of neoliberal hegemonic globalization. This sets the stage for further inquiry into globalization as a gendered process. We address such questions as: do women benefit from globalization? Are some women empowered by globalization? Addressing these questions helps to develop an analysis of the changing role of women and how they navigate their encounters with globalization. Although we make references to women around the globe, our major emphasis is on the women of Africa.

The authors of this chapter take a clear stance that neoliberal globalization is a gendered process and by its very nature eludes uniform analyses and rather deserves to be analysed through multiple lenses. We begin the chapter with an overview of the gendered nature of globalization. Globalization affects women differently as compared to men but also impacts women of different social and economic status differently. Thus, the impact of globalization on women depends on where the woman is located as far as social difference identifiers are concerned. Moreover, women are very resilient and capable of subverting the very system that marginalizes them in very innovative and creative ways that ultimately work toward their advantage. Women are navigating their economic marginalization ushered in by neoliberal globalization in ways that can best be described as complex and paradoxical. This possibility is discussed at length in a section on

D. Kapoor (ed.), Critical Perspectives on Neoliberal Globalization, Development and Education in Africa and Asia, 87–98.

CHAPTER 6

gendered globalization as a double-edged sword. We conclude by reemphasizing the fact that both devotees and critics of globalization need to pay heed to the complexities of the ways African women participate in, become drawn into, are affected by, and negotiate their encounters with contemporary forms of global economic restructuring. It is only by acknowledging these complexities that we can offer analyses which will yield a deeper understanding of the phenomenon in question.

GLOBALIZATION AS A GENDERED PROCESS: AN OVERVIEW

The gendered nature of globalization can also be referenced as the feminization of globalization. From the global South and the North, there is data available to illustrate that economic globalization is a *gendered* process. In accordance with the philosophy of neoliberal globalization, state intervention in the economic life of the people, under all circumstances, is undesirable because it is considered unproductive. Globalization subsequently entails trade liberalization, the devaluation of national currencies against 'major' currencies (especially the US dollar), and deregulation of the public sector, or simply, privatization of public utilities. These policies have resulted in the retrenchment of workers and consequently, massive unemployment, reduction in government spending on social infrastructure, cuts in government subsidies for social services wherever they are available, and increased costs of these services. Women, especially those in Africa, bear the brunt of these changes because of their already marginalized status.

Even mainstream development agencies, such as the United States Agency for International Development (USAID) and the World Bank have acknowledged negative consequences for women (Beneria, 2003; Rakowski, 2000). Research shows that the effects on women are both in the market (such as an increase in women's labour force participation or changes in the nature of their employment) and in the household as a result of division of labour within the home (Beneria, 2003). Women's participation in the labour force, especially employment in *maquiladoras* (sweatshops), has received substantial media attention, and is the focus of some of the debates surrounding globalization. Journalist Nicholas Kristof has been one of the advocates of sweatshops as a *better* alternative than no jobs, or worse jobs, in developing nations. Others point out that jobs with few rights, or even outright abuse, that do not contribute to any meaningful ticket out of poverty, are not worthwhile (Miller, 2007). Relative to women in Asia and Latin America, women in Africa, particularly sub-Saharan Africa, have not been affected by the growth in factory jobs in the same ways. Multinational corporations are investing in sub-Saharan Africa at a much slower rate, and in addition to less direct foreign investment, sub-Saharan Africa also suffers from slower growth, lower education levels, and higher poverty than other parts of the world (Miller, 2007).

However, this is not to say that globalization of manufacturing and the increase in competition has left African women unscathed. Besides farming, many of Africa's poorest people depend on trade for their daily bread and welfare. As a result of neoliberal globalization, established and large companies such as TNCs bring in and sell their finished goods at much cheaper prices than those of native manufacturers, thus forcing many local industries to close down. In Zimbabwe, the clothing sector has taken the worst toll with the closure of the local Cone Textiles, with several layoffs. Most of these workers, being breadwinners, lost their ability to provide for their families. In Kenya, the women who were involved in manufacturing famous sisal bags were negatively affected when these bags were produced in mass quantities in Japan and sold in East Africa and surrounding countries at low prices. Additionally, a company in Lesotho was required to lay off 50% of its work force – all the women workers. Massive unemployment is a common phenomenon in Africa. In Zimbabwe, retrenchments and liquidations have led a staggering number of over 200,000 people out of employment over a period of five years since 1992 (Muyale-Manenji, 1998). Botswana, Malawi, Kenya, Uganda, Tanzania and other African countries demonstrate the same pattern. Often it is women who are the first to lose their jobs, as they are the most vulnerable workers (Darkwah, 2007; Muyale-Manenji, 1998).

The unemployment levels have had a direct impact on African culture and in the division of household duties. In many African countries, it has always been the responsibility of the man to work for his family. This has changed as men and women both leave home in search of available work. In fact, in some cases where there are massive retrenchments, you now find men at home while the woman goes to work. This has affected household responsibilities, where you find a change of roles when a man has to wash and look after the children. In cases where the man goes to work, the woman is forced to become involved in supplementary activities such as sewing, selling vegetables and knitting to complement her husband's salary. In African countries, women have suffered disproportionately from the impact of globalization (Darkwah, 2007).

Additionally, globalization has led to male partners and older boys migrating distances for work, increasing hardship on women left behind. Migrant worker programs can also be associated with other problems such as human trafficking and 'brain drain'. However, it is not just men who move in search of employment. An increasing number of women are becoming migrant workers. The United Nations Development Fund for Women (UNIFEM) states that women are over half of the migrant workers in Asia and Latin America, and labour in the worst jobs with the lowest wages and least protections (Sen, 2007).

Women in agriculture and from rural areas face an equally difficult situation. Agriculture in the developing world has been hit both by economic restructuring that focuses on export industries, and the unfair trade practices of US and European Union agricultural subsidies. This is what derailed the 2003 World Trade Organization Doha round in Mexico. There are many reasons why the poorest nations have been unable to succeed in export trade, but certainly a core issue is that they aren't operating on a level playing field, especially in agriculture. For example, cotton is a key crop in central and western Africa, yet the global price of cotton is 20% lower than it could be without US cotton subsidies (Kripke, 2007). Would the removal of these trade barriers and subsidies be a panacea for West African and developing nations? Baker and Weisbrot (2007) suggest otherwise.

A major source of livelihood for most indigenous African women is subsistence farming along with the commercialization of a relatively small proportion of the produce to buy soap, salt and other commodities that cannot be grown on the farm. Historically, development agencies, as well as African governments, have ignored women's roles in agriculture or land ownership. Africa's farmers are mostly small landholders, who depend on basic technologies, rainfall, and few inputs or services. Many of the labourers are women, yet agriculture and food policies have generally ignored the rural women (Thomas-Slayter, 2003). The commercialization of agriculture and the advance of the cash economy have eroded some traditional privileges of women who work the land. For example, privatization of the land results in women losing access to commonly held open-access resources.

In Kenya, when men are given the deeds to land, it implies that they are the heads of households, and though women are legally able to own land, only 4-5% of women in Kenya do so (Thomas-Slayter, 2003). Women often suffer from less access to agricultural resources. For example, if men control the tools of transportation and ploughing, women are dependent on men both to initiate the planting season, as well as to market their produce. Thomas-Slayter (2003) observes that in some places with "increasing specialization, out-migration, and dependence on the market, gender entitlements to resources are becoming more asymmetrical than ever" (p. 262). For example, in Zimbabwe women constitute 60% of communal farming (Muyale-Manenji, 1998). Due to liberalization, the supply of credit and agricultural inputs such as fertilizers has been minimal and the marketing of women's produce from their subsistence farming has been at the mercy of businessmen whose main interest is profit maximization. Consequently, food security in Africa and for African women has been threatened by such interventions unleashed by neoliberal globalization that accentuates these divides. The result has been rural-urban migration and an increase in the numbers of "squatters" and crime in the urban areas. This has more severe impacts on women and children than other members of society (Davis, 2006).

Another contributor to the decline in food production per capita among African nations is the HIV/AIDS pandemic. The pandemic also exacerbates problems faced by women (Thomas-Slayter, 2003). Infection rates of women are high and women bear the brunt of caring for the sick and orphans, as well as dealing with the lost labour. The neoliberal emphasis on individual solutions over communal ones is evident in international campaigns to combat HIV/AIDS. These campaigns tend to focus on individuals changing their behaviour and fail to consider women's limited control over their sexuality (Elliott, 2008). Uganda has been a success story in HIV prevention, and has followed an ABC (Abstinence, Be faithful, use a Condom) strategy. However, the effectiveness of the program has varied by gender, with far more women than men becoming infected since the implementation of ABC (Weisberg, 2007). The phenomena of migrant workers and cross-border trade encouraged by the neoliberalization of the economy (see Islam and Mitchell in this collection) have also worsened the AIDS pandemic. In Zimbabwe, Ghana and other African countries, some women have resorted to cross-border trade. The social and cultural repercussions are that children are left without parental care with a subsequent increase in the number of rape instances (in Zimbabwe, four in a day). There have also been reports of married women getting involved in extra-marital affairs once they cross the border. Spouses left behind also indulge in sexual activities with women other than their partners, complicating and worsening the AIDS pandemic (Muyale-Manenji, 1998).

As caregivers in the home, women face a disproportional burden in relation to the impacts of neoliberal reforms. Their labour in the home is unpaid and thus not 'counted' in the cost/benefit analysis of economic reforms. Under structural adjustment policies (SAPs) (see Emeagwali in this collection), states are required to reduce public spending. Privatization of public services and increased prices of services (such as healthcare, public transportation, and education) are particularly felt by women. In most African societies, it is the responsibility of the women to take care of the health not only of themselves, but also of the children in the home. A USAID report notes that policies such as removal of subsidies (say on food) results in women spending more time "organizing consumption" (Rakowski, 2000, p. 121). The report also acknowledges that increased health-care fees are compounded with declining nutrition, unhealthy babies, and fewer women receiving prenatal care.

The education sector in African countries has also felt the impact of globalization. Muyale-Manenji (1998) mentions that many girls have dropped out of school because their families could not afford to pay the school fees. Zimbabwe has not yet felt the extent to which this can go, but people from Ghana or Uganda who have lived under SAPs for many years and whose countries have been quoted by the World Bank as 'success stories' will testify that the majority of a whole generation have not been to school (many of whom are women) because of lack of funds. In Africa, there is a limit to your capacity to enjoy your rights if you have not been to school. It means that you may not get a job and therefore your economic rights (which are basic human rights) are affected. Education must empower women with knowledge of their rights and how to seek redress should such rights be violated. The policies of neoliberal globalization have resulted in a reversal of the gains in gender equality that was made possible through the education of women (Carnoy, 2000; McGinn, 1997; Stromquist & Monkman, 2000).

Many of these gender impacts of neoliberal globalization are arguably unintentional. It is perhaps more troubling to know that some economic planners deliberately use women's role as 'shock absorbers' or rely on 'fill in the gaps' solutions based on women's labour and low cost contributions (Elliott, 2008; Rakowski, 2000). Indeed, some compensatory programs to ameliorate the negative impacts of neoliberal globalization on the poor, seek to channel resources through women. On the one hand, this could be viewed as the deliberate targeting of women as 'shock absorbers'. We know that women will make sure the children eat before they do, and will sacrifice themselves for the wellbeing of their household. On the other hand, real resources are put in the hands of women that serve to alleviate poverty. Ultimately, however, these programs target women essentially as welfare recipients and dependents; they fail to address structural problems of

91

poverty or generate income. Income generating projects that are offered are ones that reinforce women's roles as 'housewives' (such as gardens, handicrafts, or sewing). Yet, some women do prefer this type of productive activity since it allows them to concentrate on what they value – the care of their children (Rakowski, 2000). Overall, globalization benefits those poised to benefit. As persons already disadvantaged in society (via lack of education and resources such as technology and credit), women are not likely to be the beneficiaries.

GENDERED GLOBALIZATION AS A DOUBLE-EDGED SWORD

Critical analysis of neoliberal globalization does not go unchallenged in the literature. First is the assertion that the economic reforms themselves are not wholly negative, and in fact, may be positive in some contexts. Second is the argument that the economic hardship (under austerity measures) has actually led to the empowerment of women. Both challenges require moving beyond the typical critique of neoliberal globalization to a more contextualized examination, and at the same time, broader perspective of what globalization might entail.

Is it possible that women benefit from their new economic roles in globalized economy? The first challenge to the gendered critique of globalization is the argument that economic reforms can actually put economic power in the hands of women, and thus may be a source of empowerment for them. Feminist scholars note that a low income is better than no income; control over productive resources is the most important source of relative power in capitalist societies and globalization has given women workers more choices, resources, and elevated status at home (Elliott, 2008; Rakowski, 2000). Rakowski (2000) gives some examples:

> In Latin America and Africa, studies have documented how even low income wage-work takes women out of households and the control of men, provides them with new experiences for capacity building, brings them into the company of other women, helps them differentiate their multiple roles (mother, friend, worker) and gender roles in general, and encourages them to think more about themselves and their aspirations as individuals (Korzeniewicz, 1997; Gadio and Rakowski, 1998). One study in Nigeria found that a fee payment for previously free services contributed to women's sense of empowerment as "consumers" with rights to demand changes in the type and quality of services they purchase. (Blumberg et al., 1995, p. 126)

Few would assert that these benefits are always present, so context becomes crucial. The evidence for negative impacts for women versus opportunities for women varies across countries and regions (Beneria, 2003; Rakowski, 2000). Rakowski (2000) notes that one would find it difficult to argue that the expansion of the market in Middle Eastern countries has resulted in improvements of women's status. Instead, women have even faced physical attack because of their role as wage labourers and their increased household duties. In Africa and Latin America, however, research supports the idea that in some countries and some groups, women's status improves with their increased workloads. Thus, a key point is that the impacts of globalization on gender are not uniform but rather must be contextualized in terms of race, ethnicity, class, education and place of residence (Beneria, 2003; Rakowski, 2000). Thus, middle class women working in the public sector are at highest risk of job loss, and rural women are hit worse than urban women, except in Mexico. Even in a small geographic area, like the Caribbean, the impacts of assembly work vary greatly. Miller (2007) gives the example of export sector workers in sub-Saharan Africa to illustrate the importance of education to competition in the global marketplace. He cites a study done in the late 1990s comparing Mauritius' successful export industries with Ghana's unsuccessful ones. A more educated and productive workforce in Mauritius allowed their workers to garner ten times as much as those in Ghana.

In Nigeria, Ghana and other parts of Africa, women are among the groups that are most affected by the direct impact of policies that negatively affect social services. This is so because women in Africa are considered the domestic gender. They are saddled with traditional roles that include domestic chores and reproductive activities. They are also the ones who occupy the lowest rank of the societal ladder; they are the least educated, and are usually employed in low-paying jobs. Just like other African women, the SAPs of the 1980s, which led to the removal of health care subsidies and the retrenchment of the workforce, have taken a toll on the Ghanaian woman. On the other hand, there are pockets of women of higher socio-economic status with decent educational backgrounds that have been able to make ends meet in the global economy, albeit with some stumbling blocks. For example, the removal of price and import controls, a simplification of tariff schedules, and the abolition of the ten percent sales tax, as well as the legalization of foreign exchange transactions, have made it much easier for Ghanaians (mostly business women) to start lucrative import businesses (Aryeetey, 1994). However, the majority of African women are uneducated and are mostly subsistence farmers. For these women, in order to benefit from the impact of capitalist neoliberal globalization, there has to be a trickledown effect, which has been too long in coming.

Using Nigeria as a case, Okechukwu (n.d.) discusses the cultural marginalization of women due to the prevalent patriarchal ideology, which has resulted in the miserable socio-economic conditions of the Nigerian woman. Okechukwu asserts that while men and women in the developing countries suffer economic disadvantages as a result of neoliberal economic policies, women, because of their culturally constructed position as domestic gender, suffer an even heavier burden. This cultural and economic marginalization of African women has been further exacerbated by structural adjustment policies. Also noteworthy is the fact that age-long cultural gender-bias and practices in Africa have led to the devaluation of womanhood by patriarchy; in 'domesticating' the woman, she has been relegated to a diminished social status. These cultural and societal factors emphasize that globalization is a gendered process and also unmask the predicament of women vis-à-vis globalization as neither being straightforward nor merely economic in nature. It is rather complex and contradictory.

The ethnographic studies reported in a book edited by Gunewardena and Kingslover, (2007) portray the ways in which some marginalized women perceive and manage what may seem hopeless at first glance. For example, Ghanaian female traders, like Sisi (profiled in an ethnographic study by Darkwah, 2007), who represent a long historical tradition of female trading in West Africa, take up transnational trading as a means of surviving the compressive effects of structural adjustment and find ways to take advantage of trade liberalization policies. Sisi, who is a fairly accomplished business woman, was able to attain relative success because of her socio-economic status, educational level and the ties she had with the outside world. Her business (in the "Ghana-London-New York Trade" made possible in part by globalization) was fairly lucrative because she had other advantages such as being able to stay in New York while shopping without paying hotel bills because her husband worked and resided in New York.

Portrayals of women like Sisi and others described in various studies (Moran, 2007; Naples & Desai, 2002) illustrate the varied impacts of neoliberal policies on their survival capacities and social positioning. A disproportionate number of African women, like women of other parts of the world, bear the brunt of globalization but they are affected differently based on the social difference identifiers (age, educational level, socio-economic status, and geographical location, race, ethnicity, etc.) that best describe them.

Overall, women's participation in the labour market has greatly increased under neoliberal restructuring, surpassing growth rates for men. Rakowski (2000) and Beneria (2003) note that there are varied explanations for this growth. In some places women are taking over jobs men held, while in other places there is no effect on men's employment. Women may be in more demand in some places, particularly in the export industries, but in other cases it seems that women's increased participation is supply driven (women who were not employed previously entering the labour market). Sometimes women's average wage rates have declined and sometimes they have increased. In all cases, contextualizing the effects of globalization is essential.

A second challenge to the gendered critique of neoliberal globalization is that there is growing evidence for the idea that market pressures and the social impacts of economic reforms lead women to challenge patriarchy. Even if women are negatively affected by economic reforms, the hardships they endure ultimately lead women to organize and become empowered. The very reforms that increase women's poverty and workloads have also opened opportunities. As men are less able to support households, women become increasingly important to the household and community survival. As a consequence, women's status, influence, and autonomy increase, along with their relative control over resources. The disruptions brought by neoliberal globalization can actually open up opportunities for gender equality on some fronts.

Thus, while contemporary forms of economic globalization have resulted in the subjugation of women and heightened vulnerabilities that range from threats to their survival and well being to the creation and deepening of social distance and exclusionary practices, both locally and globally, there are instances where women are actually empowered. Indeed, some studies (Ahearn, 2001; Collier, 1974; Naples & Desai, 2002; Rowbotham & Linkogle, 2001) have shown that women are finding ways of critiquing (and finding alternatives to) capitalist rationales for organizing social and economic relations and employing alternative logics successfully in resistance movements.

The very nature of women's resilience lends itself to the way they interact with and manoeuvre the impact of globalization, rendering the latter a gendered process. There are writings grounded in the formative work of feminist anthropologists on the significance of women's agency (Ahearn, 2001; Collier, 1974) in engaging in resistance practices that challenge and subvert their marginalization and subordination (Naples & Desai, 2002; Rowbotham & Linkogle, 2001). Authors such as the ones referenced here have employed the concept of navigation to capture the nuanced ways in which women of diverse social locations and identities (ethnic, racial, indigenous, caste, class, religious, political affiliations and the intersections of these) exercise their personal and collective agency in resisting and challenging the disempowering aspects of globalization that they encounter and experience. Although the concept of agency is a critical one in gender and women's studies theorizing, feminists (Abu-Lughod, 1998; Fernandes, 1997; Sunder-Rajan, 1993) have underscored how agency is far more complicated than a mere assertion of self-empowering will. Beneria (2003) points out that assumption of boundless agency may be traced to rational choice theory. These feminists, through a critical lens, have shown that not everyone is as free to choose among options as the 'rational economic man'.

Butler (1999) refers to the concept of navigation as the understanding that agency may not be conceived of as simplistic and all-transforming autonomous actions. She and others explore and document the complex, contradictory, and controversial aspects of agency as the subjects of their study often challenge the gendered power system that subordinates them, sometimes accommodating to such power structures and sometimes displaying ambivalence toward them. A case in point is Sisi, the 'business woman' of Ghana in West Africa, mentioned earlier in this chapter.

One primary vehicle through which women are empowered is in community self-help groups organized by women at the grassroots. Such groups can provide personal security for women (especially if they are working in areas outside the traditional space of the home), access to credit through rotating credit schemes, and an opportunity to pool labour or leverage and share risks. Thus, these groups are of practical service for women, but also a source of enjoyment and networking (Rakowski, 2000). For example, in diverse locations of Tanzania, Ghana, and Zimbabwe, women working in the informal economy form networks to share their resources, start credit associations, and generally form solidarities for survival (Desai, 2007).

Ultimately, the idea that reforms can inadvertently empower women should not overshadow the reality that patriarchy is pervasive and that deep barriers exist to women's awareness of themselves as individuals with separate needs from their family and community. Indeed, Elliott (2008) notes that women's participation in local grassroots initiatives may allow them voice but not necessarily power, because the efforts are too localized and fail to address structural obstacles (including national and global ones) that limit women's empowerment. Also, in some cases, the women's groups were encouraged by governments to mobilize, with the knowledge that donor groups such as the World Bank were increasingly channelling aid through grassroots organizations. From 1980-1984 in Kenya, the number of women's groups grew more than five times and membership in the groups increased eight times as part of this governmental push (Lairap-Fonderson, 2002). The impetus for the formation of these groups, however, does not necessarily condemn them to irrelevance or subservience in political terms.

This organization of women happens spontaneously at the grassroots, but it also emerges at transnational levels. Some of the transnational organizations of women have been initiated as a direct response to structural adjustment and neoliberal reforms, and are in themselves, expressions of globalization. Transnational solidarity networks for women, however, are not without their own problems, sometimes even reinforcing the very inequalities they seek to address. For example, the leadership and participation at the international level tends to revolve around women from the North and educated women from the South, discounting the voices of women from the grassroots. Funding also tends to be directed from North to South. One might also critique the NGO-ization of women's movements, which sometimes results in the mainstreaming of their message and their increasing role as contractors or players for government agendas (Desai, 2007). Even the language of empowerment has been appropriated by governments, financial institutions, and the donor community in a bid to de-politicize and undermine its' implications for these very institutions (Lairap-Fonderson, 2002). Nevertheless, Desai (2007) notes that these transnational feminist solidarities are ultimately "forged not on preconceived identities and experiences but in the context of struggle" (pp. 416-417). These feminist solidarities seek to be a counter to the hegemony of global capital, and even while not perfect, they are often aware of their own weaknesses and able to be self-reflective about them. There is potential in them to change the global political economy.

CONCLUSION

Gendered globalization or the feminization of globalization is therefore a complex process. The impact of globalization is not so straightforward as to warrant a uniform set of analyses and perspectives. This chapter illustrates the reconstructions, redefinitions, alternative representations, and reconstitutions of women's roles ushered in by the dramatic restructuring of economic and social orders. We have tried to unmask not only the gendered nature but also the lack of uniformity in the unfolding of globalization processes. The widening disparities that have resulted from globalization have affected women's lives in variant ways and have led to their divergent responses to the disempowering consequences of globalization. Women's encounters with these processes, ultimately, affirm the hegemonic nature of transnational economic structures, policies, and practices that embody neoliberal economic philosophies.

In conclusion, much like previous authors (particularly, those in the volume edited by Gunewardena and Kingslover, 2007), we have grappled with the fact that even as these new economic and social orders undermine traditional patriarchies, they often introduce novel hierarchies. This chapter has identified the gendered impact of contemporary capitalist globalization and has explored how globalization processes intersect with various, often pre-existing, forms of social inequality. There is evidence that such inequalities are inevitably aggravated by globalization and that they reproduce prior patterns of marginalization along gendered dimensions. Those who are most affected by these policies are often individuals given the least chance to say anything about the implementation of these policies and about how and where these policies will unfold in both the global North and South. Hence women in Africa, particularly those already occupying marginal social locations, due to various factors (such as having no formal credentials in education), are inevitably entangled in the related processes of disempowerment. However, in the end, our main focus has been to clarify and unveil the ways in which women in Africa participate in, become drawn into, are affected by, and negotiate their encounters with globalization. We have attempted to answer the question of how globalization impacts the changing roles of women in Africa and in answering it, emphasized the double-edged nature of gendered globalization.

REFERENCES

Abu-Lughod, L. (1998). *Remaking Women: Feminism and modernity in the Middle East.* Princeton, NJ: Princeton University Press.

Ahearn, L. M. (2001) Language and agency. *Annual Review of Anthropology, 30,* 109-137.

Aryeetey, E. (1994). Private investment under uncertainty in Ghana. *World Development, 22*(8), 1211-1221.

Baker, D. & Weisbrot, M. (2007). False promises on trade. In B. Rakocy, A. Reuss, & C. Sturr (eds.), *Real world globalization: A reader business, economics and politics* (9th ed). Boston, MA: *Dollars and Sense.*

Beneria, L. (2003). *Gender, development, and globalization: Economics as if all people mattered.* New York: Routledge.

Butler, J. (1999). *Gender trouble: feminism and the subversion of identity* (2nd ed). New York: Routledge.

Carnoy, M. (2000). Globalization and educational reform. In N. P. Stromquist & K. Monkman (eds.), *Globalization and education: Integration and contestation across cultures.* Oxford: Rowman and Littlefield Publishers, Inc.

Collier, J. (1974). Women in politics. In M. Z. Rodaldo & L. Lamphere (eds.), *Women, culture and society.* Stanford, CA: Stanford University Press.

Darkwah, A. K. (2007). Making hay while the sun shines: Ghanaian female traders and their insertion into the global economy. In N. Gunewardena & A. Kingslover (eds.), *The gender of globalization: Women navigating economic and cultural marginalities* (1st ed.). Santa Fe: School for Advanced Research Press.

Davis, M. (2006). *Planet of slums.* London: Verso.

Desai. M. (2007). Transnational solidarity: women's agency, structural adjustment, and globalization. In J. Timmons Roberts & A. Bellone Hite (eds.), *The globalization and development reader: Perspectives on development and global change*. Malden, MA: Blackwell Publishing.

Elliott, C. M. (2007). Introduction: markets, communities, and empowerment. In C. M. Elliott (ed.), *Global empowerment of women*. New York, NY: Routledge.

Fernandes, L. (1997). *The politics of gender, class and culture in the Calcutta jute mills*. Philadelphia: University of Pennsylvania Press.

Gunewardena, N. & Kingslover, A. (eds.) (2007). *The gender of globalization: Women navigating economic and cultural marginalities* (1st ed.). Santa Fe: School for Advanced Research Press.

Kripke, G. (2007). Make trade fair. In B. Rakocy, A. Reuss, & C. Sturr (eds.), *Real world globalization: A reader business, economics and politics* (9th ed.). Boston, MA: *Dollars and Sense*.

Lairap-Fonderson, J. (2002). The disciplinary power of micro credit: Examples from Kenya and Cameroon. In J. L. Parpart, S. M. Rai, & K. Staudt (eds.), *Rethinking empowerment: Gender and development in a global/local world*. London: Routledge.

McGinn, N. (1997). The impact of globalization on national education systems. *Prospects, 28*(1), 41-54.

Miller, J. (2007). Nike to the rescue? B. Rakocy, A. Reuss, & C. Sturr (eds.), *Real world globalization: A reader business, economics and politics* (9th ed.). Boston, MA: *Dollars and Sense*.

Moran, M. H. (2007). Clothing difference: Commodities and consumption in Southeastern Liberia. In N. Gunewardena & A. Kingslover, A. (eds.), *The gender of globalization: Women navigating economic and cultural marginalities* (1st ed.). Santa Fe: School for Advanced Research Press.

Muyale-Manenji, F. (1998). The effects of globalization on culture in Africa in the eyes of an African woman. Retrieved from http://www.oikoumene.org/en/resources/documents/wcc-programmes/public-witness-addressing-power-affirming-peace/poverty-wealth-and-ecology/neoliberal-paradigm/the-effects-of-globalization-on-culture-in-africa-in-the-eyes-of-an-african-woman.html.

Naples, N. A. & Desai, M. (eds.) (2002). *Women's activism and globalization: Linking local struggles and transnational politics*. New York: Routledge.

Okechukwu, U. C. (n.d.). *Globalization and the question of gender-justice: The Nigerian experience*. Retrieved from, www.codesria.org/IMG/pdf/UROH.pdf..

Rakowski, C. A. (2000). Obstacles and opportunities to women's empowerment under neoliberal reform. In R. L. Harris & M. J. Seid (eds.), *Critical perspectives on globalization and neoliberalism in the developing countries*. Leiden, Netherlands: Brill.

Rowbotham, S. & Linkogle, S. (eds.) (2001). *Women resist globalization: Mobilizing for livelihood and rights*. New York: Zed Books.

Sen, B. (2007). Legalizing human trafficking. In B. Rakocy, A. Reuss, & C. Sturr (eds.), *Real world globalization: A reader business, economics and politics* (9th ed.). Boston, MA: *Dollars and Sense*.

Stromquist, N. P. & Monkman, K. (eds.) (2000). *Globalization and education: Integration and contestation across cultures*. Oxford: Rowman and Littlefield Publishers.

Sunder-Rajan, R. (1993). *Real and imagined women: Gender, and postcolonialism in India*. London: Routledge.

Thomas-Slayter, B. P. (2003). *Southern exposure*. Bloomfield, CT: Kumarian Press.

Weisberg, J. (2007). ABCs of AIDS prevention. In B. Rakocy, A. Reuss, & C. Sturr (eds.), *Real world globalization: A reader business, economics and politics* (9th ed.). Boston, MA: *Dollars and Sense*.

B. CASE STUDIES

Formal Contexts of Education

UNDERSTANDING THE CRISIS IN HIGHER EDUCATION IN ZIMBABWE: CRITICAL EXPLORATIONS

Munyaradzi Hwami, University of Alberta, Graduate Student and Great Zimbabwe University, Instructor

INTRODUCTION

The problems facing the formerly colonized countries today generically referred to as the "South", have come to be associated with Western or developed nations' agendas and projects. Colonialism, development, and currently neoliberal globalization, it can be argued, have been Western/Northern hegemonic manoeuvres to extract the much required natural resources to satisfy hyper-consumerist aspirations and ways of living (Black, 2007; Willis, 2005). Harvey (2003) describes neoliberal globalization as the new imperialism where accumulation by dispossession is the main characteristic, and Tikly (2004) also refers to neoliberal globalization as imperialism, a form of Western global hegemony. Similarly, other scholars such as Moyo and Yeros (2007), Bond (2001) and Mamdani (2008) explain Zimbabwe's current problems, specifically in higher education, on the West and its project of domination of the countries of the South. This is manifested in the radical economic policies forced upon the South, on countries like Zimbabwe, by the World Bank/International Monetary Fund (IMF) inspired structural adjustment policies (SAPs) and more recently, the Poverty Reductions Strategy Papers (PRSPs).

On the other hand, we have critical colonial commentators and scholars such as Masunungure and Bratton (2008), Raftopoulos (2006), and Scarnecchia (2006) who view the problems in Zimbabwe as manufactured and perpetuated by the Zimbabwean government and its self aggrandizement policies. The West by virtue of its colonial past is used as a scapegoat. According this school of thought, governance is at the centre of Zimbabwe's crisis (e.g., in higher education) (Makumbe, 2002; Sithole, 2001). ZANU PF by virtue of having led the bloody and brutal liberation war in the 1970s, regards itself as having the right to rule, by right of conquest (Masunungure & Bratton, 2008), the same claim that was used by the British to exclude the majority black Africans from government during the close to a century long period of colonial rule. On the basis of this reasoning, ZANU PF does not foresee a day it will be out of power and accordingly envision an eternal grip over power. The disputed land issue and elections, the selective use of the law, political violence, corruption and the consequent meltdown of the economy should

D. Kapoor (ed.), Critical Perspectives on Neoliberal Globalization, Development and Education in Africa and Asia, 103–120.

be understood in relation to ZANU PF's attempts to be the *de facto* ruling power in Zimbabwe regardless of the results of elections every five years.

These two perspectives provide different explanations of the crises Zimbabweans and higher education are currently experiencing. Opponents of Robert Mugabe and his government blame Mugabe while on the other hand Mugabe's sympathisers blame Western imperialism and the neo-liberal agenda. Meanwhile, both nationalism and neoliberalism are foreign ideas with no local indigenous cultural origins and meaning to the ordinary Zimbabwean. It is against this background that this chapter explores the possibility that the twin trajectories of ZANU PF nationalism and neoliberal globalization may be partially responsible for the current crisis in higher education in Zimbabwe, and that the way out of this predicament calls for the people of Zimbabwe, and more importantly the university community, to construct their own ideas outside nationalist and neoliberal thinking. Before blaming outsiders who are responsible to a significant extent, Zimbabweans should define the status of their postcolonial nation and come to a consensus over issues of governance notwithstanding policy differences. Students and faculty are currently divided into pro- and anti-radical nationalist camps and this has eroded any opportunity for finding solutions bedevilling the nation in general and the university in particular.

This chapter represents an attempt at developing a critical examination of the crisis in higher education, specifically in Zimbabwe's universities. Unfortunately, most of the influential works currently available can simply be described as pro-Mugabe or anti-Mugabe. I argue that the crisis in higher education can be explained by both these contradictory and inter-dependent developments; Zimbabwe is a victim of a double tragedy of radical capitalism and radical nationalism.

The chapter addresses the crises in Zimbabwe's higher education, with specific reference to public universities, drawing upon a variety of written source, including press briefings, newspaper and secondary sources on political developments and higher education in Zimbabwe. These sources are read and interpreted from personal experiences in the Zimbabwe higher education (university) system, both, as its product and as an instructor. After considering the neoliberalization of higher education, the chapter considers the crises-making impacts of ZANU PF radical nationalism. Issues of educational quality and student victimization are then raised and examined as key illustrations of a system in crises being propelled by these twin trajectories affecting the country. This is followed by a reflective conclusion calling for honest analysis of external and internal colonial explanations for the crises and the need for new approaches to address this situation; approaches that need to consider (*critically* consider, as opposed to blind traditionalist-observance) local/indigenous approaches (traditional wisdoms) to ways out of crises—a directional proposition that will no doubt require continued engagement, elaboration and political commitment on the part of concerned students, faculty and administration, if not all Zimbabweans.

NEOLIBERAL GLOBALIZATION, PRIVATIZATION AND CRISIS IN HIGHER EDUCATION

Globalization is a contested phenomenon, one that does not lend itself easily to any single definition or characterisation. It is usually discussed in economic, political, social, cultural, educational and technological terms (Vaira, 2004), with and emphasis on interconnectedness and supraterritoriality (deterritorialisation) (Scholte, 2005); a process characterised by interdependence, flows and exchanges, the related role of new technologies, the integration of markets, and the shrinking (compression) of time and space (Appadurai, 1996). Thus, globalization is a dynamic hybridization of various interlinked processes allegedly operating on a planetary scale. However, Smith (2006) recognizes that the phenomenon of globalization can be seen as a Euro-American articulation and vision of an empire, which dates back to the Middle Ages. Most people weaker economies/nations, because of the immiseration they endure at the expense of the extravagant consumption culture found in the affluent and Euro-American world, do not hesitate to see globalization as yet another episode in Western hegemonic development and colonial control. For instance, Grosfoguel (2005) perceives globalization as capitalist and Euro-centred colonization. Along the same lines, McMichael (2005) argues that it is a "Western imperial project, a realignment of market rule, where the iron fist of imperialism and its geopolitical imperatives is ungloved" (p. 119-120). The relentless extraction of raw materials from the South, and the consequent destruction of both human and natural resources in these weaker economies, prompted Petras and Veltmeyer (2001) to argue that "it is a strange concept of globalization that describes pillage and profit in the same breath as interdependence and stateless corporations" (p. 66). Thus there is an element of unanimity among critical scholars that globalization is imperialism. It is yet another stage of Western pillaging of weaker societies' resources.

> Today's neo-colonialism/imperialism (globalization), as an advanced strain of colonialism, does not require direct political rule and occupation, as control is exercised through growing economic and financial dependencies which ensure captive labour markets in developing countries producing goods primarily for export to developed countries and secures continued exploitation of resources and environments in developing countries largely for developed country consumption. (Kapoor, 2009a, p. 3)

Thus as Zimbabwe adopts SAPs dictated by the World Bank and the IMF, devaluing its currency to attract foreign (mostly Western) investment, encouraging production for export while Zimbabweans fail to access home made products, like sugar; as it enters into agreement with Transnational Companies in the various sectors of the economy, we are witnessing neo-colonialism. The ideology of this new form of colonialism is described in terms of the espousal of a free-market ideology and is widely recognized as neoliberalism. The principles of the free market have since been adopted in higher education institutions, at the instigation of the World Bank/IMF and the government. Neoliberal ideas in Zimbabwe's universities, like in other countries, have mainly been introduced in the form of marketization. Proponents of higher education marketization (neoliberalism) have consistently argued that large scale public funding of higher education is no longer tenable and is regressive; that generous public funding of higher education undermines equitable access, efficiency and even quality (Barr, 2004; Johnstone, 2001; World Bank, 1994).

University education in Zimbabwe has become a casualty of neoliberal policies imposed on highly indebted countries of the South. Soon after attaining independence, most African governments, including the Zimbabwean government, seeking national development, borrowed money from the International Monetary Fund (IMF) and the World Bank. The Bretton Woods Institutions turned these national debts into an opportunity to impose SAPs. Indebted governments, like the government of Zimbabwe, were required "to reduce spending, to privatise industry and services, to cheapen labour, to open up markets to multinational companies, to relax controls on capital movements, to devalue their currencies etc" (Levidow, 2002, p. 8). With reference to higher education, the government was called upon to "relieve the burden on public sources of financing higher education by increasing the participation of beneficiaries and their families" (World Bank, 1988, p. 77). The above position was reinforced in 1994 when the World Bank pointed out that "the extent of government involvement in higher education (in Africa) far exceeded what is economically efficient" (World Bank, 1994, p. 9). Universities in Zimbabwe were called upon to generate revenue for their operations. Government funding started dwindling as prescribed by the World Bank (Altbach, 2004; Wangenge-Ouma, 2008). Marketization strategies have been adopted and include, among many others, formation of university owned for-profit companies, co-ventures with proprietary non-university institutions, farming, petty trade on campus and admission of full fee-paying students (Nafukho, 2004). Fee-paying students are enrolled in courses invariably referred to as parallel programs. These are normal degree courses offered in the evenings, weekends and holidays when formal university business has closed. Students in parallel programs pay full fees with no government subsidy. The introduction of parallel programs has been witnessed at the University of Zimbabwe, Midlands State University, Great Zimbabwe University and National University of Science and Technology. Parallel programs fit in with neoliberalism's treatment of higher education as a private commodity; a traded commodity to be purchased by a consumer, a product to be retailed by academic institutions (Altbach, 2004; Levidow, 2005). The reality is that only those from rich socio-economic backgrounds attend parallel programs.

ZANU PF RADICAL NATIONALISM AND THE CREATION OF CRISIS IN ZIMBABWE

The ZANU PF government has always publicly portrayed itself as patriotic, nationalist and pan-Africanist, and has always turned to nationalist rhetoric to arouse the people's feelings and obtain political support, both nationally and outside Zimbabwe's borders. According to Gellner (2006), "nationalism as a sentiment is a feeling of anger aroused by the violation of the political principle which holds that the political and the national unit should be congruent or a feeling of satisfaction aroused by its fulfilment" (p. 1). Guibernau (1996) defines nationalism as "the sentiment of belonging to a community whose members identify with a set of symbols, beliefs and ways of life, and have the will to decide upon their common political destiny" (p. 47). In the case of Zimbabwe, geographical location, language, and colonial experience that ended after a brutal war, are some of the common uniting factors that define a people as Zimbabweans, and thus arouse the sentiment of nationalism.

Nationalism, at its extreme is sometimes equated to racism or ethnocentrism, which define nationhood from social egocentrism, implying that loyalty towards the macro culture is more important than the wishes of its individual members (Hall, 1992). In Zimbabwe, since 2000, the demand for civil and political rights has been viewed and dismissed by the ruling party and government as minority and foreign concerns aimed at unsettling majority political will and reversing the gains of national independence and sovereignty (Raftopoulos, 2003). Zimbabwean nationalism cannot be divorced from Mugabe's policies, with Mugabe having been at the helm since 1980 when the country gained independence from Britain. This nationalist doctrine is termed Mugabeism by Ndlovu-Gatsheni (2009) and is described as follows:

> at one level it represents pan-African memory and patriotism and at another level it manifests itself as a form of radical left-nationalism dedicated to resolving intractable national and agrarian questions. Yet, to others, it is nothing but a symbol of crisis, chaos and tyranny emanating from the exhaustion of nationalism. (p. 154)

But others are very clear with their prognosis of Zimbabwean nationalism as practised by ZANU PF. It is seen as a policy that includes deliberate defaulting on foreign debt; pursuit of an anti-imperialist foreign policy; increased state intervention and regulation of business and a fast-track land reform program (Moyo & Yeros, 2007). Mugabe's nationalism is also viewed as championing justice for the majority who were denied justice during the colonial period (Mamdani, 2008). But the question remains: why are the peasants and ordinary Zimbabweans opposed to Mugabe's rule, in other words, ZANU PF nationalism, if it has indeed brought previously denied justice and land? The portrayal of Mugabe nationalism or Mugabeism, as dictatorial and without the support of the ordinary peasants in Zimbabwe, is well documented by Ranger (2008). The 2008 national elections, for both the parliament and President, showed a rejection of ZANU PF by the people of Zimbabwe, and more importantly the rural peasants. Others expose the authoritarianism and violence hidden behind the pan-African and anti-imperialist rhetoric of Mugabe's nationalism (Phimister & Raftopoulos, 2004; Raftopoulos, 2006).

It can be derived from Benedict Anderson's theory (1991) of nationalism, as well as from any genealogical analyses of world nationalisms, that ZANU PF's brand of nationalism, and any other form of African nationalism, was created/imagined in to being by European colonialism. Colonialism did not introduce nor promote democracy, human rights and freedom, "rather it was a terrain of conquest, violence, police rule, militarism and authoritarianism" (Ndlovu-Gatsheni, 2009, p. 1144). Colonialism therefore is seen reproducing itself, but in another form, within nationalist political movements, such as ZANU PF. The brutality of the Zimbabwean police force, even towards unarmed citizens like university students has been widely documented, and has been equated to Ian Smith's Rhodesian system (Makoni, 2007; Megan, 2006). The proposition here, as in these analyses just referenced, is that colonialism did not end in 1980 when Zimbabwe obtained its independence. This was just an end of a stage in European/Western-colonialism. Colonialism exists today in the garb of neoliberal globalization as authored and driven by the rich countries (mostly ex-colonial powers) of the world and their Transnational Companies (TNCs) (e.g., see Muronzi, 2009 and partnerships between indigenous Zimbabweans and TNCs in the case of Marange diamonds). Mugabe and his ZANU PF's alleged leftist radical dictatorial nationalism thrive on these contemporary avenues of Western hegemonic control as they provide his brand of nationalism with ready support from disgruntled people who have borne the brunt of IMF-designed immiseration.

Unemployment in Zimbabwe is currently at 80%, the rate of inflation hit record world levels in 2008 as shown in Table 1 (adapted from the Reserve Bank of Zimbabwe: Inflation Rates, 2009). The abandonment of the Zimbabwean dollar at the beginning of 2009 and the resultant adoption of foreign currencies, although it has reigned in price increases, find the majority in the communal areas, without access to foreign money, and it is reported that barter trade has been adopted in some circumstances, such as in the payment of school fees.

School dropouts due to high fees, especially in universities, spread of diseases because of no clean water, or no water at all, as was the case at the University of Zimbabwe (Makoni, 2007; The Sunday Mail, 2009) paint a grim picture of the situation. Prostitution (propelled by hardship) and consequently high risks of contracting HIV/AIDS among university students is yet another problem (Makoni, 2007). Faculty and other highly skilled personnel are leaving Zimbabwe in large numbers (Chetsanga & Muchenje, 2003; Makombe, 2009). The fact that Robert Mugabe capped only 612 out of the 4000 University of Zimbabwe students who were scheduled to graduate at the 2009 graduation ceremony illuminates the extent of the crisis in Zimbabwe, both, in general and specifically in higher education (Gumbo, 2009).

Table 1. Rate of inflation

Year	All Items CPI	Year on Year Price Increases
1990	29.6	15.5
1991	36.8	24.3
1992	52.3	42.1
1993	66.7	27.5
1994	81.6	22.3
1995	100.0	22.5
1996	121.4	21.7
1997	144.3	18.9
1998	190.1	31.7
1999	301.3	58.5
2000	469.6	55.9
2001	100.0	71.9
2002	233.2	133.2
2003	1084.5	365.0
2004	4880.3	350.0
2005	16486.4	237.8
2006	184101.4	1016.7
2007	12562581.7	6723.7
2008	35500566912457.9	231150888.87%
2009 July	91.3	1.0%

EXPLORING THE INTERSECTIONS: NEOLIBERALISM-ZANU PF RADICAL
NATIONALISM AND THE EROSION OF HIGHER EDUCATION

The period 1980 to 1990 is referred to by some as one of developmental nationalism, when the government of Zimbabwe adopted policies that aimed to satisfy the nationalist demands that had helped it galvanise people's support for the war (Ndlovu-Gatsheni, 2009). The rationale of developmental nationalism was rooted in the imperative need to redress colonial racial inequalities and the uplifting of the majority blacks to a status of dignified human beings. Colonial governments had consistently treated indigenous black Africans as sub-humans, not capable of governing themselves. The first decade was therefore characterized by phenomenal quantitative expansion in higher education.

The adoption of IMF/World Bank sponsored reforms in 1991, however, ushered in a new era in education and specifically university education. The guiding principle was the reversal of government support and the adoption of what the World Bank (1988) referred to as relieving "the burden on public sources of financing higher education by increasing the participation of beneficiaries and their families" (p. 77). It should be pointed out that the ZANU PF government was forced to adopt or was arguably perhaps even in favour of the SAPs that were adopted in higher education, as the party/officials if not Mugabe/ZANU PF radical nationalism also stood to gain (materially and politically) from some of these neoliberal interventions.

Inaccessability, Privatization of Services, Financial Duress for Students and Employment Implications for Faculty

The privatization of university amenities such as catering and accommodation services benefitted those with connections within the government or the ruling party (Muronzi, 2009). They became the new entrepreneurs in the name of black empowerment or indigenization. Foreign companies were also encouraged to invest in Zimbabwe. Thus the post 1991 Zimbabwe witnessed what some have described in other contexts as "state-corporate developmental collusions" (Kapoor, 2009b, p. 62), as the government of Zimbabwe and neoliberal policies derived from Washington, worked together in promulgating policies that marked the beginning of the crisis Zimbabwe has been enmeshed in for more than a decade now. Though the Zimbabwean government later dropped the IMF/World Bank driven structural adjustment programmes at the beginning of the new millennium, in principle the new home grown policies that were introduced are still very much neoliberal policies. The difference was that they were now authored by Zimbabweans as the business mantra found in IMF/World Bank development prescriptions had a huge presence in the so called home grown programs. The consequences for the people, such as those witnessed in higher education, were the same--privatization, marketization, and cost recovery (Slaughter & Leslie, 1997).

Thus, from 1991 to the present, the population of Zimbabwe has been under siege by the neoliberal agenda, at the behest of the ZANU PF government. The introduction of fee-paying policy in universities together with the privatization of basic amenities such as accommodation and food catering has brought untold suffering to the students, the majority of whom are from rural/peasant and working-class parentage. Studies have shown that students are finding it difficult to pay for university education. For instance a study of university students in Zimbabwe showed that most students were finding it difficult to meet educational costs (Makoni, 2007).

The crisis is also seen in the drop in salaries of university employees and this has affected the working morale of academics. There has been a mass exodus of academics, resulting in plummeting standards. The flight of lecturers has hit crisis levels (Makumbe, 2009). Makombe (2009), citing Ministry of Higher and Tertiary Education documents, reported that public universities have been hard hit by understaffing with the University of Zimbabwe having 385 out of the required 1171 academic members; Harare Institute of Technology has a 70% vacancy level with only 37 academic staff members out of a possible 123. Major push factors were low pay for academics in a collapsing economy with 165,000% inflation – the world's highest – poor working conditions, lack of transport and computers, and problems finding accommodation (Manyukwe, 2008). To add to this plethora of problems, there have been consistent increases in fees since 1991 and universities have been losing crucial donor funding, especially from the West. Only the

Chinese seem to be supporting the University of Zimbabwe and in return, the Chinese language is being taught at the institution.

World Bank and International Monetary Fund's macro-economic principles of budget deficit reduction and restricted social spending (Johnstone, 2001; Nafukho, 2004) forced the government to stop financing higher education and leave that responsibility to individuals. The adoption of the home grown development blueprint by the Zimbabwean government did not change this policy. With the abandonment of the valueless Zimbabwean dollar and adoption of multi-currencies, especially the US dollar and the South African Rand, higher education became even dearer and more out of reach (Share, 2009; Sunday Mail, 2009; ZINASU, 2009). Universities are largely underfunded and this forced universities to close doors for the whole of the second half of the 2008 academic year (Manyukwe, 2008). The University of Zimbabwe, the flagship of higher education in Zimbabwe, failed to open at the beginning of the 2009 academic year and only opened in August, and when it did open it could not accommodate first year students. Very few students turned up on opening day because of high fees ranging from US$403 to US$600. Only 68 out of 12 000 students at the institution had paid tuition fees while grants from traditional sources such as the government had either not been released or were not adequate (Share, 2009). Another worrying trend is that students are being forced to seek alternative accommodation as the college authorities cannot reopen the halls of residences citing water shortages (The Sunday Mail, 2009). The official government owned Herald newspaper quoted a university student in Harare describing their accommodation situation as follows:

> About 20 students share a guestroom in the main house and there are 11 illegal wooden cabins, which house more than 45 students. Most house owners collect between US$20 and US$40 in rentals a month from each student. These landlords are making a killing from the students' predicament. Our landlord collects over US$3 200 every month, as there are more than 80 students each paying US$30. (Share, 2009)

The marketization policies adopted under the neoliberal doctrine adopted from the West, and the continuation of these policies by Mugabe's government have brought university education down on its knees. Some blame Western nations, as well as the International Monetary Fund and the World Bank for Zimbabwe's crisis because they have been refusing to extend balance of payment support, while the government of Zimbabwe argues that it is under Western sanctions. However, critics of the government blame Robert Mugabe and his government for having stolen the presidential vote in March 2008 that effectively ruined this nation and made it difficult for any well meaning nations and donor agencies to continue to assist this country (Makumbe, 2009).

Neoliberalism regards higher education as a private commodity, a traded commodity to be purchased by a consumer, a product to be retailed by academic institutions (Altbach, 2004). University vice-chancellors and faculty deans have been turned more into business executives than the usual superintendents of pedagogical issues. In an attempt to generate revenue and fund their activities marketization has been adopted by some universities in Zimbabwe as part of the neoliberal model of privatization. Full fee-paying students are admitted over and above the students who come in with government subsidies. These students are enrolled into courses invariably referred to as parallel programmes. In most cases students enrolled in these programmes come from families that are of a higher socio-economic status and in most cases they are already professionals seeking upward mobility within their trades. This explains why at the Midlands State University, Great Zimbabwe University, National University of Science and Technology and the University of Zimbabwe, parallel programmes started in the Faculty of Business before other areas joined in. Parallel programmes help bring in much required revenue, but some perceive it as a degree buying venture that has led to the deterioration in the standards of degrees being awarded in Zimbabwe. The government considers it as empowerment of the people and a vindication of its progressive policies of educating the nation; a need the black majority Zimbabweans were denied during British colonial rule.

The policies of Robert Mugabe's government have precipitated the crisis (Raftopoulos, 2006) and Mugabe bases the rationale and justification for his dictatorial policies on Western imperialism as manifested by neoliberal globalization schemes dominating the contemporary world (Moyo & Yeros, 2007). Neoliberal policies, as first imposed by the International Monetary Fund and later adopted by the Mugabe regime cannot be absolved here. Mugabe's leftist nationalism (Ndlovu-Gatsheni, 2009), radical and exhausted nationalism (Raftopoulos, 2003) also characterised as dictatorial power grab nationalism (Meredith, 2007) is seen to be at the centre of the crisis. The crisis in higher education can be located at the vortex of neoliberal globalization and Mugabeism (authoritarian nationalism).

Quality of University Education

According to Mbembe (2002), Marxism and nationalism as ideologies gave birth to two narratives on African identity: nativism and Afro-radicalism. Mbembe (2002) defines nativism as:

> a discourse of rehabilitation and a form of defence of the humanity of Africans predicated on the claim that their race, traditions, and customs
>
> confer to them a peculiar self irreducible to that of any human group, and there to chart what might or should be the destiny of Africa and Africans in the world. (p. 629)

Mugabe's version of nationalism has been described by some as nativist. Ndlovu-Gatsheni (2009) argues that "Mugabe's nationalism despite its self-projection as 'democratic', 'radical' and progressive', is interpolated by nativism" (p. 1147).

To attain this African (Zimbabwean) reclamation or rehabilitation and renaissance, expansion in higher education was undertaken to accommodate as many people as possible. In 1980, there was only one university, the University of Zimbabwe with a student population of 2,240 (Nherera, 2005). Currently there are nine public universities with a total of 55,548 students, as per 2007 statistics (Southern African Regional Universities Association, 2009). This expansion has been quantitative and the qualitative dimension has been ignored or cannot be attained under current circumstances. With the neoliberal doctrine from the World Bank and the International Monetary Fund dictating to the indebted governments to reduce higher education funding, and the absence of corporate funding, universities in Zimbabwe were faced with the problem of undercapitalization. The impact of this has been the mass movement of faculty to other countries, particularly to South Africa and Botswana where conditions are better. Some of the new universities do not have staff at the grade of professorship except the vice and pro-vice chancellors. The natural sciences and business fields have been hard hit and most universities make use of teaching assistants with just first-degree qualifications (Makombe, 2009). They are supposed to operate under experienced professors but in some instances they are found to be in charge of courses. Due to the high demand for university education, most universities have introduced graduate programs. It is common to find holders of a masters degree teaching masters courses. Statistics show that close to 3.5 million people have left Zimbabwe since 2000 when the economy went into decline and political persecution heightened. Of these 500,000 are skilled professionals, who given the right environment, would prefer to return home (O'Dea, 2006). The Ministry of Higher and Tertiary Education has since formed the Brain Drain and Human Capital Mobilisation Committee whose mandate is to deal with the issue of skills shortages wrought by the brain drain (Jongwe, 2009). As part of this brief, the committee has been given the task of exploring various ways by which this brain drain can be turned into a brain gain. The goal of the committee is to keep more professionals here while reaping the benefits of remittances from expatriate Zimbabweans. At the time of independenc, similar shortages of teaching staff were alleviated by bringing in expatriates but today Zimbabwe is a pariah society and very unattractive even to its own citizens, let alone to foreigners. The problem of inadequate teaching staff has led to heavy teaching loads with instructors having to teach all year without a break. Since the introduction of parallel programmes, almost all the universities have programmes running throughout the year, in some cases including evenings and weekends. University vacations have been made to coincide with school holidays so as to allow school teachers enrolled in the parallel or part-time programs to attend lectures. The only time some lecturers have a break is when universities are forced to close due to strikes by students or industrial action by staff. These have been very frequent in recent years. Such closures are usually followed by crash programmes to make up for the lost time and money. The Great Zimbabwe University calendar for 2009 has three 'semesters'. Midlands State University students complained of not holding tutorials and being starved of lectures by being constantly referred to the internet for more information (Makoni, 2007). Under such stressful circumstances, and the large numbers involved, many cases of plagiarism go unnoticed and students engaging the services of others for a payment make the quality issue even worse. Similar issues of quality were noted in Kenya where cases of students taking previous research projects and slightly altering the titles and changing names, then presenting the projects as their original work have been reported (Wangenge-Ouma, 2008).

In addition to the adverse affects of a selective elite-driven economy and the consequent depressing conditions in Zimbabwe's universities, academics have faced persecution from Mugabe's increasingly dictatorial government. With the government facing challenges and its growing unpopularity, the critical voice from academe has been labelled the voice of the opposition and perceived as agents of the West aiding and seeking regime change. Such has become the politicization of the university that academic freedom does not exist. The law governing universities gives government, through the Minister of Higher and Tertiary Education control over the running of the institutions. According to Cheater (1991), "the Minister's involvement in choosing the nominees of the organisations represented on Council" (p. 202), are some of the main features of the laws that govern universities in Zimbabwe. Faculty members at that time, as cited by Cheater (1991) tried to oppose the law and the Association of University Teachers released a press statement rejecting the intention of the Bill which they saw as being there to transform the university from an autonomous institution of learning into a state (party) university.

It should be pointed out that at independence in 1980 Mugabe, when addressing a conference on the role of the university in Zimbabwe said, "To paraphrase that famous aphorism about generals and war: higher education is too important a business to be left entirely to deans, professors, lecturers and University administrators" (Chideya, Chikomba, Pongweni, & Tsikirayi, 1981, p. 6). This meant academic freedom was not going to be recognised and Mugabe's administration has been relentless and consistent.

The denial of academic freedom in Zimbabwe has nothing to do with neoliberalism. Its genealogy can be traced to the 1960s when ZANU PF was formed, an era characterized by European colonial dictatorship, and later the failure of the party to transform itself from a liberation movement into a governing political party. In an attempt to instil patriotism among the youth, educational institutions are being pressured to teach what ZANU PF calls patriotic history whose rationale is to ward off Western criticism and protect national independence and sovereignty. According to Sikhumbuzo Ndiweni, ZANU-PF Information and Publicity Secretary for Bulawayo, "the mistake the ruling party made was to allow colleges and universities to be turned into anti-Government mentality factories" (Ranger, 2004, p. 218). Such ideas are premised on the fact that the opposition parties in Zimbabwe, such as the MDC, have former student leaders and faculty members among their ranks. And by being universities, the nature of their business involves critiquing their society. Krigger (2006) observed that historians in Zimbabwe have deplored how the ruling party, ZANU PF, has been propagating a distorted version of the history of the nationalist struggle to legitimate its violent confiscation of land and repression of the opposition since 2000.

Universities are faced by a paranoid dictatorship, which defines every episode in its history as a war against the West. Western neoliberal globalization, much criticised and condemned in the South and justifiably so on many counts, has become cannon fodder on which ZANU PF feeds. Sloppy post-colonial theorists see Mugabe as an example of a pan-Africanist, an indomitable "lion" who possesses the temerity to name Western oppression and empower Africans by dispossessing European farmers of the land they held since colonial times. But the suffering that the ordinary Zimbabweans go through is ignored and all blame is heaped on the West. Within such an intimidating atmosphere, it is difficult to find any scholarship that is critical of the government. Those that have openly criticised ZANU PF, for example, John Makumbe and Takavafira Zhou, have been labelled enemies of the state and have faced persecution in the form of arrests while those who praise the government are found sitting on various boards of parastatals. The net result of all this has been a decline in the standing of university education.

State Victimization of Students

The deleterious impact of ZANU PF radical and dictatorial nationalism on one side and neoliberal interventions on the other has also been witnessed in the welfare of the students. Cases of students demonstrating in relation to Zimbabwean universities are not new as they date back to the Rhodesian days. Unfortunately, since independence, opposition to Mugabe's dictatorial practices has brewed mainly in universities, with the University of Zimbabwe being in the lead. Students are squeezed in between teething economic challenges and a government that wants them to remain silent and soldier on under the banner of nationalism and patriotism. Megan (2006) cites numerous cases of student victimization.

The laws in Zimbabwe today threaten the academic freedom of students and consequently promote student victimization. One of them is the University Amendment Act of 1999 that gives the Vice Chancellor of an institution the right to expel students for life. 101 students have been expelled since 2001 for political reasons (ZINASU, 2009), while hundreds have been victimized in the form of torture, arbitrary arrest and unlawful detentions. Several of them have had to finish their education abroad. It is a clear violation of the freedom of expression and academic freedom of students, that they can be expelled for expressing political views. While administrative authorities at tertiary learning institutions expel, fine or suspend students, the riot police, state security agents and campus security guards spearhead the physical and emotional torture of students. State security agents reportedly break into rooms of student activists or union leaders at late night or early morning hours to kidnap them for questioning or torture in order to silence them (Universities World News, 2008; ZINASU, 2009).

CONCLUDING REFLECTIONS

Colonial/post colonial studies on Africa, are generally anti-colonial and consequently, and rightly so, blame African ills on Western hegemonic projects, namely colonization, development and neoliberal globalization. The intentional result of such positioning by some scholars has been to ignore the problems inherent within African governance since the end of direct European political rule. This stream of scholarship ignores the rise and development of dictatorship, especially within the former liberation movements. To such scholars, criticizing fellow Africans is unpatriotic and reactionary, leading to labels such as "an agent of neo-colonialism". This chapter distances itself from such a blend of post-colonial African writing. Equally questionable is the critical writing, mostly written by authors from the "developed world" who are mostly sympathisers of commercial farmers whose land was taken without compensation by Mugabe's government. These have considered Mugabe's government as dictatorial, racist and fail to acknowledge the effects of Western colonial hegemonic policies, particularly poverty caused by the policy prescriptions championed by neoliberal globalization. Neo-liberal globalization feeds Mugabe's nationalist rhetoric and the subsequent portrayal of Mugabe as an African pan-Africanist hero in some quarters of the African community and generally with blacks in the diaspora.

In this chapter I have argued that both the radical nationalism of the ZANU PF government and neoliberalism (radical capitalism) are responsible for the plight of the suffering people of Zimbabwe and those who work and study in the country's universities. Consequently, the response to the crises in universities cannot be located in either of these two ideologies/analytics alone. Universities and other concerned scholars are being called upon to engage in what is described as "border gnosis; knowledge from a subaltern perspective conceived from the exterior borders of modern/colonial world system" (Mignolo, 2000, p. 11). Peters (2007) echoes the same opinion when he states:

> In non-European cultural traditions the task of the post-colonial university, may be precisely to focus upon the question of national cultural self-definition and to do so as a means of coming to terms, confronting, engaging with, or resisting forces of cultural homogeneity which threaten to erode indigenous traditions in the wake of a globalization which commodifies both word and image. (p. 48)

Local indigenous ideas need be promoted – ideas that are not only opposed to the rich First World's continuing and sustained pillaging of weaker nations' raw materials and natural resources and labour, but also critical of the breed of African leadership that has become as oppressive and dictatorial as the former European colonisers. Mignolo (2000) called such an approach "a double critique, a border thinking" (p. 67). As succinctly expressed by Grosfoguel (2005), some form of colonialism is still present in Zimbabwe today:

> Coloniality does not refer only to classical colonialism, or internal colonialism, nor can it be reduced to the presence of a colonial administration

... I use coloniality to address colonial situations in the present period. I mean the cultural, political, sexual, and economic oppression and exploitation of subordinate groups, with or without the existence of colonial administrations. (pp. 287-288)

To turn a blind eye to African leaders' excesses, including the persecution of university students and faculty and the near total collapse of universities is irresponsible scholarship. Ignoring coloniality and all the forms of suffering that accompany colonialism of all strands is unacceptable and cannot be a viable foundation from which to build higher education and indeed, Zimbabwe.

REFERENCES

Altbach, P. G. (2004). Globalisation and the university: Myths realities in an unequal world. *Tertiary Education and Management, 10*(1), 3-25.

Anderson, B. (1991). Imagined communities: Reflections on the origins and spread of nationalism. London: Verso.

Appadurai, A. (1996). *Modernity at large: Cultural dimensions of globalization*. Minneapolis, MN: University of Minnesota Press.

Barr, N. (2004). Higher education funding. *Oxford Review of Economic Policy, 20*(2), 264–283.

Black, M. (2007). *The no-nonsense guide to international development*. Toronto: New Internationalist Publishers.

Bond, P. (2001). Radical rhetoric and the working class during Zimbabwean nationalism's dying days. *Journal of World Systems Research, 7*(1), 52-89.

Cheater, A. P. (1991). The University of Zimbabwe: University, national university, state university, or party university? *African Affairs, 90*, 189-205.

Chetsanga, C. J. & Muchenje, T. B. (2003). *An analysis of the cause and effect of the brain drain in Zimbabwe*. Harare: Scientific and Industrial Research and Development Centre.

Chideya, N. T., Chikomba, C. E. M. A., Pongweni, J. C., & Tsikirayi, L.C. (eds.) (1981). *The role of the university and its future in Zimbabwe: International Conference Papers*. Harare: Harare Publishing House.

Gellner, E. (2006). *Nations and nationalism*. Oxford, UK & Victoria, Australia: Blackwell Publishing.

Guibernau, M. (1996). *Nationalisms: The nation state and nationalisms in the twentieth century*. Cambridge: Blackwell Publishers.

Grosfoguel, R. (2005). The implications of subaltern epistemologies for global capitalism: Transmodernity, Border thinking, and global coloniality. In R. P. Appelbaum & W. I. Robinson (eds.), *Critical globalization studies*. New York/London: Routledge.

Gumbo, L. (2009, November 14). President caps 612 University of Zimbabwe graduates. *The Herald*. Retrieved from http://www.herald.co.zw/inside.aspx?sectid=16379&liverdate=14/11/2009.

Hall, S. (1992). *Our Mongreal selves: New statesmen and society*. Oxford: Oxford University Press.

Harvey, D. (2003). *The new imperialism*. New York: Oxford University Press.

Johnstone, D. B. (2001). Responses to austerity: The imperatives and limitations of revenue diversification in higher education. *Education Policy Studies Series; Hong Kong Institute of Education Research*. Hong Kong: The Chinese University of Hong Kong. Retrieved from http://www.gse.buffalo.edu/org/inthigheredfinance/textForSite/AusterityRevDivers.pdf.

Jongwe, A. (2009, August 7). Ministry gears up to tackle brain drain. *The Financial Gazette*. Retrieved from http://www.financialgazette.co/zw/companies-a-markets/1543-ministry-gears-up-to-tackle-brain-drain.html.

Kapoor, D. (ed.) (2009a). *Education, decolonization and development: Perspectives from Asia, Africa and the Americas*. Rotterdam/Boston/Taipei: Sense Publishers.

Kapoor, D. (2009b). Adivasis (original dwellers) "in the way of" state-corporate development: Development dispossession and learning in social action for land and forests in India. *McGill Journal of Education, 44*(1), 55-78.

Krigger, N. (2006). From patriotic memories to 'patriotic history' in Zimbabwe, 1990-2005. *Third World Quarterly, 27*(6), 1151-1169.

Levidow, L. (2002). Marketizing higher education: Neoliberal strategies and counter- strategies. *The Commoner, 3*, 1-21.

Levidow, L. (2005). Neoliberal agendas for higher education. In A. Saado-Filho & D. Johnston (eds.), *Neoliberalism: A critical reader*. London: Pluto Press.

Makoni, K. (2007). *Understanding the effects of high educational costs and incidence of Student victimization at Zimbabwe's tertiary learning institutions*. Harare: ZINASU.

Makombe, L. (2009, November 26). Staff shortages hit tertiary sector. *The Zimbabwe Independent*. Retrieved from http://www.theindependent.co.zw/business/244433-staff-shortages-hit-teretiary-education-sector.html.

Makumbe, J. (2002). Zimbabwe's hijacked election. *Journal of Democracy, 13*(4), 88-101.

Makumbe, J. (2009, July 30). Gono, Mugabe to blame for wrecking education dream. *The Zimbabwean*. Retrieved from http://www.thezimbabwean.co.uk/2009073023219/opinion-analysis/gono-mugabe-to-blame-for-wrecking-education-dream.

Mamdani, M. (2008). Lessons of Zimbabwe. *London Review of Books, 30*(23), 1.

Manyukwe, C. (2008, October 12). Desperate universities launch income projects. *University World News: Africa Edition*. Retrieved from http://www.universityworldnews.com/article.php?story=20081010092124578.

Masunungure, E. & Bratton, M. (2008). Zimbabwe's long agony. *Journal of Democracy, 19*(4), 41-55.

Mbembe, A. (2002). African modes of self writing. *Public Culture, 14*(1), 239-273.

McMichael, P. (2005). Globalization and development studies. In R. P. Appelbaum & W. I. Robinson (eds.), *Critical globalization studies*. New York and London: Routledge.

Megan, L. (2006). Zimbabwe Cracks Down on Students After Tuition Protests. *The Chronicle of Higher Education, 52*(40), 7-8.

Meredith, M. (2007). *Mugabe: Power, plunder and the struggle for Zimbabwe*. New York: Public Affairs.

Mignolo, W. D. (2000). *Local histories/global designs: Coloniality, subaltern knowledges, and border thinking*. New Jersey: Princeton University Press.

Moyo, S. & Yeros, P. (2007). Intervention: The Zimbabwe question and the two lefts. *Historical Materialism, 15*(3), 171-204.

Muronzi, C. (2009, November 19). Minister failed to float tender for diamond partners. *The Zimbabwe Independent*. Retrieved from http://www.theindependent.co.zw./business/24433-minister-failed-to-float-tender-for-diamond-partners.html.

Nafukho, F. M. (2004). The market model of financing state universities in Kenya: Some innovative lessons. In P. T. Zeleza and A. Olukoshi (eds.), *African Universities in the twenty first century*. Pretoria: University of South Africa Press.

Ndlovu-Gatsheni, S. J. (2009). Making sense of Mugabeism in local and global politics: 'So Blair, keep your England and let me keep my Zimbabwe'. *Third World Quarterly, 30*(6), 1139-1158.

Nherera, C. M. (2005). *Globalization, qualifications and livelihoods: Shifts in the educational structure of Zimbabwe following economic liberalization*. London: Institute of Education, University of London.

O'Dea, U. (2006, November 2). Zimbabwe courting expat lecturers to tackle skills gap. *Times Higher Education*. Retrieved from http://www.timeshighereducation.co.uk/story.asp?storyCode=206504&sectioncode=26.

Peters, M. A. (2007). *Knowledge economy, development and the future of higher education*. Rotterdam/Taipei: Sense Publishers.

Petras, J. & Veltmeyer, H. (2001). Globalization as ideology: Economic and political dimension. In J. Petras & H. Veltmeyer (eds.), *Globalization unmasked: Imperialism in the 21st century*. Halifax: Fernwood.

Phimister, I. & Raftopoulos, B. (2004). Mugabe, Mbeki and the politics anti-imperialism. *Review of African Political Economy, 101*, 385-400.

Raftopoulos, B. (2003). The state in crisis: Authoritarian nationalism, selective citizenship and distortions of democracy in Zimbabwe. In A. Hammar, B. Raftopoulos, & S. Jensen (eds.), *Zimbabwe's unfinished business. Rethinking land state and nation in the context of crisis*. Harare: Weaver Press.

Raftopoulos, B. (2006). The Zimbabwean crisis and the challenges for the left. *Journal of Southern African Studies, 32*(2), 203-217.

Ranger, T. O. (2004). Nationalist historiography, patriotic history and the history of the nation: The struggle over the past in Zimbabwe. *Journal of Southern African Studies, 30*(2), 215-234.

Ranger, T. O. (2008). Lessons of Zimbabwe: Letters. *London Review of Books, 30*(24). Retrieved from http://www.lrb.co.uk/v30/no24/ letters.html.

Reserve Bank of Zimbabwe (2009). *Inflation rates*. Harare: Reserve Bank of Zimbabwe.

Scarnecchia, T. (2006). The 'fascist cycle' in Zimbabwe, 2000-2005. *Journal of Southern African Studies, 32*(2), 221-237.

Scholte, J. A. (2005). *Globalization: A critical reader*. New York: Palgrave Macmillan.

Share, F. (2009, November 11). Accommodation crisis forces University of Zimbabwe students to live in slums. *The Herald*. Retrieved from http://www.herald.co.zw/inside.aspx?sectid=16874&livedate=11/11/2009=3.

Sithole, M. (2001). Fighting authoritarianism in Zimbabwe. *Journal of Democracy, 12*(1), 160-169.

Slaughter, S. & Leslie, L. L. (1997). *Academic capitalism and the entrepreneurial university*. Baltimore: John Hopkins University Press.

Smith, D.G. (2006). *Trying to teach in a season of great untruth: Globalization, empire and the crises of pedagogy*. Rotterdam/Taipei: Sense Publishers.

Southern African Regional Universities Association (2009). *SARUA Handbook 2009: A guide to public Universities of Southern Africa*. Johannesburg: SARUA Publications.

Tikly, L. (2004). Education and the new imperialism. *Comparative Education, 40*(2), 173-198.

The Sunday Mail (2009, May 3). University of Zimbabwe on the verge of collapse. Retrieved from http://www.sundaymail.co.zw/inside.aspx?sectid= 18096&cat=09.

Universities World News (2008, February 10). Zimbabwe universities close ahead of elections. Retrieved from http://www.universityworld news.com/article.php?story=20080208090045413.

Vaira, M. (2004). Globalisation and higher education organisational change: A framework for analysis. *Higher Education, 48*(4), 483-509.

Wangenge-Ouma, G. (2008). Higher education marketization and its discontents: The case of quality in Kenya. *Higher Education, 56*, 457-471.

Willis, K. (2005). *Theories and practices of development*. London: Routledge.

World Bank (1988). *Education in Sub-Saharan Africa: Policies for adjustment, revitalization, and expansion*. Washington, DC: World Bank.

World Bank (1994). *Higher education: The lessons of experience*. Washington: The World Bank.

Zimbabwe National Students' Union (March 2009). *Monthly briefing paper*. Retrieved from http://www.zinasu.org.

NEOLIBERAL GLOBALIZATION, MULTILATERAL DEVELOPMENT AGENCIES AND HIV AND AIDS EDUCATION IN SOUTH AFRICA: LOOKING BACK TO LOOK AHEAD

Faisal Islam, PhD, McGill University, Montreal, Canada

Claudia Mitchell, James McGill Professor, McGill University, Montreal, Canada

INTRODUCTION

As one of the most destructive epidemics in human history, AIDS has claimed more than 25 million lives since 1981 (UNAIDS, 2009) and is the leading cause of death in Africa, where some 15 million Africans have died since the epidemic was first acknowledged (AVERT, 2009). According to some estimates, 70% of the world's infected population live in sub-Saharan Africa, which is home to 10% of the world's population (Pillay, 2003). In 2008, more than 14 million children in sub-Saharan Africa had lost one or both parents to HIV and AIDS (UNAIDS, 2009).

When it comes to addressing this epidemic in Africa and elsewhere, there is no consensus among multi-lateral development agencies and national governments, although there is still lip service paid to the idea that education, as a 'social vaccine', has a significant role to play in curbing and combating the spread of HIV and AIDS (Bakilana, Bundy, Brown, & Fredriksen, 2005; UNFPA, 2008). Based on a 'looking back' review of the programmatic literature on HIV and AIDS education initiatives being undertaken by multilateral development actors and international financial institutions, this chapter suggests that the educational contribution to HIV and AIDS prevention being advanced by many multi-lateral agencies has been inadequate as framed within a neoliberal globalization agenda, and has fallen short of its potential for addressing the epidemic. What we hope is that our analysis could prove to be instructive for educational initiatives undertaken by agents of the state, civil society actors and even progressive elements within these dominant development institutions (or their funded partners) who are concerned with the links between the need for greater political-economic democratization and the struggle against the epidemic.

In the first section of the chapter we consider the historical background of the neoliberal economic and political agenda in Africa and the exacerbation of HIV

D. Kapoor (ed.), Critical Perspectives on Neoliberal Globalization, Development and Education in Africa and Asia, 121–134.

and AIDS. We then provide a review of dominant agency-supported HIV and AIDS education programs such as current perspectives on Life Skills and abstinence-only education and their limitations in dealing with HIV and AIDS prevention. In this section, we also discuss how the donor-driven agenda is still influencing local prevention efforts, and we consider the educational silences typified by neoliberal approaches to HIV and AIDS education and posit alternative directions for HIV and AIDS education. In this section, we also suggest shifting HIV and AIDS prevention education from narrowly-focused individual fixations as imposed by agency-led development to local collective responses in accordance with community needs, initiatives and culture.

NEOLIBERAL GLOBALIZATION AND HIV&AIDS IN AFRICA: LOOKING BACK, PART 1

In 1949 at the beginning of the post-colonization era, US President Harry S. Truman set a roadmap of development by declaring:

> We must embark on a new program for making the benefits of our scientific advances with industrial progress available for the improvement and growth of the underdeveloped areas. (Seabrook, 2003, p. 61)

The message conveyed to the 'underdeveloped' world was that the only way to make progress was to follow the Eurocentric model of development. International Financial Institutions (IFIs), including the World Bank and the International Monetary Fund (IMF) were created and transnational companies were given a pivotal role in institutionalizing development. The recession of the 1970s, coupled by a phenomenal hike in the oil price adversely affected the economy of the African countries. This provided opportunities for the IMF and the World Bank to intrude in local economies using loans as a tool to influence the economic and social policies in these countries (Seabrook, 2003). African countries were compelled to take more loans to repay their debts and to accept the conditions of the Structural Adjustment Programs (SAPs) to stabilize the economy. However, the diagnosis was counter-productive. The region was mired in more trouble. The total debt of sub Saharan African in 1970 was USD 16.3 billion which subsequently increased to USD 280 billion in 2000 (Geda, 2003).

The current phase of 'development' is influenced by globalization, which has legitimized neoliberalism and consolidated capitalism (Herd & McGrew, 2002). Indeed, a key to the neoliberal development framework is the idea of transforming the world into a single market entity through the creation of free markets, elimination of spatial barriers, and initiation of structural changes (Herd & McGrew, 2002). Multinational Corporations (MNCs), aided by the IFIs and the rich countries were given a key role in spearheading the global capitalist order through production and investment. A survey in the year 2000 found that out of the 100 largest world economies, 51 are corporations and 49 are the countries. Further, the top 200 corporations' sales are growing at a faster rate than overall global economic activity (Anderson & Cavanagh, 2000). MNCs have not only accumulated massive profits, but are also steering the world economy. The richer governments (for example G-8 countries) have taken the responsibility to protect the interests of global corporate capital and the IFIs. IFIs were created to negotiate with and influence individual countries, so that their environment would be conducive to global corporate investment and capital movement with minimal or no government control (Bond, 2006; Broad, 2002; Held & McGrew, 2002). It has now been more than 50 years since US President Truman promised to help the 'underdeveloped' world, and yet the dream of 'development' is still far from reached. The inequality and poverty between the world's richest and poorest nations are at a historic level and are worsening as the benefits of globalization are spreading unevenly across the globe and within countries (Held & McGrew, 2002).

The issue of HIV and AIDS in Africa cannot be fully comprehended unless it is understood in relation to neoliberal globalization and its impacts on socio-economic and political life. It is important to understand the role of the corporate sector, especially the pharmaceutical companies and the failed policies of IFIs, which have played a critical role in spreading HIV and AIDS in Africa. The corporate sector has a high stake in Africa. For example, its contribution, as listed on the Johannesburg Stock Exchange, falls between 36 and 54 percent of the South African GDP (Malherbe & Segal, 2001). Yet this sector is not willing to play its part in the fight against HIV and AIDS. A survey of multi-national firms working in East Africa observed that only one-third of the surveyed firms invest in HIV and AIDS prevention (Ramachandrana, Shahb, & Turnerb, 2007). Similarly, a 2004 WEF (World Economic Forum) Executive Opinion Survey, in which a total of 7,789 high-level executives from firms in 103 countries were contacted about how concerned they were about HIV and AIDS, observed that "fewer than 6% have formally-approved written HIV policies" (Bloom, Bloom, Steven, & Wetson, 2004, p. 1). In the same survey only 16% of the surveyed firms reported that they provide information to their employee about the risk of the infection (Bloom, Bloom, Steven, & Wetson, 2004).

Not only is the corporate sector unwilling to play its part, People Living With AIDS (PLWAs) face discrimination in the workplace. In the first place PLWAs may not be offered jobs, and even if they secure employment, they may experience a reduction in a company's contributions to health benefits. Rosen and Simon (2002) observe that one large employer, in South Africa, has curtailed its ceiling for HIV-related claims from ZAR100,000 to just ZAR 15,000 per family. Further, citing a survey carried out by the Johannesburg Chamber of Commerce and Industry, the authors observed "40 percent of the responding firms had moved to lower-premium medical aid schemes that provided fewer benefits" (p. 3) to PLWAs. The same study found that HIV-positive people are at greater risk for being dismissed from their jobs. A textile firm in South Africa, for example, reported that it carried out HIV and AIDS tests for their employees without informing them, and those who were found to HIV positive were dismissed from the jobs (Rosen & Simon, 2002). In Zimbabwe during 1997, there was widespread evidence of illegal pre-employment testing of job applicants and screening of applicants to avoid hiring those with risky lifestyles. In addition, many South

African firms are outsourcing the jobs to private contractors and independent companies to avoid benefits which have to be offered to potential full-time employee (Rosen & Simon, 2002). While these examples may be read as somewhat dated ('that was then and this is now') we cite them nonetheless as evidence of a particular climate of inequality and one that is likely to have long lasting effects on attitudes and practices, even in terms of workplace policy change.

The role of pharmaceutical companies in relation to HIV and AIDS is even more dismal. Despite the devastating effects of HIV and AIDS, it seems that relatively little progress has been made in finding a cure, although the development of treatment through Antiretrovirals (ARVs) and access to them has improved in some areas. When ARVs were first discovered in 1990, dramatically reducing the number of HIV-infection related deaths in the San Francisco Bay area, people for the first time saw the opportunity of turning the epidemic into a manageable disease (Usdin, 2003). However, after two decades since ARVs were discovered, they are still out of reach, especially for the poor. In sub-Saharan Africa where more than 60% of HIV and AIDS infected people live, only 44% of people who needed the treatment were receiving it in 2008 (AVERT, 2010). The chief hindrances are the cost and patent issues that hamper the affordability and accessibility of the drug. In 2001, for example, ARVs cost USD 1200 to USD 2500 and in some countries more than USD 10,000 per year for patented therapy. Because of the high cost, only a fraction (30,000) of affected people (28 million) in sub-Saharan Africa in 2001 was able to receive the drug (AVERT, 2005). Pharmaceutical companies, in defence of the astronomical prices, regarded the high cost of research and development (R&D) in the field of HIV and AIDS as a chief reason for the high cost of ARVs. This argument was contested on several counts: First, evidence suggests that the pharmaceutical companies' spending on R&D is as low as one-fifth of what they claimed. Second, much of a company's R&D budget goes into lifestyle drugs (i.e., non-medical drugs that can alter physical appearance) such as skin treatment (drugs that are more common in Europe and North America) and only one-tenth of the R&D goes into global diseases such as HIV. Third, the spending of pharmaceutical companies on advertizing and marketing is much higher than on the R&D budget (Usdin, 2003). In contrast, the high prices of drugs, especially on life saving drugs, help the companies to earn massive profits. In 2000, the pharmaceutical industry was the most profitable industry in the United States and the combined worth of the top five pharmaceutical companies was twice the GDP of all the sub-Saharan African countries (Usdin, 2003).

NEO-LIBERAL GLOBALIZATION AND HIV&AIDS IN AFRICA: LOOKING BACK, PART 2

In this section, we offer a brief historical look at the situation of ARVs with the idea of deepening an understanding of the slow progress in addressing HIV and AIDS in sub-Saharan Africa. In South Africa, in particular, there has been a spate of recent publications, which provide an analysis of what went wrong (see Geffen,

2010; Iliffe, 2006; Nattrass, 2007; Steinberg, 2008). And although, there have been recent changes, and there are many reasons for optimism within the HIV and AIDS policies of the Zuma government, the point of our analysis is to deepen an understanding of how a neoliberal agenda can (and has) contributed to fuelling the spread of AIDS. Ironically, the pharmaceutical companies have not only insisted on keeping higher prices, but have also in recent history blocked the availability of generic drugs. Generic drugs are much cheaper and can reduce the cost of ARVs by 50 to 70. The WTO Agreement on Trade-Related Aspects of Intellectual Property Rights (TRIPS) introduced intellectual property rules into the world trade. Although TRIPS protects the intellectual property right, it also has flexible clauses that enable governments to protect the public health through use of 'parallel imports' (i.e., patent drugs can be imported from other countries where the patent drugs are cheaper) and issuance of 'compulsory licenses' (i.e., in case of health emergencies copies can be made of patent drugs without the approval of the patent holder). But when the South African government in 1997 passed the Medicines and Substances Amendment Act, allowing the government to use parallel imports and compulsory licenses (using the legal flexible clauses of TRIPS), the pharmaceutical companies filed a lawsuit against the government (Martorell, 2002). To pressurize the government, some of the pharmaceutical companies even threatened to boycott the supply of drugs to South Africa and to pull out their investment from the South African drug market. After partially losing the case and gaining much negative publicity from this incident the pharmaceutical companies retreated and withdrew their case (Martorell, 2002).

Vulnerable groups in society such as the poor, women, and children are at high risk and are at the mercy of market-led forces for their survival. All traditional mechanisms of support, for example public funding and state-led responses, were systematically eliminated. In the quest for free-markets, IFI policies and projects under the guise of economic development, have had negative impacts on the lives of vulnerable groups. For example, during the pre-colonial era, the education system was indigenous, focusing on transmitting the 'accumulated wisdom' and 'knowledge of society' from one generation to next generation whereby preparing young people to participate in the maintenance and development of the society (Abdi, Puplampu, & Dei, 2006). Moletsane (in press) and others have cautioned us against romanticizing the past in trying to understand sexuality education, but for better or worse, colonization annulled African traditional education systems (Abdi, Puplampu, & Dei, 2006). Even the new form of education (based on a Eurocentric formal education system) was still popular, with high enrolment in primary, secondary and higher education, until the arrival of the World Bank and IMF initiated Structural Adjustment Programs (SAPs) in 1980. SAPs severely destroyed the state's ability to treat education as a public good. SAPs are considered as a turning point in the growth and development of Africa. Abdi, Puplampu, and Dei, (2006) termed the SAP era as a 'lost decade' and describe the situation as follows:

> Sub-Saharan Africa's growth rates were good, actually, robust in the first decades after independence (4.3 in the 1960s and 4.2 in the 1970s), [yet] it is

also true that since the reign of SAPs, Africa has consistently seen severe economic and social decline on all fronts. (p. 22)

The SAPs drained the national government's ability to provide support and services to its vulnerable populations. To avoid economic hardships, the developing countries sought loans from developed countries and IFIs. The IFIs provided conditional loans and grants which demanded cutting government spending, elimination of subsidies on agriculture, health, education, and other social services. To enable transnational companies to penetrate the local economy, SAPs specifically required the government to cut back its role and spending and to promote privatization and deregulation (Stromquist, 1999). Historically, national governments were responsible for catering to the needs of its citizens, but after the advent of SAP and similar programs, the government's role was diminished to disciplining citizens to meet the requirements of globalization (Held & McGrew, 2002). The impact was devastating in the case of the HIV and AIDS pandemic. Vulnerable groups, who depend upon government support were left to the mercy of discriminating markets and corporations. In Zimbabwe, for example during the 1990s, SAPs reduced social expenditures and subsequently, the availability of condoms (Parker, Easton, & Klein, 2000).

Besides limiting the government's role, IFI-supported projects affected family structures by encouraging migration, a contributing factor in the spread of HIV and AIDS in Africa (Brummer, 2002). Migrant workers and their families are more vulnerable to HIV and AIDS, and the movement of people from high incidence areas to low incidence areas contributes to the spread of the disease. The construction of mega-development projects (for example hydro-electric dams funded and advised by IFIs), often displaced people from their land and/or livelihood, which resulted in the separation of families, and the alteration of traditional social patterns (Brummer, 2002; Parker et al., 2000). Away from their partners, the isolated migrant workers were more inclined to seek multiple sexual partners, mainly sex workers, hence putting themselves at risk. When workers returned home, they also increased the vulnerability of their communities to HIV AND AIDS. Parker et al. (2000) cite Decosas' (1996) analysis of how the creation of Akosombo dam in Ghana, one of the largest dams in Africa with the full support of the World Bank, has contributed to the HIV and AIDS pandemic in Krobo's community in Ghana. The creation of Akosombo dam in 1960 destroyed the agricultural base of the Krobo community. Krobo men went to the project site to work and the Krobo women provided services, including sexual-economic exchanges in the project area. These women and later their daughters turned to sex work and went abroad. The remittances received from these sex workers were the main source of Krobo's economy in absence of an agriculture base, destroyed by the dam. Two generations of Krobo women had one of the highest HIV and AIDS prevalence rates in the country during 1980s and 1990s (Parker, et al., 2000). Similarly, a research study of Bosatho mineworkers in South Africa illustrates how migrant workers were vulnerable to HIV and AIDS (Brummer, 2002). In interviews of the mineworkers, it was revealed that most of the mineworkers lived in single-sex hostels with up to 20 people sharing a single room. There were no recreational facilities in the hostel and the workers had to go to neighbouring areas to seek all kinds of recreation, including fulfilling their sexual desires (Brummer, 2002).

MULTILATERAL DEVELOPMENT AGENCIES AND HIV AND AIDS EDUCATION: NEOLIBERAL COMPULSIONS AND PSYHO-CULTURAL AND BEHAVIORAL FIXATIONS

One of the fundamental objectives of education, as per the neoliberal framework, is to prepare labor for the workplace and market needs. The World Bank, one of the largest external funders of education projects in the global south views education as an instrument for economic growth.

> The World Bank's support for education has a dual focus: to help countries achieve universal primary education and to help countries build the higher-level and flexible skills needed to compete in today's global, knowledge-driven markets, what we call Education for the Knowledge Economy. (World Bank, 2009)

Since 1963 when the World Bank started to fund education projects, its approach to education has been limited to increasing human productivity for economic growth, and to building the skills of labor to meet the requirements of the free market. The World Bank focused more on primary (and sometimes early childhood) education, agricultural extension education, and vocational or continuing education (Bakilana, et al., 2005). In all three sectors, the common denominator is the highest rate of return, especially in terms of macroeconomic productivity and growth. The emphasis on primary education is based upon the World Bank's own research assumptions that early education has the best rate of return. Adult education and education as a key to social change or as a human right hardly ever received World Bank attention. During the 1980s, the World Bank was so focused on the 'economic fruits' of primary education that it put primary education above higher education and opposed non-formal and adult education. The World Bank even threatened not to participate in the Jomtien conference if the focus of EFA remained on adult education (Klees, 2002). The case of the World Bank's support for HIV and AIDS education is no different from its overall approach to education. It did not recognize HIV and AIDS as a development issue until researchers proved that HIV and AIDS could have a drastic impact on macro-economic growth, especially on the GDP. Most of the World Bank's funding in HIV and AIDS, between 1992 and 1996, was through sector investment projects, and in 1996 the Bank shifted its policy towards investing more on building children's life skills through schools (Bakilana et al., 2005).

The focus on individual behavior and acquiring life-skills has become a dominant strategy for most of the bilateral and multilateral agencies. For example, UNICEF (2002) focuses on the following five key focus areas to improve its HIV and AIDS education programs: learner (health and concentration on learning);

content (curriculum and materials); process (design and the delivery of the programs); environment (school and classroom); and outcomes (learning achievements). Similarly, WHO in collaboration with Education International (EI) and Education Development Center (EDC) launched a teacher-training program to protect teachers, students, and communities from HIV and AIDS in 17 African countries. Funded by the Center of Disease Control and Prevention (CDC), the partnership was started in 1994 and was later joined by UNICEF, UNESCO, and the World Bank. The project has reported that so far more than 130,000 teachers have been trained in approximately 22,000 schools. Given the outreach of the program and the support from large organizations in the field of development, the project focused on: i) providing teachers with the knowledge and skills to protect themselves from HIV and AIDS and to train other teachers; ii) training teachers and students to advocate effective HIV prevention efforts in schools; iii) helping young people to acquire knowledge and skills to prevent from HIV (UNC, 2005).

Though we do agree that teaching life skills can help in reducing vulnerabilities and increase awareness for self-defense, we have seen that too many of the donor-driven models are based on an assumption of 'one size fits all'. For example, Boler and Archer (2008) observe that "Curriculum materials on HIV and AIDS look similar across many parts of Africa, Asia, and Latin America—despite differences in epidemiology and culture—because they have been designed in North America or Europe" (p. 171). The authors further argue that these materials have lacked several elements, which have made them less effective. First, in an effort to avoid potential conflict with the more conservative elements in society, many programs do not explicitly discuss sex or sexual relationships. This has made the curriculum 'acceptable to all' but not 'effective for all'. At the same time, these programs have compromised quality, especially with respect to the limitations to expose the silences and the power dynamics that keep the silences. This is particularly the case in relation to addressing gender and power, sexual relationships and the issue of puberty itself. Second, Life Skills are often seen as a simple set of behavioral skills that can be taught in mechanistic ways, ignoring deeper and broader factors that make young people vulnerable. Many of the complicated skills, such as assertiveness and empathy, are considered as simple to teach in classroom settings, even though they are not as simple to teach. Third, Life Skills are intended to be participatory, allowing students to raise questions and challenge prevalent notions and stereotypes. However, participatory methods of teaching life skills often do not conform to the current pedagogy in many schools, which is didactic, less flexible and exam-driven (see for example De Lange & Stuart, 2008; Raht, Smith, & MacEntee, 2009). This highlights the difficulty of how to implement participatory approaches to Life Skills when teaching styles in other subject areas are not as open and receptive. Fourth, the Life Skills curriculum is often designed as an add-on activity and regarded (by teachers, learners, and parents) as being imposed from the outside. These challenges result in the limited scope and coverage of the Life Skills curriculum and have led to the difficulties in its implementation (Boler & Archer, 2008).

In our work in teacher education in rural schools in South Africa, we have observed how the broader environment limits individuals' (especially school-age girls') strategies and choices when it comes to avoiding sexual relationships that can lead to HIV and AIDS (Moletsane, Mitchell, Smith, & Chisholm, 2008). In an interview with a prominent local educator and activist, she discusses why it is important that prevention effort not be limited to behavioral change:

> Building life skills is not going to work unless we understand the broader environment, including household structures and socio-economic conditions. Most of the learners in our areas are orphans and live with poverty-ridden extended family members. The issue is not about if learners get the refusal skills, the issue is about how to keep the perpetuators away from the female learners. Even if learners learned new skills at schools, the environment at home and in the larger society is very different. Most of the pregnancies in our area are unwanted and most of the cases are resulted because of rape and violence. (Islam, 2007)

Ironically, the neoliberal prescription to address the pandemic is narrowly focused on individual prevention-led strategies. This is in line with the neoliberal market-based agenda, which warrants developing an individual who is an 'enterprising and competitive entrepreneur', working for himself while ignoring others (Apple, 2001).

Though agency-led skills-building approaches fall short of addressing all the dimensions of HIV and AIDS, attempts to insist on abstinence-only education programs, as massively advocated by the United States during the Bush era also led to providing limited and distorted knowledge about HIV and AIDS (Boler & Archer, 2008). Based upon the conservative agenda of the religious right and the US Republican government, the controversial abstinence-only approach focused on the ABC-model (Abstain; Be faithful; and use Condom). PEPFAR (President Emergency Plan for AIDS Relief) was initiated during the Bush regime with a USD 15 billion budget for five years beginning in 2003, making it the largest single contribution by any country for HIV and AIDS. The PEPFAR model was exported world wide, especially in Africa with a focus on abstaining from sexual relationships until marriage, being faithful to one partner, and using condoms in the case of high-risk groups such as sex workers. The insistence on an abstinence model by the US government politicized the worldwide efforts to fight HIV and AIDS. Given the US's high stake in international development and politics, this approach also influenced the policies of other donor agencies. The result was a decline in the funding for condoms and other efforts that were not compatible with ABC approach. For example, in 2002 the US stopped funding of USD 34 billion to UNFPA, the largest condom donor in the World, based on the allegation that UNFPA was supporting forced abortions in China (Boler & Archer, 2008).

Unfortunately, as Boler and Archer (2009) observe many important international declarations and commitments fell short in addressing HIV AND AIDS education in a comprehensive way. We have already discussed how the World Bank influenced the Jomtien framework to emphasize primary education at the cost of

129

adult and popular education from EFA. The case of Millennium Development Goals (MDGs) is also critical. In September 2000, the Millennium Declaration was adopted by 191 countries in the United Nations General Assembly Special Session (UNGASS) with a pledge to end poverty (Amin, 2006). While enlisting poverty eradication, education improvement, and combating HIV AND AIDS as important goals, the UNGASS failed to duly recognize the responsibilities of all key players and make them accountable to find just and equitable solution (Christian Aid, 2006). Ignoring the adverse policies of the IMF, the World Bank, and the corporate sector and their role in generating poverty, they all became key partners in the plan to achieve MDGs along with local governments, the UN-agencies, and Civil Society Organizations. While tough monitoring mechanisms have been introduced for local governments, the private sector was just asked to demonstrate their 'corporate social responsibility' with no follow-ups or mechanisms to judge their performance. When no substantial progress was being made and many of the targets missed (Christian Aid, 2006), critics started to question the very basic purpose of the MDGs. For example, Amin (2006) argued that MDGs were 'ideological cover for neoliberal initiatives' proposed by the triad (the United States, Europe, and Japan) and co-sponsored by the International Financial Institutions. Most of the goals are too ambitious with no connection to the broader environment and the means to achieve them. He argued that goals 4, 5 and 6 in particular, which are related to child mortality; maternal health; and HIV and AIDS and other diseases respectively, were meant for extreme privatization, with full recognition for the intellectual property rights of the multinational companies (Amin, 2006).

Since 1945, modernization theory has had a dominant influence on development policies focusing on capitalist development through reliance on private enterprise and the market. It is now clear that these policies have not benefited the poor and are counter-effective (Youngman, 2000). There is a need to seek alternative development to redress the inequalities and flawed policies. In the case of HIV and AIDS, one devastating impact of the neoliberal agenda in relation to the pandemic is a shift of efforts from a human development approach to an individualistic clinical and behavioral remedy.

In the absence of material resources and increasing inequalities between rich and poor as O'Manique (2004) observed, none of these strategies will work. Thus, there is a contestation of the fact that prevention-only-strategies were advanced as the only affordable approaches for the poor, while ARVs were readily available for their European-counter parts (Boone & Batsell, 2001). Geshekter and Turshen (2000) pointed out, for example, that a mix of different ARVs could allow an infected person to live with AIDS but at a cost of USD 12,000 per annum, while in Africa, in 1993, the average person had only fourteen cents to spend on health care. The deep inequalities in health care were also observed by Ansari (2002), when he noticed that South Africa has a unique health system: the world's best for the rich; and the world's worst for the poor blacks in rural areas. Further, many of the health professionals, including doctors and nurses are unable to provide even basic health care services in rural areas because of the absence of necessary resources and equipment (Ansari & Phillips, 2001).

A first step is to bring back the focus of the pandemic from an individual's body to the social context (O'Manique, 2004; Mitchell & Pithouse, 2009). A people-driven transformation is the key to ensuring indigenous and communal efforts to comprehensive approaches to addressing HIV and AIDS. For example, Mindry (2008) explores how small local NGOs, in the rural areas of KwaZulu-Natal, South Africa, which has one of the highest HIV-prevalence rates in the region, are working to address the challenge of HIV and AIDS in their own ways. Citing an example of a small NGO, CINDI (the Children in Distress network), the author reported that the organization has extended critical mental, educational, and material support to infected children and their communities. CINDI is also running awareness strategies at the grassroots level, mobilizing local support and ensuring that no child, especially orphans, faces discrimination in schools, clinics and society at large.

Similarly, in our work with several rural schools in South Africa, we have observed that one of the schools in collaboration with a local NGO has established a multi-purpose service center for the learners (Islam, 2007). The center provides counselling, medicines, and food parcels to the learners. A three-member committee, made up of regular school staff has volunteered to run the center. The committee gets candies, biscuits, and snacks at a wholesale price from the town and sells them through the school tuck shop at a slightly higher than market rate. Parents and learners know that the price is a bit higher as the profit goes to the center. The center occasionally gets food parcels from the local NGO, Gifts for Us. But since neither local NGO nor the school have the resources to sustain all the functions carried out at the center, the activities of the center are often limited to counselling services (Islam, 2007). However, their localized struggle needs linkages and support with civil society at a broader level for a widespread change at the macro-level.

There is evidence that suggests grassroots engagement coupled with activism at the macro-level can challenge and reshape dominant discourses and practices. For example, Treatment Action Campaign (TAC), one of the largest civil society organization in South Africa, has been striving to ensure the availability of HIV treatment as a matter of social justice. Established in 1998, it quickly became a nationwide popular movement. In July 2001, when the South African government unfairly decided to launch a program for preventing mother-to-child transmission of HIV in selected locations of South Africa, the TAC challenged the government and compelled it to expand the program to other needy areas of South Africa. Similarly, TAC successfully won a battle against a German vitamin-maker and a multi-national entrepreneur, Matthias Rath, who publicly questioned the effectiveness of HIV medications and introduced his nutrition supplement as an alternative. Rath's action was not only a big blow for those advocating affordable antiretroviral therapy, but also a guise to earn massive profits on its nutrition supplement by deceiving HIV-infected people. With the then Mbeki South African government's backing, Rath extensively used print media and other forms of state-funded advertising, including billboards to promote his message and convince people to take his supplement as a cure for HIV and AIDS. TAC swiftly approached and lobbied with the South African Advertising Authority and succeeded in banning Rath's advertisements. In addition, TAC also sued the government as it failed to stop Rath's Foundation's illegal activities such as 'unauthorised pseudo-medical experiments' on people, selling unregistered drugs, and misleading people about antiretroviral drugs (Geffen, 2010; Leclerc-Madlala, 2005). TAC also exposed and challenged the Mbeki government of AIDS denialism, which created confusion and doubts over what causes AIDS and hence deprived a majority of affected people from ARVs (Geffen, 2010).

During the parallel import and compulsory licensing crises (under TRIPS) in South Africa as discussed earlier, South African liberal civil society played a key role in blocking the nefarious designs of the pharmaceutical companies and challenged them legally as well as on the streets. When the South African government passed laws for parallel import and compulsory licensing, the pharmaceutical companies took the South African government to court, threatening to divest from the country, and put sanctions on South Africa. The country's largest trade union along with grassroots organizations teamed up and launched a popular alliance to challenge this neoliberal agenda. With wider global networking and support from international organizations such as ACT Up and Doctors Without Borders, the national alliance was able to extend their protest worldwide. As a result of this immense pressure and fierce resistance along with the legal weakness of the case, the pharmaceutical companies withdrew their stand and surrendered the case (Usdin, 2003).

CONCLUSION

In this chapter, we have argued that HIV and AIDS education has to be understood in relation to the wider social, political and economic context. Drawing on the recent history of neoliberalism and globalization, we looked at HIV and AIDS as a developmental issue that has to be understood within a social context. Attempts to isolate the educational response to HIV and AIDS within the neoliberal articulation of self-improvement and individualistic fixations have not provided comprehensive prevention. The individualistic approach, as insisted upon under the neoliberal agenda, is a way to divert attention from failed policies and the distortion promoted by market-led forces and the greed for profit of MNCs, which control the drugs and their affordability, and are now influencing HIV and AIDS education. The lack of a supportive environment, which includes opportunities for health, education, and quality of life and market-led socio-political policies and practices have played an important role in exacerbating the spread of the pandemic. Efforts towards behavioral change cannot fully address the pandemic unless supported by an enabling broader environment. We argue for a 'looking back' approach with the idea that such forms of critical analysis can contribute towards 'looking ahead', specifically in terms of informing people-centered policy development.

REFERENCES

Abdi, A., Puplampu, K., & Dei, G. (eds.) (2006). *African education and globalization critical perspectives*. New York: Lexington Books.

Amin, S. (2006). The millennium development goals: A critique from the South. *Monthly Review*, 1-16. Retrieved from, www.monthlyreview.org/0306amin.php.

Anderson, S. & Cavanagh, J. (2000). *Top 200: The rise of corporate global power*. Institute of Policy Studies.

Ansari, W. E. (2002). Community development and professional education in South Africa. In S. Mitchell (ed.), *Effective educational partnerships: Experts, advocates, and scouts*. Westport, CT: Praeger Publishers.

Ansari, W. E. & Phillips, C. J. (2001). Partnerships, community participation and intersectoral collaboration in South Africa. *Journal of Interprofessional Care, 15*(2), 119-132.

Apple, M. (2001). Comparing neo-liberal projects and inequality in education. *Comparative Education, 37*(4), 409-423.

AVERT (2005). *Providing drug treatment for millions*. West Sussex: Avert.

AVERT (2009). *Sub-saharan Africa and HIV & AIDS statistics*. West Sussex: UK: Avert. Retrieved from http://www.avert.org/africa-hiv-aids-statistics.htm.

AVERT (2010). *Universal access to AIDS treatment: targets and challenges*. Retrieved from http://www.avert.org/universal-access.htm.

Bakilana, A., Bundy, D., Brown, J., & Fredriksen, B. (2005). *Accelerating the education sector response to HIV/AIDS in Africa: A review of World Bank assistance*. Washington, D.C.: The World Bank HIV/AIDS Global Program. Retrieved from http://siteresources.worldbank.org/INTHIVAIDS/ Resources/375798-1103037153392/EducandAIDS.pdf.

Bloom, D., Bloom, R., Steven, D., & Wetson, S. (2004). *Business and HIV/AIDS: Who me? A global review of the business response to HIV/AIDS*. Geneva: Global Health Initiative. Retrieved from http://data.unaids.org/Topics/Partnership-Menus/wef-ghi_businesshiv-aids_(short)_04_en.pdf.

Boler, T. & Archer, D. (2008). *The politics of prevention A global crises in AIDS and education*. Ann Arbor, MI: Pluto Press.

Bond, P. (2006). *Looting Africa: The economics of exploitation*. London: Zed Books.

Boone, C. & Batsell, J. (2001). Politics and AIDS in Africa: Research agendas in political science and international relations. *Africa Today, 48*(2), 3-33.

Broad, R. (2002). *Global Backlash Citizen Initiative for a Just World Economy* Lanham: Rowman and Littlefield Publishers.

Brummer, D. (2002). *Labour Migration and HIV/AIDS in Southern Africa.*: International Organisation for Migration Regional Office for Southern Africa. Retrieved from http://www.aidsmark.org/ipc_en/ pdf/sm/hr/mwmp/Labor%20Migration%20and%20HIV-AIDS%20in%20Southern%20Africa.pdf.

Christian Aid (2006). *UNGASS+5 Empty promises: Funding HIV prevention, treatment, and care*. London; Christian Aid.

De Lange, N. & Stuart, J. (2008). Innovative teaching strategies for HIV & AIDS prevention and education. In L. Wood (ed.), *Dealing with HIV & AIDS in the classroom*. Cape Town: Juta.

Geda, A. (2003). The historical origin of African Debt crises. *Eastern Africa Social Science Research Review, 60 XIX*(1), 59-89.

Geffen, N. (2010). *Debunking delusions: The inside story of the Treatment Action Campaign*. Cape Town: Jacana Media.

Held, D. & McGrew, A. (2002). *Globalization/anti-globalization*. Polity Press: Cambridge: Polity Press.

Iliffe, J. (2006). *The African AIDS epidemic: A history*. Athens: Ohio University Press.

Islam, F. (2007). *Teacher education in the age of AIDS: Dispelling illusions* (A participatory evaluation of the Rural Teacher Education Project in 3 schools in Vulindlela District in the province of KwaZulu-Natal, South Africa). Unpublished report. McGill University/University of KwaZulu-Natal.

Islam, F. (2009). *Teacher education for rural schools: A struggle for change* (An evaluation of the second phase of the Rural Teacher Education Project (RTEP) in two rural schools in Vulindlela district of KwaZulu-Natal). Unpublished report. McGill University/ University of KwaZulu-Natal.

Klees, S. J. (2002). World Bank education policy: new rhetoric, old ideology. *International Journal of Educational Development, 22*, 451-474.

Leclerc-Madlala, S. (2005). Popular responses to HIV/AIDS and Policy. *Journal of South African Studies, 31*(4), 845–856.

Malherbe, S. & Segal, N. (2001). *Corporate governance in South Africa.* OECD Development Centre Discussion Paper. Retrieved from http://www.tips.org.za/publication/

Martorell, J. (2002). How drug companies subordinate human life to profit. *Capitalism, Nature, and Socialism, 13*(1), 105–113.

Mindry, D. (2008). Neoliberalism, activism, and HIV/AIDS in postapartheid South Africa. *Social Text, 26*(1), 75-93.

Mitchell, C. & Pithouse, K. (eds.) (2009). *Teaching and HIV&AIDS.* Johannesburg: Macmillan.

Moletsane, R. (in press). Culture, nostalgia and sexuality education in the age of AIDS. In C. Mitchell, T. Strong-Wilson, K. Pithouse, & S. Allnutt (eds.), *Memory and pedagogy.* London and New York: Routledge.

Nattrass, N. (2007). *Mortal combat: AIDS denialism and the struggle for antiretrovirals in South Africa.* Pietermartizburg: University of KwaZulu-Natal Press.

O'Manique, C. (2004). *Neoliberalism and AIDS crises in sub-Saharan Africa: Globalization's pandemic.* New York: Palgrave Macmillan.

Parker, R., Easton, D., & Klein, C. (2000). Structural barriers and facilitators in HIV prevention: A review of international research. *AIDS, 14*(suppl 1), S22-32.

Pillay, R. (2003). *Using GIS to spatially portray the prevalence of HIV/AIDS and Tuberculosis and its demographic consequences in selected countries in sub-Saharan Africa.* Retrieved from http://www.gisdevelopment.net/application/health/overview/ma03096abs.htm.

Ramachandrana, V., Shahb, M. K., & Turnerb, G. L. (2007). Does the private sector care about AIDS? Evidence from firm surveys in East Africa. *AIDS, 21*(suppl 3), S61–S72.

Raht, D., Smith, J., & MacEntee, K. (2009). Engaging youth in addressing HIV&AIDS: Creative and participatory approaches in the classroom. In C. Mitchell & K. Pithouse (eds.), *Teaching and HIV & AIDS.* Johannesburg, South Africa: Macmillan.

Rosen, S. & Simon, J. (2002). *Shifting the burden of HIV/AIDS.* Boston: Center for International Health: Boston University.

Seabrook, J. (2003). Mechanisms of impoverishment. In J. Seabrook (ed.), *The no-nonsense guide to world poverty.* London: Verso.

Steinberg, J. (2008). *The three letter plague.* Cape Town: Jonathan Ball.

Stromquist, N. (1999). The impact of structural adjustment programmes in Africa and Latin America. In C. Heward & S. Bunwaree (eds.), *Gender, education and development: Beyond access to empowerment:* Zed Books.

UNAIDS (2009). *AIDS epidemic update.* Geneva: UNAIDS and WHO.

UNC (2005). *Teachers confronting the HIV epidemic: skills for teaching and survival.* Center for Disease Control and Prevention.

UNFPA (2008). *Education: A 'social vaccine' to prevent the spread of HIV.* Retrieved from, http://web.unfpa.org/news/news.cfm?ID=1172.

UNICEF (2002). *Lessons learned about life skills-based education for preventing HIV/AIDS related risk and related discrimination.* UNICEF.

Usdin, S. (2003). *The no nonsense guide to HIV/AIDS.* Toronto: Verson Books.

World Bank (2009). *Education and the World Bank: What is the World Bank doing to support education?* Retrieved from http://go.worldbank.org/TJAXOI2A50.

Youngman, F. (2000). The political economy of adult education and development. London: Zed Books.

GLOBALIZATION, MEDIA AND YOUTH IDENTITY IN PAKISTAN

Al-Karim Datoo, Assistant Professor, Aga Khan University, Pakistan

INTRODUCTION

Youth have been identified as a social group, most influenced by the phenomenon of globalization, especially cultural globalization, through media (Dolby & Rizvi, 2008). They increasingly engage with different kinds of media, movies, news channels, the internet – which in turn, are linking their identities to the currents of globalization and political economies of culture that flow across and around them. The same holds true for the majority of youth living in Pakistan. In Pakistan, the youth population is estimated to be around 83 million, of which, 41 million are between the ages of 15-29 years (Qamar, Umrani, Fatima, & Bashir, 2010). Social shifts/change are increasingly more evident as in the case of gender relationships and the rising incidence of unmarried couples (youth) from working class and lower-middle income backgrounds and/or the shift from extended family to the nuclear family structure, especially in urban contexts (Hasan, 2010), to reference but a few examples. Moreover, Pakistani youth, from urban as well as rural contexts, are actively engaged with media and information technology despite the digital divide.

Being active consumers of media and other forms of information technology, youth are likely developing a transnational subjectivity, which in turn is placing them 'betwixt and between' the global and the local, between the world out there, and the world at home/family. This chapter explores ruptures or breaks that are experienced by youth when they interact with global media, specifically in terms of their normative interpretations of the social world and related processes of socialization.

This chapter draws from an ethnographic study of a group of urban high school going Pakistani youth living in Karachi (a metropolis of Pakistan, with a population of 18 million people from diverse ethnic and linguistics backgrounds) and their engagement with the global media and their responses to it, especially with respect to Bollywood and other global news channels. The data was collected through participant observation in and outside the school and classrooms (including some home visits), focus group discussions around youth engagement

D. Kapoor (ed.), Critical Perspectives on Neoliberal Globalization, Development and Education in Africa and Asia, 135–149.

with the media and internet (including social media: Facebook and Orkut; social networking sites) and semi-structured interviews.

The analysis shared here focuses on the performance of a drama-skit by research participants, namely high school youth. The skit was a re-make of an old Indian/Bollywood film titled *Mughal-e-Azam* (translated as the great Mughal), which is an epic tale around the story of the Mughal emperor Akber and his son Salem's love affair with a courtesan called Anar Kali. The script performed by the youth was re-named Anar Kali (explanations follow below). The performance offers a satire, a cultural critique on the way globalization in general and media globalization in particular, is influencing Pakistani youth attitudes towards socialization and their family norms and values. A brief discussion centered around a particular data-set is analyzed in order to understand and demonstrate how the global media is influencing youth Muslim identity. The chapter elaborates on select critical ethnographic insights into the ways that media is functioning as a key globalizing force and the manner in which youth agency reacts/acts towards it.

Four related sections are considered. The first section presents theoretical/analytical references; specifically, the theoretical notion of "disjuncture" proposed by Appadurai (1996), to explore 'breaks'/ruptures caused by interactions of various types of 'scapes' and the notion of 'structuration' – a synthesis explaining the interrelationship between structure and agency (Giddens, 1986) to analyze how youth respond to media. The second section presents ethnographic data around the performance of a skit by the youth, as cultural 'text' produced by the youth themselves, 'text' which acts as a 'critique' of the dominant media in a globalizing world. The third section engages a critical analysis of the skit-text with the view to highlight the nature and complexity of local-global cultural dynamics and the ensuing 'disjuncture' experienced by the youth in question. The final section is a deliberation on the emergent data-theory connectivities and some related conclusions.

MEDIA AND YOUTH AGENCY: LOCAL-GLOBAL DYNAMICS AND DISJUNCTURE

Media and migrations have been identified as key globalizing forces (Appadurai, 1996). Through these forces global cultural flows across and around 'borders' – geographical, socio-psychological as well as cultural, influence the way individuals relate the self with the world. In this section, the focus is on discussing the youths' interaction with the global media, especially with reference to some ruptures that they experience and respond to as a result of their exposure to the media. In order to understand youth interaction with global cultural flows through media, the notion of 'disjuncture' as espoused by Appadurai (1996), will be used as theoretical construct to help analyze the complex processes and interrelationship involved in the youths' interaction with global media.

Notion of 'Disjuncture': Theoretical Foregrounding

Globalizing forces are generating processes of global cultural flows that are characterized by the interaction of various kinds of 'scapes' (Appdurai, 1996). These 'scapes' include: a) *Ethnoscapes* that refer to the 'borderless' world and people on the move (through migration or travel) which in turn are influencing people on the move (through migration or travel) who in turn are influencing social, political and economic scenarios; b) *Mediascapes* which refer to the context created by the flow of images, ideas and narratives of life-styles across the world through the electronic medium – these moving images and texts trigger 'new' desires and possibilities of being in the world; c) *Technoscapes* signify exchanges of machines, devices and information (techniques/knowledge) across time and space regarding development and the application of manufacturing and production processes in society; d) *Financescapes* refer to the complexities of the global capitalist economy, affecting local currency markets, national stock exchanges, and commodity prices; and e) *Ideoscapes* refer to the set of ideas and ideologies that are often rooted in a philosophical outlook promoted in the period of the Enlightenment. These could be ideas/ideologies pertaining to notions such as: nation, democracy, freedom, rights and so forth, which are often deployed while addressing political motives/projects articulated by various social groups.

These 'scapes' are not only interactive in nature, but are at the same time disjunctive. The disjuncture is generated due to the overlapping and intersecting of 'scapes' in a multidimensional and asymmetrical manner; a kind of rupture or break between the contexts and contents of 'scapes'. The notion of disjuncture – as a complex rupture-creating experience – and its multidimensionality provides a partial analytical optic to understand the complex processes that are involved in the way the youth group in the study encounters and responds to the global media. This rupture refers to an occurrence that is disjunctive when different 'scapes' interact. For example, a certain way of dressing (fashion) promoted by the media, financed by trans/multi-national capital enterprise, may not be seen as acceptable within a particular mind-set/context as has happened recently on Facebook when certain actions by some (hurting Muslim sensitivities), disturbed Muslim sensibilities across the world to such an extent that in Pakistan (at the time of writing), Facebook was officially blocked, at least temporarily. This example illustrates how the media-scape can generate emotional and ideological 'disjuncture'.

A second point to keep in mind in relation to the analysis discussed here is an awareness regarding the notion of 'scapes', i.e., particular perspectives engaged relative to a certain location from where 'viewing' is done. Therefore, like globalization, media too is not viewed by all from the same vantage point but rather from different historical, political and ideological locations from where youth exercise their agency. It is in these disjunctive nodes where 'difference' gets generated (in terms of meanings and ways of socialization and which in turn influence identity-making) in the youth-media encounter. In the case addressed here, analysis of interaction between two 'scapes' will be considered specifically, i.e., the disjunctures between media and ideo-scapes. The disjuncture between media-scape and local ethno-scape/identity references or for that matter, between media-scape and local idea-scape or among media-scape, finance-scape and agency, generates a world that now seems "rhizomic, even schizophrenic, calling for theories of rootlessness, alienation and psychological distance between individuals and groups on the one hand, and fantasies (or nightmares) of electronic propinquity on the other" (Deleuze & Guattari, 2005, p. 10). Furthermore, Dolby and Rizvi (2008), find that "media-scapes not only provide a resource out of which social agents "script" their own "possible lives" but also the "imagined lives" of others living elsewhere" (p. 19). Therefore, agency is not only influenced by the media-text that it receives from various scapes, particularly media-scapes through the forces of cultural globalization, but youth are also active and innovative agents, manoeuvring the same media-text for their sake by creating spaces of their own (Bourdieu, 1977; Giddens, 1986). With regards to the active role played by agency in and through the forces of cultural globalization as Giddens (1986) and Bourdieu (1977) point out, media-scapes have become vehicles for cultural power (Dolby & Rizvi, 2008) and globalization is thus characterized by competing tendencies of cultural homogenization (convergence) and heterogenization (divergence). In such a context, culture becomes a contested terrain, a site of power negotiation and production.

With this in mind, the structuration perspective proposed by Giddens (1986) provides a suitable framework for representing these tensions within the ongoing debates on global-local dynamics and in relation to the active role of agency. The structuration perspective views the global as partial (Giddens, 1986). It argues that the global is experienced, contested, appropriated and re-articulated in the local (Arnove & Torres, 2003; Sassen, 2003). Hence, this view presumes a dialectical relationship between the local and the global. It acknowledges the role of the particular in its historic, political, and cultural expressions and manifestations. It presumes interpenetration between the local and the global, viewing the relationship between the global and the local as dialectic and not binary, opposite, or un-dialectical. This view accommodates the notion of a fluid cultural dynamics, which is central to this inquiry. It perceives globalization as a process inherent with tensions, contradictions and countervailing forces and interests, having multiple centres and peripheries and therefore, multiple globals and locals. Hence, in light of the above, agents/youth are not passive recipients of the dominant structures of media-scapes but are creatively using and reinventing media spaces for self-representation.

For instance, Abu-Lughod (2002) observes how generational conflict emerges in modern Egypt in the wake of the global and local dynamic by referencing popular cultural songs and their commercialization on national media as indicative of this phenomenon. In contrast, Ginsburg (2002) points out that different communities, traditionally the objects of ethnographic representation, are now taking up media to screen their memories and thus, are creating an indigenous media. Ginsburg, Abu-Lughod and Larkin (2002) go further to assert that:

[the structuration perspective] offered an exciting way to rethink some of the questions about reception, reflexivity, and the politics and poetics of representation that have been central to visual anthropology ... indigenous media opened up thinking about the role of media as a dimension of cultural activism in identity-based social movements and became a major preoccupation. (p. xv)

The above remark is central to the theory of structuration. It highlights the important role that the structuration perspective offers to ethnographic representation of how power oscillates between structure and agency in the contested terrain of cultural production and reproduction. Moreover, it further emphasizes the neglected participation and space of "subjects" as central actors for cultural production and as generators of social and cultural activism. Above all, the works devoted to the role of media in cultural globalization seldom portray "the dialectic between the disciplinary power of technology ... and the unexpected way technologies are reworked within local cultural logics" (Ginsburg, Abu-Lughod, & Larkin, 2002, p. xv).

The following section deploys these theoretical/ conceptual constructs in an analysis of a media-text, i.e., a drama-skit performed by the youth during the school's annual function that I attended as a participant observer in relation to the development of this ethnographic study.

Exploring the Remaking of a Postcolonial Drama-Skit: A Tale of Anar Kali

For the purposes of the analysis that follows, I have selected 'text' data of a drama skit performed by the high school youth who were key informants in my research. The drama skit is a satire on the current influence of media (especially the impact of Bollywood films and Indian drama serials telecasted through channels like Star Plus, Zee and Sony television channels) on Pakistani society, especially with reference to its impact on socialization of youth and gender roles/relationships and on the traditional institution of the family (where elders typically have authority). Before sharing the skit-text, a brief background of the actor-participants is shared in order to give the reader some understanding regarding the location of these youth actors/agency in order to provide a sense of where they are acting out/critiquing/interpreting the world "from".

The group that directed and performed the skit included nine high school youth or five girls and four boys. These students were in their final years of higher secondary studies in the medical sciences track. Most of the students were aspiring to be medical professionals/doctors, except for a few who wanted to shift their field of studies from science to business management (in the near future). A majority of these students had had an opportunity to travel abroad to the US or Middle-Eastern countries and/or have relatives living there. One of the students had returned to Pakistan after living in the US for five years. Taken together, they represented four ethnic and linguistic groups. All the students were Pakistani nationals at that point in time. The students were active consumers of media; they were watching Western and Bollywood movies, as well as soaps and drama serials produced by local and global media. While the students could be seen as consumers of media, they were not passive participants but active ones, who critiqued the media.

This critique was enacted/performed through a skit presented by the students titled *Anar Kali*. Anar Kali was one of Mughal King Akbar's courtesans – Akbar's son, Salem, fell in love with her. She met a tragic death on the path of this love, as the King buried her alive as punishment. Based on this love story, the Indian film industry (Bollywood) produced a film called *Mughl-e-Azam* (The Great Mughal). The skit was named *Anar Kali* by the students and was part of the activities presented at the school's Founder's Day celebration, an event that the school celebrates every year and where students and alumni get together.

The performance was video recorded. Below, I have re-constructed an account of the performance based on the field-notes and a viewing of the recorded video.

The students begin the skit with an announcement stating that they will transport the viewers to the olden days through the movie *Mughal-e-Azam*. The movie, *Mughal-e-Azam*, the students tell the audience, is a film lover's delight. The students add that for those who haven't seen the movie, they will bring them up-to-date with this classic love story and proceed to do so. The female MC (master/mistress of ceremonies) asks the audience to imagine what would happen were this story to be portrayed in modern times. Soon the following number gets played in background "We will, we will rock you!" as King Akbar comes on to the stage.

The skit begins with the booming voice of King Akbar who is shouting for his son, Salem. Prince Salem, dressed in jeans, a hooded T-shirt, and wearing Nike shoes enters the stage, dancing to the popular Bollywood song: *Bachna ae hasino lo main agaya* [watch out beautiful ones here I come].

The music stops, and Prince Salem turns to his Father, "Hey Pops, I wanted to talk to you," he says, "I want you to meet someone. Her name is Annie; she has a strange name, Anar Kali."

At this very moment, Anar Kali or Annie enters the stage to a Punjabi song in the background: *Pitche pitche* [As I look for my nose ring, he follows me]. Annie is wearing a *gharaara* [long flowing skirt with a short tunic and a *dupatta* (shawl)]. She yells at Salem in Punjabi. Salem introduces Annie and the King to each other in English. Music with another popular Bollywood song: *Chand mera dil Chandni Ho tum* [Sweetheart you are my moon] is heard in the background. The King, falling in love at first sight, starts dancing to the tune chasing Annie around in circles in typical Bollywood fashion. Salem responds by saying "Hey dad, what you doing?" The King replies by telling Salem in Urdu: "Don't you have any work to do, go away." When Salem refuses, Akbar commands him to leave utilizing the excuse of sending him to get a CD so that he can be with Annie.

Salem leaves and another Bollywood song is heard in the background, depicting the romance between King Akbar and Annie. Annie flirts with the King, telling him in Punjabi, not to feel too bad, that it isn't his fault but it is just the magic of her beauty that burns everyone.

Salem comes back, complaining to his father about his behaviour. He says to his father: "Hands off, this is my girl!" His father responds by saying in Urdu that he (Salem) would find many more beauties and wasn't that the reason why he had sent Salem to America? "Bring a woman from America, this one is mine. Can't you make this one sacrifice for your *pitah* (father)? Think how she would look in your mother's role." Salem protests, "But Dad, this is my girl!" Akbar responds with "So what?" (Actors start laughing and both actors exit the stage).

Birbal (Akbar's *Vazir,* his minister) enters the stage, meets Annie, while in the background a Bollywood song is heard and a new romance begins. The skit ends with Birbal and Annie going off together (field-notes, August 6, 2006).

Based on the above representation of the experiences of the high school youth as a result of global cultural flows and disjuncture in particular, the following is an analytical discussion pertaining to the above skit performed by the research participants.

ANALYZING NODES OF DISJUNCTURE: LOCAL-GLOBAL DYNAMICS

Disjuncture is experienced by agents when their own values, ideas, meanings of the world and the self, meet a counter narrative of the same, produced by the media. The skit issues a statement about the present state of socio-cultural affairs whereby, the media-scape has greatly influenced the domains of concepts of love and fidelity which in turn shape contemporary social relationships, values, authority structures and roles within the family (which is seen as a fading social structure in the local context among these youth). Hence, the skit demonstrates existing tensions between local perceptions concerning the social structure of the students' context and the global projection of multiple cultural spaces. I elaborate on this tension in the following segment by drawing on more details pertaining to the skit.

The Role of Women in Traditional and Modern Societies

The *Anar Kali* skit presented by the research participants portrays shifting images of the gendered self and social values in contemporary society. One of the dimensions highlighted in this data is the image of a modern woman represented through the character of Annie, who expresses herself openly and flirts with three males, irrespective of their social positioning: the son (the Prince), the father (the Emperor) and a minister (the *Vazir*). Such a portrayal attempts to reflect contemporary social dynamics between male and female members of the society. Such a depiction generates a disjuncture between the media projected global image of a woman and the local perception of the image of a woman. Moreover, related to the image, is a disjuncture represented between the manner in which gender and social dynamics and relationships are enacted in contemporary society and the locally held norms and perceptions about inter-gender social interactions and relationships.

In this regard, during a focus group discussion, when asked how she felt about Annie having three affairs, one female participant responded:

So what's wrong with that? Haven't you heard the famous saying ... survival of the fittest? So Annie flirted with Salem [the son], Akbar [the father of Salem] and Birbal [the *Vazir*/minister], and she found Birbal the fittest ... so she went with him. (Focus group discussion, September 7, 2006)

This survival of the fittest image, where a woman exercises her choice in selecting or rejecting men, seems to be conveyed by the very immediate media-context with which the students interact, especially the Bollywood films and dramas.

These media sources can be accessed very easily through the local cable operators. Some examples of such drama series that are very popular among the students are telecast products by a popular TV channel "Star Plus." Some examples include: *Kuon Kay Saass Bhi Kabhi Bahuu Thi* [Because mother-in-law was once a daughter in law], *Kahin to hoga* [Somewhere someone will be there], and *Kahani Ghar Ghar Ki* [Story of every home]. These media texts portray such images where a woman may have multiple relationships during her lifetime. Apart from the above, both locally and globally produced TV commercials expose females as highly contributing members, both, at home and at places of work and also show men as subordinate. Thus the image of the woman is represented as self-sufficient, confidant and an opposite equal to men – a depiction that often comes into conflict with the local gender-based social structures.

Perceiving the role of woman in the local societal context, one male student remarked, "In Eastern culture, woman does home-management work and man goes outside to work." In reaction to the question that why that happens in the context of Eastern culture an interesting answer was produced: "According to our culture they are still less competent than males ... [but] I am not saying that females should not work." As a result of this apologetic remark, a debate ensued with respect to the nature and competency of women. Some male members of the group were of the opinion that the role of woman is confined to do certain chores and not others because according to one group member: "she is biologically weak", as "she cannot lift the bag/sack", for example. One girl reacted to this statement forcefully and said, "She can lift [the sack] if she wants to." The reference to biological 'weakness' was also somehow equated as referring to a lack of competence and hence, a justification for the limited role of women. Female group members reacted sharply and argued "Women can do everything. Women are joining military forces." One male member added, "Women are also becoming pilots today" (Focus group discussion, October 31, 2006).

The discourse then went on to contrast the role of women in the West with the role of women in the local context. A female participant pointed out the following:

A Western woman has to work at home as well as outside. In the East, a woman's priority is her house and they don't actually have to work, they are not made to work, but it is an option for them if they want, but there is a compulsion in the West. (Focus group discussion, October 31, 2006)

The Image of Islam and Muslim: Disjuncture between Mediated and Lived Realities

Another aspect (beyond the skit now) that the students were quite critical about was the way global media in general and Western media (BBC and CNN) in particular were seen to be distorting the image of Islam and Muslims. The students were concerned about the narrow and misleading portrayal of Islam as negative, as a religion of conflict/terror, neglecting its broad and rich socio-cultural and lived diversity.

The media was critiqued for equating 'Islam' with terrorism and portraying 'Muslims' as suicide bombers/terrorists. This caricaturing of Islam/Muslim hurt the sensibilities of the Muslim youth students in this research and generated some strong emotions and reactions against the Western media. The students regarded these media-based images as a disjunction—a disjunction between what is portrayed by the media on the one hand and what was their perceived reality, where they felt the majority of Muslims were peace-loving, kind and ethical.

The Media and Islamophobia

Frustrated by this predicament, the students shared the following perspectives in a focus group discussion: One student said, "Media has blamed us, media tells, we are terrorists". One of his colleagues added, "Those who keep beard are labelled as terrorist" (Focus group discussion, September 14, 2006). This was said in the context of the way the 'beard' has been politicized in and through media. Also, these stereotypes were confronted in travel practices/experiences or observed by some of the students, where it is a well known fact that often Pakistani citizens (with Green passports) in general, and those who wear beards are reported to have been treated suspiciously by the immigration authorities or during visa processing. The youth were well aware of these issues, and were blaming the media for manufacturing such images that could lead to such stereotypical thinking.

On a similar point, one female student lamented the media's portrayal of Muslim women wearing the veil, since, according to her, such an image is depicted as a "sign of backwardness." She went on critiquing this tendency of Western media by adding that "it is my choice whether I wear a scarf or not. I should have that freedom" (Focus group discussion, September 14, 2006).

Such media images of Muslim women were reproducing social stereotypes in the very locality where the students were situated, and were influencing intra-local socializing. Paradoxically, quite often, the peers in the school were seeing the boys who wore beards or the girls who wore *hijab* (scarf) with some sense of ridicule. As one girl who was wearing *hijab* lamented:

> In our class those girls who wear scarf are known as "Talibans". People think *mere baarey mai; ke is bandi se baat nahi karna, agar karo gey to chamat (slap) maar dey gi*" [People think that we should not talk to this girl. If we do, she will slap us].

Her peer, a male student, interjected, "We call them Ninja Turtles" and the whole group laughed (Focus group discussion, September 14, 2006).

The disjuncture experienced by the students was between the way the media depicts Islam and Muslim identities and the students' own lived experience of Islam and being a Muslim in the contemporary world. However, paradoxically, as illustrated above, although the majority of the students critique the Western media and its portrayal of Islam and Muslims (especially females), they themselves are not immune to the rhetoric, as some of them were making fun of their own female peers wearing scarves and were seeing them through a media-shaped/consistent stereotypical lens, while all along being aware of the critique.

RE-CONCEPTUALIZING GLOBAL-LOCAL DYNAMICS AND THE MEDIA FLOWS: THEORETICAL REJOINDERS

Erosion of Socio-Cultural Values: Disjuncture between Modern and Traditional

The performance of *Anar-Kali* by the students can be regarded as a satire of their own contemporary society and culture. The performance produces two parallel and comparative discourses. It juxtaposes the old and the new narratives of *Anar-Kali*, each in its own way, reflecting a clash between what ought to be and what is. The clash can be seen in the realms of the modern and the traditional impacting socio-cultural norms and values pertaining to the father-son relationship, gender social interaction and relationships and the notion of love and fidelity.

Tension between Modern and Traditional

Describing the relevance of the skit *Anar-Kali* in a focus group session, the students mentioned that "it was re-made for modern times" (Focus group discussion, September 14, 2006). When asked what they meant by the term modern, one of the skit writers defined the term as that which is "current and in fashion and full of entertainment." Tradition, on the other hand, was anything that was "old and out of fashion" (Focus group discussion, September 14, 2006).

For the students, the notions of modern and traditional were also embodied in the names of the characters. Anar Kali, for example, was perceived as an old name, hence, as one student said smilingly:

We changed the name of Anar-Kali to Annie, because Anar-kali is a very old fashioned name, and Annie is short and mode. Here in our school also people use their nick, for example, Talat Jawed [one of the teachers] is called TJ and my friends call me Musfi. So the name should be short, because it sounds good and takes less time to call, as in today's modern times everybody is so busy. (Focus group discussion, September 14, 2006)

In this manner, the student expressed a perceived difference between modern and traditional as binary terms, where the difference is expressed through the temporal and social dimensions of their lives.

Role of Women: Disjuncture between Global and Local Images/Roles

Many changes were observed in the students' understanding of the gendered self, particularly relating to the role of women. Different opinions were pronounced about the role and social positioning of women in societies. The images that are globally circulated of a modern woman and the local perception of the image and role of a woman did not seem to align with each other, for some. Within this debate, the female participants were inclined towards adapting the modern role charged with the discourse of human rights in general and women's rights in particular. Some resonance of such a debate can be seen in the reform case of the Hudood Ordinance that some female participants thought worth mentioning. This law reform was tabled by the Musharraf government as part of an effort to bring gender equality to Pakistani society. This event is a manifestation of the interplay between the local (Islamic legal discourse) and the global (international and domestic laws, human and women's rights) discourses. In other words, this demonstrates a case where the Hudood Ordinance, which is based on Sharia (traditional Islamic law), has been appropriated, as being aligned with the modern global discourse of human rights.

Conversely, some male members of the group attempted to define the role of women in the light of locally prevalent socio-religious norms and practices, arguing for the re-claiming of the traditional role of women in society. It is interesting to note that both the female and the male participants were using history of Islam as a reference to advocate their respective perspectives (which again depended on their subjective readings of the past). The female members considered the origin of modern human rights discourse to have originated from Islamic teachings and hence, by doing so, authenticated their modern role. On the other hand, the male participants were doing the same to validate their own arguments against their female peers.

'Liquid' Relationships: Destabilization of the Local Social-Normative References of Father-Son Relationships

In the play, the contemporary relationship between father and son is described as being more informal and casual, even bordering on being disrespectful. This is acted out by the students through the use of slang, informal diction and through the very content of the dialogue. Salem tries to be modern and his sense of modernity is defined by speaking English, wearing Western clothes and adopting a casual attitude towards his father. His father, while claiming Eastern-ness through his dress, his speech and never having travelled abroad, demonstrates his perception of modern norms through his open flirtation with a young woman who is currently dating his son, his openness in replacing his wife for the younger woman and openly discussing his plans with his son. With true dramatic irony, neither of the characters is aware of what he is projecting; however, the student actors and the audience certainly are. The disjuncture is manifested by this clash of perceptions – lived, imagined and influenced by media.

Notions of Marriage, Love, and Fidelity

Through the dramatization of *Anar Kali*, the students were able to juxtapose two opposing perspectives: the traditional and the modern, and to explore their struggle to reconcile these perspectives. In the traditional world, the social institution of marriage, and the concepts of love and fidelity are solidly defined. Marriage, for example, is permanent and forever. One pledges one's love and fidelity to a single person. Contemporary times, however, have challenged these notions and the students' exposure to the media has enabled them to imagine more complex and fluid relationships. More importantly, the distribution of gender power that defines the institution of marriage and the traditional concepts of love and fidelity are also challenged. The data below explore three themes: 1) the understanding of marriage, love and fidelity; 2) challenging gender roles as defined by religion; and 3) the role of women in society.

The reconstructed narrative of *Anar-Kali*, demonstrated the fluidity of social relationships in the modern world. It debunked the previously held social norms and notions of love and fidelity as commitment to one and only one relationship. The students, again, largely blame this fluidity in relationships on media portrayals of the same. Explaining how they had envisioned the new *Anar Kali*, the modern *Anar Kali*, one of the student actors asked me:

> Have you seen *Khushi*, a drama on Star Plus, where the girl Khushi got married to three men in her life [sic: after the death of each preceding partner]? So we thought why not we do the same with Annie [Anar-Kali], and therefore we came up with the idea that Annie flirts with Salem [the son], Akbar [the father] and Birbal [the minister]. (Focus group discussion, September 14, 2006)

To this explanation, one male group member reacted strongly by asking: "But then, where is the loyalty in love? Our tradition doesn't allow it. Woman has to be sincere and loyal." He went on to blame Bollywood for creating such images of women and influencing what he called "our cultural values." He remarked "*Bollywood ne rishton ka satyanas kar diya haye*" [Bollywood has destroyed relationships]. "Have you seen that movie *Kabhi Alvida na Kahena*? In that, husband – wife relationship has been destroyed. If one follows that, then anybody can have an affair with anybody else. This is crazy!" (Focus group discussion, September 14, 2006).

The institution of marriage and the notions of love and fidelity clash, when the students try to reconcile the notions of the past with the modern. Neither model seems to fit comfortably with the students as they try to re-define what marriage, love and fidelity mean to them. The resulting disjuncture occurs in trying to reconcile two opposing modes of behaviour.

The disjuncture causes further discord in the realm of religion, which also defines social relationships. When I asked the students how they felt about this new flirtatious Anar Kali as compared to the old one, one of the female students responded (as stated earlier in this chapter): "So what's problem with that. Haven't you heard the quote of Darwin 'survival of the fittest'? So Anar Kali went [ultimately] with Birbal [the minister] as he was the fittest" (Focus group discussion, September 7, 2006).

Image of Islam and Muslim Identity

The research participants were also articulate about global media misrepresentations when projecting Islam. For them, the West portrays distorted images of Islam as a religion whose followers are terrorists. Edward Said (1977) voiced similar observations:

> Much of what one reads and sees in the media about Islam represents the aggression as coming from Islam because that is what "Islam" is. Local and concrete circumstances are thus obliterated …. [It] obscures what "we" [the West] do, and highlights instead what Muslims and Arabs by their very flawed nature *are*. (p. xxii)

The above view clearly identifies what the students themselves were observing in their context concerning the power of representation that the West (global) has over Islam and Muslims (or local) (Ahmed & Donnan, 1994). It seems that the process of orientalizing the other is still in progress. A female participant recalled one such event, where a high school youth was teasing girls who were wearing *hijab* (scarves), by labelling them as Ninja Turtles – characters in a globally acclaimed cartoon series. This shows how locals (local-self) see themselves through the lens of the global (others), which Sen (2006) describes as the projection of a reactive identity. In summary, the research identified a disjuncture experienced by the students between the globally mediated image of Islam and Muslims and their self-perception of being Muslims. Furthermore, paradoxically, the mediated image of the Muslim, at times, also becomes a standard lens through which a fellow Muslim is seen and judged.

CONCLUSION

This chapter re-presented the students' interaction with the global cultural flow through media-scapes, where they experienced disjuncture: a sense and experience of rupture between the haves and have-nots, extra-local foreign norms and values and the local norms and values, imagined possibilities and realities between the global and the local. The high school youth participants experienced disjuncture mainly in the realms of socio-cultural values, their self-image as Muslims, between their past and present and a sense of the loss of local culture and heritage. Most of the students were experiencing ambivalence due to the disjuncture caused by local-global cultural interplay (Bauman, 1991). They seem to find tradition as a burden and modernity and modernization as direction-less and chaotic. Such a scenario depicts a sense of ambivalence, a characteristic feature of "liquid modernity" (Bauman, 2000), as solid social structures and relationships in which agency used to anchor itself remains solid no more but is in fact becoming fluid, which in turn generates a sense of ambivalence; a state of confusion and in-between-ness for the students (Bhabha, 1994).

Hence, as a result of the above disjunctures or ruptures, the chapter considers the interrelationship and the dialectic between the media-scapes and urban high school youth agency. In this regard, the chapter argues that the structuration perspective is at play between the media-text and the response-text, co-constructed by the students' agency (Bourdieu, 1977; Giddens, 1986) More so, it represents how global-local interaction is destabilizing a normative sense of values: the role of women in society is debated, boundaries of the modern and tradition are being blurred or the way tradition is reinvented to fit with the modern or how being modern is legitimized with appeals to religious tradition on occasion. Furthermore, in this a a astruggle, students are using media-text to critique the global media, drawing normative reference from Mughals who again, are taken as representative of normative authorities; as the values of those times are revered (as implied by the meanings students seem to associate with the discourse). The very shift of AnarKali to Anny, as an Anglo-Saxon reconstruction of the signifier has come to be understood and reckoned with as a marker of modernity; a notion rooted in Western/modern global/colonial power dynamics and a colonization of the mind.

Hence, it can be concluded that the globalization of values is one of the most contested zones within processes of cultural globalization, where local is universalized through a re-invention of tradition or the traditional (for example, Islamic history and the role of women). In addition, 'value paradoxes' are sites of cultural production and a field of inquiry vis-à-vis the other aspects of global/colonial inquiry (political-economic, for instance) along with the various discourses related to globalization (Gannon, 2008).

The values-related paradoxes studied in this exploration suggest that the audience/youth agency is reconstructing media to use the medium to carry out their own projects of self/identity. In this way, the very tools of globalization (e.g. media) are used to counter global/hegemonic narratives of norms and being (competing narratives of self). Therefore, the global media flow is creating both, a sense of anxiety and ambivalence of identity while nevertheless unleashing a reinvention of tradition, through a reinterpretation of history and values and a re-articulation of the same to mobilize some aspects of life – deploying a disjuncture which has emerged as a result of cultural globalization to rejuvenate local conceptions. In this sense, the structuration of global/local self, generates and perpetuates the dynamics of culture and power in which the self is reinvented and re-imagined and local/societies at large are reconfigured.

REFERENCES

Abu-Lughod, L. (2002). Egyptian melodrama – Technology of the modern subject? In F. D. Ginsburg, L. Abu-Lughod, & B. Larkin (eds.), *Media worlds – Anthropology on new terrain*. Berkeley: University of California Press.

Ahmed, A. S. & Donnan, H. (eds.) (1994). *Islam, globalization and postmodernity*. London: Routledge.

Appadurai, A. (1996). *Modernity at large: Cultural dimensions of globalization*. Minneapolis: University of Minnesota Press.

Arnove, R. F. & Torres, C. A. (eds.) (2003). *Comparative education: The dialectic of the global and the local* (2nd ed). Maryland: Rowman and Littlefield Publishers.

Bauman, Z. (1991). *Modernity and ambivalence*. Cambridge: Polity.

Bauman, Z. (2000). *Liquid modernity*. Malden, MA: Blackwell.

Bhabha, H.K. (1994). *Location of culture*. London: Routledge.

Bourdieu, P. (1977). *Outline of a theory of practice*. Cambridge: Cambridge University Press.

Deleuze, G. & Guattari, F. (2005). *A thousand plateaus: Capitalism and schizophrenia*. London: Continuum.

Dolby, N. & Rizvi, F. (2008). *Youth moves: Identities and education in global perspectives*. New York: Routledge Taylor & Francis Group.

Gannon, M. J. (2008). *Paradoxes of culture and globalization*. Los Angeles: Sage Publications.

Giddens, A. (1986). *The constitution of society: Outline of the theory of structuration*. Berkeley: University of California Press.

Ginsburg, F.D. (2002). Screen memories: Resignifying the traditional in indigenous media. In F. D. Ginsburg, L. Abu-Lughod, & B. Larkin (eds.), *Media worlds – Anthropology on new terrain*. Berkeley: University of California Press.

Ginsburg, F. D., Abu-Lughod, L., and Larkin, B. (eds.) (2002). *Media worlds: Anthropology on new terrain*. Berkeley: University of California Press.

Hasan, A. (2010). The emergence of new societal values. In R. Husain (ed.), *Karachiwala: A subcontinent within a city*. Karachi, Pakistan: JAAL.

Qamar, S., Umrani, S., Fatima, S., & Bashir, T. (April 2010). Symposium at Peshawar. *ASK Development Newsletter*. Lahore, Pakistan.

Said, E. (1997). *Covering Islam*. London: Vintage Books.

Sassen, S. (2003). *Spatialities and temporalities of the global: Elements for a theorization*. In A. Appadurai (ed.), *Globalization*. Durham, NC: Duke University Press.

Sen, A. (2006). *Identity and violence: The illusion of destiny*. New York: W.W. Norton and Company.

**Contexts of Adult Learning/Education,
Community Development and/or Social Action**

CHAPTER 10

SOCIAL MOVEMENT LEARNING IN GHANA: COMMUNAL DEFENCE OF RESOURCES IN NEOLIBERAL TIMES

Jonathan Langdon, Assistant Professor, St. Francis Xavier University, Antigonish, Nova Scotia, Canada

INTRODUCTION

The "globalization project" (McMichael, 2008, p. 21) is inextricably intertwined with neoliberalism, and has had a dramatic effect on the people of the Global South. Neoliberal globalization has been devastating for rural populations pushed off their lands in order to make way for extractive industries, export-oriented cash crops, and/or national development plans, while encouraging a burgeoning "planet of slums" (Davis, 2006) in urban centers. Drawing upon research with a rural movement in Ada (Ghana) defending communal access to a salt-producing lagoon (with occasional and contrasting reference to an urban-based resource defence movement or the National Coalition against the Privatization of Water or NCAP-W), this chapter advances the proposition that neoliberal globalization is most vulnerable to resistance in rural contexts. The participatory study of social movement activism and learning in Ada demonstrates that the strongest movements contesting neoliberal globalization in Ghana are embedded in the defence of rural communal resources, movements whose strength rests on the material (livelihood) and the epistemic (and cultural) value of these resources to the movement communities. The research also suggests that the way movements are organized, led, and learn is critical to their regeneration, as well as towards ensuring that this regeneration remains rooted in the material/livelihood and epistemic/cultural critique of neoliberal globalization.

WHERE NEOLIBERAL GLOBALIZATION TOUCHES THE LIVES OF GHANAIANS: PARTICIPATORY RESEARCH AND SOCIAL MOVEMENTS

Recent literature suggests that globalization has its most profound impact and generates greatest resistance in locations where globalized capital aims to extract resources (Cowen & Shenton, 1998; Ferguson & Gupta, 2002; McMichael, 2006; Peet & Watts, 2004). In describing the emergence of huge urban slums throughout the Global South, Davis (2006) points to the massive influx of rural dwellers to urban centres as a result of displacement due to extractive industries, shifts to export oriented cash crop production, and/or large-scale national development projects. While being cognizant of the ways in which this displacement and rural

D. Kapoor (ed.), Critical Perspectives on Neoliberal Globalization, Development and Education in Africa and Asia, 153–170.

impoverishment are linked to these slums (slumization), it is also critical to focus on the points of origin of this displacement and the ways in which processes behind these displacements are generating resistance (McMichael, 2006). In this sense, following McMichael (2006), one can envisage a different "Agrarian question" (p. 465) that does not see rural life as anachronistic and in need of being incorporated into the global market, but rather as an 'epistemic challenge' to this manner of global organizing and restructuring. Kamat (2002), for instance, has suggested that much writing on protest movements in the South has tended to focus on urban-based movements and where it has focused on rural movements, there has been a tendency to categorize these movements too quickly as either identity based movements, or class based movements. Kapoor (2007) meanwhile has demonstrated how Adivasi (forest dweller) movements in the Indian context contest the penetration of capital, and state disciplining on multiple registers that include material and cultural/epistemic grounds. Peet and Watts (2004) have further elaborated on how the defence of communally owned and managed natural resources is a strong base for building local movements.

Cowen and Shenton (1998) have discussed how, in the African context, the colonial and post-colonial state has been deeply implicated in managing rural African populations to suit the needs of capital. Similarly, Ferguson and Gupta (2002) note how neoliberal globalization in the African context has constituted a new topography of power, where the streamlined neoliberal state is reconfigured as either an enabler of capital, or is by-passed by transnational capital altogether. They call this process transnational governmentality, a term which builds on the work of Foucault (1991), and that focuses on the "mentality," or the "how" of governance (Dean, 1999, p. 2). Importantly for the Ghanaian case study or the subject of this chapter, it is the way in which this neoliberal transnational governmentality enables the emergence of new forms of capital that is the basis of the current challenges faced by the Ada movement. Likewise, and here building on Foucault's (1980) notion of subjugated knowledges as the way in which disciplining systems such as transnational governmentality are resisted, it is argued below that it is the coupling of epistemic contestation with livelihood protection that lends rural movements, such as in Ada, their strength.

This last point echoes McMichael's construction, but also builds on other literature that has noted this combination; for instance, Taussig's (1980) work documenting the way in which Columbian and Bolivian peasants used local legends to develop explicit critiques of capital. More explicitly, Mignolo (2000) has connected the Foucauldian notion of subjugated knowledges to his idea of local histories that contest global designs, such as neoliberal globalization. Mignolo (2000) further links this framework to subaltern studies. Kapoor (2007) has noted the significance of subaltern studies in underlining material and epistemic challenges to corporate-state power. For instance, Partha Chatterjee (1982) describes the importance of local religion as "an ontology, an epistemology" through which "subalterns act politically", and where "the symbolic meaning of particular acts – their significance – must be found in religious terms" (p. 31). In this sense, there is a strong emergent case for examining the ways in which capital is being reconfigured in local spaces, often either by using or by-passing the state, and the myriad ways in which local movements are emerging to contest attempts to enclose, privatize or expropriate communal resources.

The participatory study that informs this chapter builds upon this dialogue. However, the insights being shared in this chapter are not just a product of a review of the most recent critical literature just alluded to but are emergent from the rich experience of the participatory collective that were at the core of this study (for a more detailed discussion of the study's methodology please see Langdon, 2009b). The study builds on a strong tradition in social movement learning literature in using participatory approaches while adding to the few studies on an under-researched African movement context (Hall & Turray, 2006; Walter, 2007). The study examined a number of social movements/dynamics in Ghana since the country returned to democracy in 1992, while specifically assessing the manner in which these movements learned throughout this period (Langdon, 2009a). The research brought together 27 activist-educators (in 2007 and 2008) who were/are active in different Ghanaian social movements, including the women's movement, the socialist movements of the 1980s, the democracy movement, various student movements, the anti-privatization of water movement (NCAP-W) and local anti-neoliberal natural resource defence movements – such as the Ada case examined in this chapter. Of this larger group, a core group of 5 worked with the author to collectively analyze the emergent themes from participatory dialogues, as well as decide on future actions suggested by the research. This approach follows a participatory research technique developed by Fine, Torre, Boudin, Bowen, Clark, Hylton, Martinez, "Missy," Rivera, Roberts, Smart, and Upegui (2004). This core group is referred to as the participatory research (PR) group in this write-up and includes Kofi Larweh, Al-Hassan Adam, Gifty Emefa Dzah, Tanko Iddrisu and Coleman Agyeyomah.[1]

A key finding of the PR group while drawing on reflections from 20 years of activism in the Ghanaian democratic context is that when the livelihoods of Ghanaians are threatened directly by neoliberal globalization, related movement resistance is the strongest. Kofi of the Ada movement, notes "when people's livelihoods are at stake, then they see that, look we have to do something, that is when the movement becomes strongest, and so there is a little spark and then it goes off" (PR group meeting, February 23, 2008). However, it is not the livelihood issue alone that reveals why rural spaces are among the most important sites of resistance to neoliberal globalization. In fact, the PR group saw the livelihood question as having implications for both rural and urban populations and not some thing that was only specific to rural contexts. For instance, in the urban context, the privatization of social services has generated much activism and resistance. A case in point, as shared by the PR group, is Ghana's National Coalition Against Privatization of Water (NCAP-W) (cf. Prempeh, 2006). Al-Hassan, a key figure in the NCAP-W, notes the movement is currently successfully drawing thousands of urban dwellers out to contest the management contract the previous National Patriotic Party (NPP) government put in place for water, which has seen partial-privatization lead to massive service-cost hikes with no commensurate

155

improvement of service (PR group meeting, February 23, 2008). Yet, despite this important example of urban contestation, the PR group put forward the understanding that while urban resistance could generate much pressure, it remained locked in debates around modernization, where social change is dominated by Eurocentric models of change (either by the state or market). As such, these debates tend to remain rooted in public/private infrastructure development and ownership dichotomies.

This dichotomy is most tellingly revealed in the shift in development discourse in Ghana in the mid-1980s, when a purportedly socialist revolutionary state transitioned from a state-interventionist model to embrace a market-led structural adjustment program called the Economic Recovery Programme (ERP) – a quintessential cornerstone of neoliberal globalization's architecture in Ghana. Suddenly state rhetoric transitioned from state-led planning to export-oriented market-led development. An important piece of this transition was the downsizing of the public sector, including massive lay-offs in state-run industries, and the selling off of these industries to private capital (Hutchful, 2002). Additionally, this transition was predicated on major relaxation of restrictions on foreign investment, a regulatory shift that saw a 500% rise of foreign mining company activity (Hilson, 2004). With the transition to democracy, the access of foreign mining firms has continued to increase, culminating in the recent opening of protected forest reserves – another public asset – for mining exploration and exploitation by the previous government (Tienhaara, 2006). In this sense, the choice faced by Ghanaians has been between a state-led or market-led model of development, yet both of these models have appropriated assets (such as land and natural resources) through different discourses of the national good – a process indicative of the topographies of power (Ferguson & Gupta, 2002; Harvey & Langdon, 2010; Langdon, forthcoming). Suffice it to say, Ghana's current democratic constitution continues a long tradition dating back to colonial times where government intervention has consistently benefited the interests of capital (foreign and domestic) over the interests of local communal approaches to land and resource use.

In contrast to this, rural ways of being in the Ghanaian context are often (but certainly not always) founded on different value systems. For instance, the communal access and control of natural resources remains an important feature of the land tenure system in much of Ghana (Songsore, 2001). As Hilson (2004) has noted, this is why the socio-cultural as well as economic implications of extractive industries on land is so problematic:

> [The] perpetual expansion of mining and mineral exploration activity has displaced numerous subsistence groups outright and destroyed a wide range of cultural resources. Operations have caused widespread environmental problems, including excessive land degradation, contamination, and chemical pollution. (p. 54)

One of the key cultural resources that is at stake in such mining activities is the collective relationship with, and access to land and other resources. However, in threatening these relationships, mining activity is also strengthening rural community resistance. As Al-Hassan[2] notes, "anti-neoliberal movements are stronger when you have collective access to assets" (PR group meeting, February 23, 2008).

The strength of this defence of collective assets was significant in the PR group's analysis of Ghanaian movement dynamics, and encouraged the group to focus specifically on the movements that evolve from processes of resource defence, and the manner in which neoliberal globalization is contested. In shifting to focus on anti-neoliberal movements defending communal assets, the PR group echoes the analysis of McMichael (2006) and others in locating the greatest challenge to neoliberal globalization not in urban movements like the NCAP-W, but rather, in movements that challenge not only the policy directions of neoliberalism but its' very epistemic foundation. In the Ghanaian context, these are "Unbranded ... Indigenous or organic movements ... which [are so localized that they] don't have any names," who resist because their way of life is challenged (Al-Hassan, PR group meeting, February 23, 2008). Kofi explains, "These [communal defence] movements are embedded in people's livelihoods" (PR group meeting, February 23, 2008), meaning that it is in the communities where the direct effects of neoliberalism are being felt that organic unbranded movements are mobilizing. And as Kofi notes above, it is this threat to livelihoods that "sparks" movement mobilization and generates its strength. Here, critique of the global and national economy is intertwined with the issue-based critique of the rights of rural communities to land and decision-making concerning their land and natural resources. When this is coupled with strong spiritual and ancestral connections to these resources and land, as well as deep localized knowledge about the land and resources, it becomes clear that what is at stake are not just the implications for livelihoods but also the prospects for cultural reproduction. Coleman connects this point to other anti-neoliberal rural-based movements, such as those generated by the effects of mining activity. He notes, "Most of the farmer based associations [in mining areas] have turned overnight into anti-neoliberal movements. They are doing that because it has been necessitated in the current [neoliberal] environment" where their livelihoods have been destroyed (PR group meeting, February 23, 2008). These movements are emerging in communities affected directly by mining activity, where displacement from land, destruction of sacred sites and the poisoning of water sources has had a dramatic effect on rural communities (Hilson, 2004; CHRAJ, 2008).

From these discussions of communal resource defence movements, an emergent understanding from the PR group is that the strength and resilience of movement resistance to neoliberal globalization in these instances is rooted in threats to the erosion of cultural ways (cf. Boateng, 2008; Langdon, 2009a; Owusu-Koranteng, 2007). The Ada salt flat defence movement – a name generated by the PR group as it is unnamed – is a perfect example of just such an organic, unbranded movement which subsequently became the focus of analysis and praxis, stimulating discussion that began in 2008 and this is on-going in relation to directions for action and participatory reflection with the concerned movement constituencies.

The Ada movement is discussed here utilizing three primary and two secondary sources. First, there are the collective deliberations of the PR group through which a common understanding of general dynamics of social movements in Ghana since 1992 is articulated. Connected to this is an analysis of the Ada movement drawn from the direct experience of a PR group member who has been involved in the Ada movement since its inception, as well as tangential experience of other PR group members. Second, there are the deliberations drawn from an initial meeting between PR group members and Ada movement members. Third, this movement description is further contextualized by a radio documentary on conflicts surrounding the Songor salt lagoon that interviewed key figures in the movement. Additionally, two academic secondary sources are used to historicize the situation in Ada as well as the emergence of the resource defense movement.

It is hoped that the analysis and description of the movement will be deepened through the process of the emerging participatory research currently being designed. As such, a key caveat to the snapshots and interpretations presented here is that they do not capture all the complexity of the movement's context; they are grounded in only a dozen voices connected with the movement. It is hoped that over time the dialogue this process engenders will provoke not only a deeper engagement with this issue, but also a reflective process on movement priorities, identity, structure and learning. In this sense, the participatory research will ultimately be movement owned and directed, and as such will serve movement purposes – something Kapoor and Jordan (2009) have noted is an important ethical dimension for PAR work with social movements.

THE ADA MOVEMENT

Ada is a collection of coastal communities located roughly 150km from Ghana's capital, Accra, and surrounding the Songor lagoon. It is also the hub of the traditional Ada state (Manuh, 1992). Unlike many other coastal peoples whose livelihood is dependent on fishing, according to Amate (1999) the Adas rely heavily on winning salt from the Songor lagoon for their livelihood. Amate (1999) notes: "The Songor lagoon is by far the single highest income-generating natural asset ... of the Ada nation ... its inexhaustible natural salt yielding capacity ... is unique" (p. 166). The Songor salt flat is also an integral part of the Ada peoples' spiritual identity and history. The lagoon is the home of the Libi spirit – a key deity connected to salt formation who is mediated by the Libi *Wornor*, the spirit's high priest. Historically, generations of Adas have defended their ownership of the Songor lagoon, its deity, and the salt it yields, through pre-colonial wars, colonial attempts at expropriation, and contemporary struggles against government and private capital attempts to enclose the lagoon (Amate, 1999; Manuh, 1992). While these efforts at defence have been to ensure ongoing communal access to the salt flats by the Adas, this access in both historical and contemporary times has never been limited to only the Adas. Albert Apetorgbor, a member of the older generation of the Ada movement, describes how "People from all walks of life come to the Songor Lagoon for salt. Some come from as far as Tamale, Ewe land,

Kumasi and other places" (Radio Ada, 2002, p. 3).[3] This openness has led members of the movement as well as the PR group to describe the traditional salt flat management system as an alternative model to national capitalist and statist expropriations of natural resources (Songor group meeting, March 20, 2008; PR group meeting, February 23, 2008).

In attempting to describe the Ada movement it is important to begin by focusing on the history of the Ada people as well as the Songor lagoon. "In the past," notes Manuh (1992), "the process of collecting salt from the lagoon demonstrated community management of a natural resource" (p. 104). Amate (1999) describes the precolonial authority structure associated with the Songor, as well as in the Ada nation more broadly: "The early kings of Ada were ... not free agents. Their areas of competence and activity were circumscribed by the parameters laid down for them by the high priests" (p. 41). This was especially true of the Songor, where the Libi *wornor*, the Songor high priest, and the Tekperbiawe clan from which he came were "accepted from time immemorial by all the Ada clans" as the main authority of the lagoon (Amate, 1999, p. 166). Yet, at the same time, Kofi notes how the traditional resource management system was based on a sense of collective ownership and access:

> The [Songor] movement is deeply rooted in the culture of the people, why? Because of the way ownership is conceived. Ada is made up of different clans, ... and one clan [the Tekperbiawe,] is seen as the owner of the water body. And there are four others who are owners of the surrounding lands. You look at the wisdom in this ... So when you say the owner of the water body is there, and the surrounding lands have also got owners it is a convenient agreement for joint ownership. (PR group meeting, February 23, 2008)

In this sense, no one clan can claim *outright* ownership of the resource. This collective tradition of ownership not only benefits all those living in the Ada area, but also other Ghanaians – underscoring the point raised above that the Songor is a "national asset" (Kofi, PR group meeting, February 23, 2008).

Amate (1999) also describes the evolution of chieftaincy in the British colonial period (1868-1957), especially in connection with the Songor as the main livelihood generator. He notes that despite its precolonial acceptance, the Libi *wornor's* authority "began to be seriously challenged" in the colonial period (1999, p. 166). Much like Geschiere's (1993) account of British manipulation of "customary law" (p. 151) in Cameroon, where the British used their position as mediators between different leadership factions to destabilize local authority, Amate (1999) describes repeated mediation by the British with regards to the Songor, where alternatively the Libi *worno's* authority was reinforced, and then eroded through subsequent decisions. This historical context is crucial in understanding how competing claims of authority over the Songor continue today, such as ongoing attempts to enclose and privatize the lagoon in the interests of capital. However, in order to fully elaborate on the historical factors that set the stage for the emergence of the Ada movement, we would need to consider the dramatic effects of one of Ghana's largest national development projects on the lagoon.

Manuh (1992) has described how the decision to build a major dam on the Volta River by Ghana's first (statist) government in the 1960s led to a dramatic change in the ecology of the Songor salt flats and lagoon in the 1970s. This intervention led directly to a 7-year drought on salt formation, as the yearly flooding of the Volta no longer occurred (Songor group meeting, March 20, 2008). According to Manuh, it is partially as a result of this dramatic change that a local traditional chieftaincy authority, the Ada Traditional Council, decided to grant leases of land to two companies in the 1970s with the hopes that these companies would bring investment and jobs to the area – not try to prevent access to the resource. Kofi notes:

> The discussion was for a small parcel, but on paper it was something huge. Ok, that was one of the reasons for the [formation of the movement] because what was discussed was not what was put on paper, and the people were being prevented from winning salt even from the larger portions that was for the local people. (PR group meeting, February 23, 2008)

Amate (1999) adds that the entire leasing process was fraught with competing claims, and lawsuits between different elements in the chieftaincy and priestly authority structures. However, in the years following this concession, the prevention of access to the lagoon by one company in particular, Vacuum Salt Limited (VSL) largely precipitated the formation of the Ada movement. Also instrumental to the formation of this movement were the shifts in power at the national level, when a socialist military uprising in 1981, led by the Provisional National Defence Council (PNDC), took control of the country from a civilian administration. Its leader Jerry Rawlings declared the PNDC espoused socialist goals meant to "transform the social and economic order of [the] country" (cited in Shillington, 1992, p. 80).

This shift, according to Manuh (1992), opened the door for one of the local People's Defence Committees (PDCs) "formed in communities and workplaces following the events of 31 December 1981" to take "over the operations of Vacuum Salt Limited" (p. 151). However, when the PNDC and Rawlings later took an abrupt right turn in 1984, introducing Ghana's first structural adjustment policy (the ERP discussed above), the tables were turned. The owners of Vacuum Salt Limited returned and again prevented access to the lagoon, but this time with the backing of local police and military forces. It was at this point that many of those involved in the PDCs left the PNDC and began to work with local salt-winners to organize a loose co-operative. While many other cooperatives existed at the local level in Ghana during this period – a tacit connection to a leftist rhetoric by the PNDC – the salt co-operatives were different and "arose from the struggle of Ada people ... to regain sovereignty over the lagoon" (Manuh, 1992, p. 115). At its height, the main co-operative boasted 3200 members, and also fostered many smaller collectives (Manuh, 1992). In contemporary times, despite the much looser organizational framework, this history of struggle along with the co-operatives that emerged help to ensure the ongoing presence of the movement – though its existence is largely unnamed, indicating its unbranded nature (Al-Hassan & Kofi, PR group meeting, February 23, 2008). In this sense, the co-operative structure provided the mechanism through which a movement could be formed, even in an era where many of those opposing the new neoliberal focus on deregulation were targeted, tortured and imprisoned (Haynes, 1991). It was through this cooperative that the growing arrogance of VSL and the Apenteng family that owned it were resisted.

In recounting this resistance, it is best to draw on the perspectives of members of this era of resistance. Apetorgbor describes how:

> The late Apenteng, especially his son Stephen, would not allow anybody to win salt, let alone keep it in stock around the Lagoon for a better price. One day … he brought some soldiers to the Kasseh market some 20 kilometres away from the Lagoon… The soldiers started beating all the women selling salt at the market and all the vehicles loaded with salt were attacked. (Radio Ada, 2002, p. 3)

The violence used by VSL helped spark the formation of the cooperative. It also provoked an intervention by the local priests, the Libi *worno*, who guarded the spiritual essence of the lagoon (Manuh, 1992). Apetorgbor further describes how the local knowledge of preserving the salt formation to ensure equitable distribution as well as maintenance of the ecosystem became a rallying point during the conflict with VSL (Songor group meeting, March 20, 2008). The practice of fetish priests placing sticks in the lagoon in order to indicate a "ban on entering the lagoon" was used to symbolically challenge the use of the lagoon by VSL (Manuh, 1992, p. 113). When the company removed the sticks, it sparked large-scale anger and acts of resistance against the company and its local police and military allies (Songor group meeting, March 20, 2008). These acts included burning "a heap of salt kept in storage … most of which belonged to Apenteng [of VSL]" (Radio Ada, 2002, p. 5). As a result, Apetorgbor describes how:

> Anybody found in the Lagoon was arrested … They were sent to the Vacuum Salt Company's office. The suspects were given salt to chew and salt concentrates to drink. They were given other unspeakable punishments, as Apenteng directed. Thereafter, they were taken to … Accra, where they were put in cells for three weeks. (Radio Ada, 2002, p. 5)

On May 17, 1985, the violence of VSL against the people of Ada culminated in the death of Maggie Lanuer – a pregnant woman killed by a stray bullet fired by a raiding police officer. After her death, the government formed a commission to investigate the complaints being made by Ada residents, and ultimately banned the VSL owners from operating in and around the lagoon (Manuh, 1992; XXX commission, 1986).

Yet, this victory was hollow, as the legal control of the Songor simply passed from the company to central government hands. Instead of returning the management of this resource to the communities and people who had been successfully maintaining, defending, and sharing it for generations, the PNDC government enacted law 287, whereby the Songor and its salt would be considered like any other natural resource, and therefore come under the control of the central PNDC government to be held in trust for all Ghanaians. Furthermore, this law significantly informed the country's 1992 constitution (Langdon, forthcoming). Yet, as Manuh (1992) notes, this control is actually for hire, as the central government changes sides in local conflicts based on the the interests of transnational capital. This unpredictability worries those fighting for local control of the Songor lagoon. For instance, Maggie Lanuer's husband, Thomas Ocloo, states that "it was the death of my wife that led the former President [Rawlings] to make a law to take over the Songor and hold it in trust for the people of Ada"; yet, "the [previous New Patriotic Party] government and for that matter the [previous] President Kufuor [did] all he [could] to take over the resource completely to deprive the Adas of ownership" (Radio Ada, 2002, p. 6). As a result of this unpredictability, Ocloo states, "The Adas want the government to hand over the resource to them" (p. 6). According to Al-Hassan, the Songor struggle suggests they are not just fighting the government of the day, but "fighting against the constitution" (PR group meeting, February 23, 2008). At the same time, as will be discussed below, the struggle is also now with local chiefs who would undermine the collective control of the lagoon. It is precisely this larger implication that makes the Ada Songor movement so important, as the movement's struggle has implications not only for the ongoing history of defending this resource, but also for the national framework through which neoliberal globalization is enacted.

CONTRASTING SOCIAL MOVEMENT APPROACHES TO ORGANIZATION AND LEADERSHIP

A key aspect of the Ada story and of the story of other unbranded organic movements is the way movements are organized and led. For instance, the Ada movement – touched on more in a moment – displays what the PR group described as a dialogue-based approach to organization and leadership, where leadership is decentralized, and where movement priorities are constantly in dialogue with the felt-needs of the wider movement (Langdon, 2009a). Wright and Wolford (2003) have noted how a diffuse approach to leadership has been key to the success of Brazil's Landless People's Movement – also rural based, and founded on collective access to the land. The PR group contrasted this more horizontal typology of movement organization with one that is strategic and didactic, where decision-making is centralized in a core of movement leaders. The PR group further noted this horizontal, dialogue base is especially difficult to maintain in urban contexts. Al-Hassan notes that despite its foundation in a "horizontal organization," NCAP-W is "beginning to face [institutionalization] … because NCAP[-W] is becoming more elitist" (PR group meeting, February 23, 2008). Tanko underscores this emerging elitism by revealing shifts in movement priorities:

There was a point in time, where we were opposed to privatization of water, but you hear ... muted voices within the NCAP[-W] fraternity who said, "look, if it is nationals who have money and can ..." so then the principle is not against privatization, but that we don't want some foreigner coming in. (PR group meeting, February 24th, 2008)

Suddenly what has been a modernization debate over public or private infrastructure ownership becomes reconfigured as a conflict between capitalist elites – national or foreign. The potential for this type of cooptation is a reality for any social movement mobilization; yet, what is at issue here is the way the centralization of decision-making, as well as a failure to advance an epistemic challenge to modernization, leads the movement to easily disconnect from the very real material issues it purports to represent. As Coleman describes it, leadership in this context decides "what is best for the people" rather than these priorities emerging from the wider movement itself (PR group meeting, February 23, 2008).

Organization and Leadership in the Ada Movement

Returning to the Ada case, the dialogue-based typology helps highlight the ways in which power within this movement is diffuse: there are no particular leadership names that surface when the movement is described, even as the movement remains itself unnamed/unbranded. Instead, there is a description of actions that emerge from struggle. For instance, the salt burning Apetorgbor describes revealed the pluralistic character of the movement. He notes, "Some of those arrested came from Matsekope, Luhour, Kopehem, Koluedor and some of the coastal villages" (Radio Ada, 2002, p. 3). This is an important indication of how this movement connected with community felt-needs across the Ada spectrum. It is also captures the diffuse, organic and pluralistic nature of the movement that Manuh's description outlined, where the emergence of other salt winning co-operatives complemented and challenged the first co-operative. This multiplying of co-ops both mushroomed the activism around the salt lagoon, making it more difficult for one particular group to be targeted by police, and also helped ensure that power of the first co-op was constrained. Wright and Wolford (2003) describe a similar dual logic in the case of the landless movement, where diffuse leadership both provides protection and limits individual power.

Yet, the groundedness of this movement does not go without its challenges. The current situation faced by the movement is a perfect illustration of these challenges, even as it underscores the dialogue-based nature of the movement. Kofi describes this new challenge:

[The other day] there was a big meeting [that] has to do with this cannibalization of the lagoon by some of the new chiefs who see that "I am a chief and there is no collective resource that I am controlling so let me, once I know that I have part of the resource of the lagoon as one let me bring in some crude technology [to make salt]". So what the companies [such as VSL] are doing some of the chiefs have started ... [S]o it is bringing conflict, so local people who can walk into the lagoon to win salt are finding it difficult because the surrounding lands that produce salt are now all being controlled. (PR group meeting, February 23, 2008)

This cannibalization, known locally as "Atsiakpo", involves enclosing the lagoon in private salt-wining pans. A segment of youth associated with the movement destroyed some of these enclosures and were subsequently arrested, and the older generation of activists were quite slow in coming to their aid (Harvey & Langdon, 2010; Langdon, 2009a). This has led to tensions within the movement between an older generation that has worked with as well as challenged chieftaincy institutions, and a younger generation that sees challenging them as critical part in contesting attempts to disinherit the collective ownership of the resource. Al-Hassan points out how much of this tension stems from the way in which chieftaincy has been co-opted by colonial and capitalist interests in Ghana:

> The introduction of private capital control, which was being encouraged by the chiefs ... people have that kind of recognition of leadership rule by chiefs and clans, once, you just gave us the history of the place, which from the beginning there was nothing like chieftaincy, and chieftaincy is a recent creation. (PR group meeting, February 23, 2008)

Al-Hassan illustrates how the tendency to respect the institution of chieftaincy, even where it clearly "is a recent creation," enables unscrupulous connections with private capital that undermine collective asset control. While the older generation of revolutionaries and salt-winners contested decisions made by chiefs they still mostly respected the institution; for instance, Manuh (1992) notes that the main salt-cooperative sometimes even paid the upkeep costs of the chiefs. With certain chiefs now behaving like VSL, the younger generation has reinterpreted chiefs as a threat to access and therefore livelihoods *and* the epistemic origins of the traditional collective resource management system. Revealing an emergent tension between the actions of the youth and the more respectful dialogue of the older generation, community members have largely supported the analysis of the youth. Indicating the dialogue-based nature of this movement, these community members, as well as users of the resource from outside the Ada area have all been using the medium of community radio to air their concerns. Kofi describes this deep level of community concern in his description of ongoing calls to the radio:

> In fact, on Monday of this week, part of the morning program, part of the morning breakfast show was what is happening in the Songor because we have had calls, and people have been calling in on some other programs that we have organized in the community people have hinted, and so they say ... if action is not taken, if people do not, if the people who are cheating us are not prevented there will be war in the Songor. (Kofi, PR group meeting, February 23, 2008)

It is through informal dialogue processes such as these that the actions of the youth are being supported, and pressure is being brought to bear on the cooperatives to reconsider whether to even negotiate with chiefs. The tension at the heart of the relationship between the movement and chiefs is reflected in statements like this one by Apetorgbor:

> We bow today, reminding the elders of the Traditional Council that they are occupying their stools as our heads. Without us, they are nothing ... In yesteryears, our forefathers went to war, but today there are no such wars ... The new war is not the usual use of guns and cutlasses; it is a war of malicious schemes and the lure of money to deprive the Adas of their birthright. The elders must be firm and resolute. They must not give themselves up to be lured. I wish to remind them again of their oath. (Radio Ada, 2002, p. 7)

LEARNING RE-EMBEDDED IN STRUGGLE

In addition to these organization and leadership questions, the PR group also concluded that the dialogue-based typology is grounded in fundamentally different approaches to learning within movements. Where strategic and didactic movements determine specific ways of conceiving of their struggle – stifling dissent through authoritative structures – dialogue-based movements are grounded in a framework of ongoing discussion that resists ownership of learning, and democratizes it. This differentiation has important implications for the ways in which movement members *learn to struggle*.

Learning to struggle is one of three analytical lenses of informal learning within social movements that emerged in the PR group analyses – all three of which build on the work of Griff Foley (1999) and his conception of "learning in struggle" (p. 9). For Foley, studying the often-overlooked informal learning that emerges in social movement struggles and actions is critical to understanding the challenges movements face and the implications of the strategies they use to grapple with these strategies. Foley (1999) argues that analyzing learning in struggle can reveal the "complex, ambiguous and contradictory character of social movements," (p. 143) where a successful campaign may stop a particular project, but may also entrench new forms of neoliberal power in a movement. Foley's (1999) approach focuses on the effects of capital, but also recognizes the importance of what he calls "people's everyday experiences," and like the subjugated knowledges described above, he sees these as being the source of "recognitions which enable people to critique and challenge the existing order" (p. 4). Importantly, it is through processes of informal learning in the face of struggles that he sees these recognitions emerging, even if their emergence can have ambiguous consequences. In the analysis of the PR group "learning in struggle" was kept as the way to describe the long term process of movement learning in social action; meanwhile, "learning through struggle" was advanced as a way to describe the particular and often ambiguous learning that occurs during the course of a particular conflict or event (i.e., a strike, a campaign, or a particular demonstration), and "learning to struggle" emerged as a way to describe the normative thoughts on, as well as

165

processes through which, movement members actually learn to engage in struggle (Langdon, 2009a/b).

In this sense, "learning to struggle" captures both thinking on *how* movements *should* learn to struggle, as well as reflections on *how* movements *do* learn to struggle. In combining both of these inflections, the PR group identified unbranded and organic movements – with their dialogue-based organizational and leadership structure – as a key source of inspiration for the ways in which movements not only *do* learn, but *should* learn to struggle.

Snapshots of Learning to Struggle in the Ada Movement

Broadly speaking, three snapshots of learning to struggle in the Ada movement have emerged in discussions between movement members and members of the PR group. These snapshots have yet to be interrogated and deepened through a PAR process still in the making. Nonetheless, these snapshots provide a useful illustration of learning to struggle.

First, the revolutionary youth and workers of the first days of the PNDC who had briefly taken over the running of the VSL compound joined with local salt-winners in contesting and then resisting the return of the VSL owners in 1984. In challenging both company and hired police and military, this new alliance formed strong bonds, yet these bonds remained pluralistic as the first salt cooperative mushroomed into the formation of other cooperatives. A key component to the mobilization around this learning in action and struggle was the manner in which defending the traditional management as well as the spiritual significance of the resource, drew support from broader community members. While the most telling demonstration of this was the collective reaction to the company's removal of the sticks placed by the Libi *Wornor* in the lagoon, it is also clear that part of the mobilizing force was also a defense of collective access to a livelihood source and the way in which VSL restricted this. The key point here is that the traditional resource management system provided an important rhetorical platform, with both epistemic and livelihood roots, from which this pluralistic group argued for local control of the resource (Manuh, 1992).

Second, over time, the group of salt-winners and former members of the local revolutionary core have used the rhetorical link with the traditional resource management system to conduct a dual set of engagements. On the one side, this older core has been involved in trying to convince the central government to cede the resource to local control (Manuh, 1992); on the other, this core has worked on chiefs to respect their custodial roles, and not overstep them. This second aspect is reflected in Apetorgbor's statement above. However, this second approach has been configured more as an appeal to chiefs, even as it reminds them of the history. In contrast to this approach that still respects the authority of chiefs, the youthful element within the movement has taken a much more radical stance in identifying chieftaincy as a threat to communal access (Kofi, PR group meeting, February 23, 2008). This disconnection between the older generation of movement leaders and youth has emerged as a major challenge to the movement's continued relevance. It has also emerged as an important moment where the movement membership is regenerating, and thereby re-learning to struggle. This process of challenge and potential regeneration remains open-ended.

However, the third emerging snapshot of learning to struggle suggests the direction that this regeneration between generations might take. The reaction of community members to this most recent threat to communal ownership of the salt flats indicates the analysis and actions of the youth are more deeply grounded in the current felt needs of the wider community. This connection with felt needs also has potential rhetorical recourse to a reconfigured concept of ownership of the lagoon which draws on precolonial societal structures where it is not chiefs but rather the Libi *worno* who have the authority over lagoon access (Amate, 1999; Apetorgbor, Songor group meeting, March 20, 2008). This is a key re-articulation of the epistemic challenge the movement and the Libi *worno* launched against VSL, where chiefs along with the Libi *worno* were accorded a place; now this challenge is being re-configured to contest expropriation attempts by local chiefs on the basis of challenging the foundations of their authority. With this argument beginning to emerge in public discourse, the older generation of movement leaders is already beginning to reconfigure their relationship with the broader chieftaincy system (Kofi, personal communication, July 2009). The re-articulation will certainly be necessary to remain in dialogue with the articulated felt needs of the broader community to maintain communal access to the salt flat.

This most recent moment of learning to struggle is particularly significant, as collective access to the resource is a cornerstone of the movement's strength. If the movement becomes didactic, and turns a deaf ear to this latest effort to mobilize, the very heart of the movement could disappear.

Nonetheless, these snapshots taken together illustrate how the Ada movement is well positioned to learn to struggle in new ways because it is rooted in the ongoing collective defense of community felt needs; yet this process is not straight forward, nor is it without its own ambiguous power dynamics. What this example demonstrates is the potential for collective rural resource defense movements to challenge not only the material reality but also the epistemic logic of neoliberal globalized resource alienation. It also reveals the very real power stratification of the local, where the realities of globalization are felt, and where these realities can lead to cooptation of resistance.

CLOSING REFLECTIONS ON GLOBALIZATION AND RURAL SOCIAL MOVEMENTS

Rural resource defence movements, such as Ada's, provide an example of significant contestations of the epistemic and livelihood implications of neoliberal globalization. For instance, the initial mobilization period was sparked by the dual challenge of VSL to communal access to the natural resource, and the longstanding and balanced natural resource management system deeply informed by the regenerative spirit of the lagoon as interpreted by the Libi *worno* – the guardian of this spirit. This management system belies logics of outright land ownership and rather places responsibility for resource use and maintenance in collective hands – entrenching a custodial rather than exploitative relationship with the resource. It is not surprising that this first challenge arose at the dawn of the neoliberal age, when structural adjustment programs, such as Ghana's ERP, were clearly privileging and encouraging the penetration of extractive and exploitive relationships with land and resources over alternative logics. Following on from this, it is also not surprising that in the contemporary era, as neoliberal globalization has reconfigured capital's topographic relationship with African states through transnational governmentality, it is local elites who are leading the latest efforts of resource enclosure – in much the same way that it should not be surprising to see certain members of NCAP-W beginning to suggest local capital control is as good as keeping water a public asset. Yet, despite the fact that in the Ada case these elites are members of chieftaincy structures, the strength of the dialogue-based movement process is ensuring local analysis of this new strategy of capital: it is an attempt to reconfigure the communal nature of this resource, and, regardless of their position, the behavior of these chiefs contravenes the pre-colonial balanced approach to resource ownership. The mobilizing strength of this challenge is telling, as one recent Radio Ada caller said, "If this situation is not addressed, there will be war in the Songor." In this sense, both in the recent past and in contemporary times, the connection between the defense of communal assets and a long-established alternative way of being and valuing the world provides the strength for challenges to neoliberal globalization in the Ada case, in particular, and the Ghanaian context, more generally; after all, the Ada case not only contests material attempts to enclose the lagoon, but also the constitutional framework used to determine who should control *national* assets. This has important implications for other similar movements in Ghana, such as those in mining affected areas.

Challenges to neoliberal globalization are most pointed, most embedded in peoples felt needs and alternative epistemologies/ontologies in rural locations in Ghana. In this sense, the Ghanaian-centered research presented here, as exemplified by the Ada case, augments the insights of other contemporary research and theorizing that sees agrarian locations as resisting the logic of neoliberal capitalist resource extraction and as the greatest challenge to neoliberal globalization – precisely because these are the spaces where the compulsions of capital are the most pressing and where their discursive and material power are weakest, as people still have recourse to other ways of knowing, being and building livelihoods.

Studies of globalization must focus not only on resistance emerging in urban contexts, where it is often most visible but also in rural locations where capitalism exploits resources – and where the logic of this resource extraction is being questioned by unbranded and unnamed movements and communities with alternative and regenerative relations with their land.

NOTES

[1] The identity of all other participants in the study, with the exception of those involved in the Ada movement, cannot be identified. For the purposes of clarity, and to underscore their pivotal role in the generation of the analyses that follow, members of the PR group, when quoted, will be referred to by their first name.

[2] In order to highlight the contributions of members of the PR group, their first rather than last names are used, after they have been introduced.

[3] This description implies the wide-scale national use of this resource since Tamale is in Ghana's North, while Ewe-land refers to Eastern Ghana, and Kumasi is in the middle of the country.

REFERENCES

Amate, C. O. C. (1999). *The making of Ada*. Accra: Woeli Publishing Services.

CHRAJ (2008). *The state of human rights in mining communities in Ghana*. Accra: Commission on Human Rights and Administrative Justice.

Cowen, M. P. & Shenton, R. W. (1997). Agrarian doctrines of development: Part II. *Journal of Peasant Studies, 25*(3), 31-62.

Davis, D. (2006). *Planet of slums*. London: Verso.

Dean, M. (1999). *Governmentality: Power and rule in modern society*. Sage: London.

Ferguson, J. & Gupta, A. (2002). Spatializing states: Toward an ethnography of neoliberal governmentality. *American Ethnologist, 29*(4), 981-1002.

Fine, M., Torre, M. E., Boudin, K., Bowen, I., Clark, J., Hylton, D., et al., (2004). Participatory action research: From within and beyond prison bars. In L. Weis & M. Fine (eds.), *Working method: Research and social justice*. New York: Routledge.

Foley, G. (1999). *Learning in social action*. London: Zed Books.

Foucault, M. (1980). *Power/knowledge: Selected interviews & other writing*. New York: Pantheon Books.

Foucault, M. (1991). Governmentality. In G. Burchell, C. Gordon, & P. Miller (eds.), *The Foucault effect: Studies in governmentality*. Chicago: University of Chicago Press.

Geschiere, P. (1993). Chiefs and colonial rule in Cameroon: Inventing chieftaincy, French and British style. *Africa, 63*(2), 151-170.

Hall, B. L. & Turray, T. (2006). *A review of the state of the field of adult learning: Social movement learning*. Ottawa: Canadian Council of Learning.

Harvey, B. & Langdon, J. (2010). Re-imagining capacity and collective change: Experiences from Senegal and Ghana. *IDS Bulletin, 41*(3), 79-86.

Haynes, J. (1991). Human rights and democracy in Ghana: The record of the Rawlings' regime. *African Affairs, 90*(360), 407-425.

Hilson, G. M. (2004). Structural adjustment in Ghana: Assessing the impact of mining-sector reform. *Africa Today, 51*(2), 53-77.

Hutchful, E. (2002). *Ghana's adjustment experience: The paradox of reform*. Geneva: UNRI.

Kamat, S. (2002). *Development and hegemony: NGOs and the state in India*. Oxford: Oxford University Press.

Kapoor, D. (2007). Subaltern social movement learning and the decolonization of space in India. *International Education, 37*(1), 10-41.

Kapoor, D., & Jordan, S. (2009). International perspectives on education, PAR, and social change. In D. Kapoor & S. Jordan (eds.), *International perspectives on education, PAR and social change*. New York: Palgrave Macmillan.

Langdon, J. (2009a). Democracy and social movement learning in Ghana: Reflections on 15 years of learning in the democratic terrain by Ghanaian activist-educators. Unpublished PhD Dissertation, McGill University, Montreal, Canada.

Langdon, J. (2009b). Learning to sleep without perching: Reflections by activist-educators on learning in social action in Ghanaian social movements. *McGill Journal Of Education/Revue des Sciences de l'Éducation de McGill, 44*(1). Retrieved from http://mje.mcgill.ca/article/view/2946/3049.

Langdon, J. (Forthcoming). Democratic hopes, transnational government(re)ality: Grounded social movements and the defence of communal natural resources in Ghana. In D. Kapoor & D. Caouette (eds.), *Beyond development and globalization: Social movement and critical perspective reader.* Ottawa: University of Ottawa Press.

Manuh, T. (1992). Survival in rural Africa: The salt co-operatives in Ada district, Ghana. In D. R. F. Taylor & F. Mackenzie (eds.), *Development from within: Survival in rural Africa.* New York: Routledge.

McMichael, P. (2006). Reframing development: Global peasant movements and the new agrarian question. *Canadian Journal of Development Studies, 27*(4), 471-483.

McMichael, P. (2008). *Development and social change* (4th ed.). Chicago: Pine Forge Press.

Mignolo, W. (2000). *Local histories/global designs: Coloniality, subaltern knowledges and border thinking.* New Jersey: Princeton University Press.

Owusu-Koranteng, D. (2007). Petition against the international bridge-builders award to Mr Wayne Murdy, the CEO of Newmont. Retrieved from http://www.globalresponse.org/content/Letter%20to %20DU%20Chancell or%20from%20 WACAM%20%20Ghana.pdf.

Peet, R. & Watts, M. (eds.) (2004). *Liberation ecologies: Environment, development, social movements* (2nd ed.). London: Routledge.

Prempeh, E. O. K. (2006). *Against global capitalism: African social movements confront neoliberal globalization.* Burlington, VT: Ashgate.

Radio Ada, (2002). *Radio Ada oral testimony documentary: Resource conflict – The Songor Lagoon.* Ghana: Radio Ada.

Songsore, J. (2001). The economic recovery program/structural adjustment program: Its likely impact on the "distant" rural poor in Northern Ghana. In Y. Saaka (ed.), *Regionalism and public policy in northern Ghana.* New York: Peter Lang.

Taussig, M. (1980). *The devil and commodity fetishism in South America.* University of North Carolina Press: Chapel Hill.

Tienhaara, K. (2006). Mineral investment and the regulation of the environment in developing countries: Lessons from Ghana. *International Environmental Agreements, 6,* 371-394.

Walter, P. (2007). Adult learning in new social movements: Environmental protest and the struggle for the Clayoquot Sound rainforest. *Adult Education Quarterly, 57*(3), 248-263.

Wright, A. L., & Wolford, W. (2003). *To inherit the earth: The landless movement and the struggle for a new Brazil.* Oakland, CA: Food First Publications.

CRITICAL PERSPECTIVES ON DEVELOPMENT AND LEARNING IN COMMUNITY ACTION IN BANGLADESH AND THAILAND

Bijoy Barua, Associate Professor, East West University, Bangladesh

INTRODUCTION

Over the last four decades, the economic growth model has neglected diverse local economics and indigenous knowledge in order to modernize ethnic communities in the southeastern part of Bangladesh and northeast/northern Thailand. Such conventional interventions have been accelerated through the processes of industrialization, construction of dams, implementation of forestry programs, land control, and the framing of rules and regulations in the name of investment, growth and the extension of the market model. This massive process has been designed to regulate the lives of ethnic communities/minorities and hill tribes (e.g., the *Marma, Chakma, Issan-Lao* speaking people, and *Karen*[1]) through a scheme of centralized development policies that have undermined local decision-making, participation, creativity, knowledge, and livelihoods in parts of Bangladesh and Thailand (Barua, 2009; Buergin, 2000; Dewan, 1993; Korten, 1990; Poffenberger, 2006; Sato, 2000; Trakarnsuphakorn, 2007). Despite the huge extension of this growth model of development intervention, there has been increasing social and cultural resistance by various ethnic communities in these areas to revitalize their cultural knowledge, rights and livelihoods through a localized participatory development approach (Barney, 2007; Barua, 2010; Darlington, 1998, Missingham, 2003). Simultaneously, the proclamation of the World Decade for Cultural Development (WDCD) in the mid 1980s, the Social Summit in Copenhagen in 1990 and the Earth Summit of Rio in 1995 have also helped promote a consciousness among dominant agents of development regarding the significance of indigenous culture, knowledge, and sustainable development within dominant development interventions (UNESCO, 1995; United Nations, 1990).

In keeping with these developments, I concur with the observation that "a strongly holistic tradition and tendency to identify with the indigenous peoples (or ethnic communities) provide anthropologists (sociologists and development specialists), with a unique perspective on development process" (Wilson-Moore, 1997, p. 486) – one that needs to be seriously deployed in the interests of a more honest process of people-centered-development. If development is to play a useful role in the lives of people, it is important to value the perspective of ethnic communities in the construction of knowledge within the process of development. This chapter advances a of critique conventional assumptions about dominant

D. Kapoor (ed.), Critical Perspectives on Neoliberal Globalization, Development and Education in Africa and Asia, 171–186.

imported development models and approaches that have dislocated ethnic communities, local knowledge, and livelihoods in parts of southeastern Bangladesh and northern Thailand. Specifically, based on my practical observation(s) and field research experience(s) (Barua, 2007, 2009; Barua & Wilson, 2005), I attempt to construct knowledge from the socio-cultural perspective of a Buddhist society as the people of these regions practice *Theravada* Buddhism, which does not advocate *pseudo-desire* and *unbridled desire* (*tanha*) among the people (Barua, 2009; Goulet, 1993) or material and cultural aspirations that are central to the market model promulgated in contemporary dominant development interventions. The analytical perspective/discourse of the Buddhist notion of development as one that promotes an *eco-centric* development approach which nurtures diversity for sustainable livelihoods is what is deployed here to critically assess the dominant modernization-oriented development interventions in these regions (Barua & Wilson, 2005). Buddhist traditions, in fact, grew as a spiritual power against social injustice and oppression (including oppression in the name of modern developmentalism) and emerged as a "movement of renouncers" in ancient India (Wijayartna, 1990, p. 1). The discussion here is limited to the issues and problematics raised by Buddhist analytical perspectives and related post-colonial development discourses/debates pertaining to peoples' knowledge, dams, forests and livelihoods, development interventions, and socio-cultural concerns. For the convenience of discussion, the terms 'ethnic minorities', 'ethnic communities', 'Buddhists' 'forest communities', and 'hill tribes' are used interchangeably in the chapter. The terms 'modernization' and 'globalization' are also used interchangeably since they are deeply rooted in development discourse and vice versa.

DEVELOPMENT DISCOURSES AND POST-COLONIAL AGENDAS: TOWARDS EUROCENTRISM OR PEOPLE-CENTERED DEVELOPMENT?

The post-colonial nation-state emerged with the hope and aspiration of attaining rapid economic growth similar to the west after the end of formal colonialism in Asia and Africa. Bilateral development agencies were founded in the 1950s to continue to implement processes of colonial control and modernization, i.e., the western-style development model in Asia, Africa and Caribbean Islands (Burkey, 1993). Similarly, modernization theory emerged in the late 1930s with the initiatives of colonial administration. It became more dominant in the late 1950s and the early 1960s (Parpart, Connelly & Barriteau, 2000). The theory of modernization is deeply ingrained in the environment of western society and culture. The central concern of the modernization model is that development is a natural, linear progression away from traditional socio-economic practices and toward economic growth. Socio-cultural values are seen as fatalistic and endemic to traditional societies, values that retard the prospects for such progress (Barua, 2010). Additionally, the process of modernization was seen as creating a space for each individual for higher economic growth (Rostow, 1960). The model of modernization was adopted with the understanding that it would improve the standard of living of all people in the developing countries regardless of their gender and ethnic identity. The main focus was on economic growth through a process of rapid industrialization in order to ensure cultural, social and behavioural change in society (Learner, 1958). However, the economic growth model suppressed the core issues of life by diverting the communities with symbolic surrogates such as money, materialism, consumerism, status, and power (Loy, 2003).

The growth-oriented modernization model was augmented by the 'human capital' approach in order to develop human resources (Rathgerber, 1990; Schultz, 1961). In this effort, education and training have long been considered essential preconditions for the modernization of an economy through the introduction of technology and behavioral change (Hallack, 1990). Modernization theory claims that economic, socio-cultural and political changes are mutual and coherent in their impacts with respect to change (Inglehart, 1997). Education is perceived as the provider of modern values in order to change the cultural practices and customs of people in developing countries (Barua, 2009). In most cases, modernization theory favoured the approach of a *transfer of technology* in order to diffuse western values among people in rural societies, while indigenous knowledge and culture was considered backward and irrational (Selener, 1997). This modernization model was pushed forward by the western-dominated nation states after World War II, replicating the socio-cultural values of the corporate economy that eventually forced the post-colonial nation states to assimilate western values and traditions in a passive manner (Parpart, Connelly & Barriteau, 2000). As Pieterse (2001) elaborates:

> modernization is essentially social engineering from above and an operation of political containment rather than democratization. American modernization projects such as community development and the Green Revolution exemplify this character of White revolution. (p. 23)

That is, modernization policies tend to demobilize existing social capital and displace local economic resources in pursuit of economic growth in order to construct artificial social fabrics through the application of liberal productivism in developing countries. Over the years, this economic growth model has not improved the quality of life; it has created an environmental disaster and widened social and economic inequality within the social structure of developing countries.

Northern versus Southern Discourse

In the 1960s, social scientists in Latin America raised critical questions about modernization theory due to the continuing under-development of their region. Among these proponents, Frank (1969), Amin (1976) and Rodney (1982), rejected the Eurocentric model of modernization. They argued that underdevelopment was mainly the result of unequal and exploitative economic relations between the northern states and the southern states (Handelman, 2003). Dependency theory openly questioned the assumed mutual benefits of international trade and development stressed by European and American proponents of modernization and growth theories. The key argument of dependency theory was that socio-economic dependency (neo-colonialism) created under-development within the rural peripheries in Latin American nations in the name of modernization (Burkey, 1993). The dependency theorists outwardly rejected the acceptance of the western model of development in southern countries. They argued that underdevelopment was caused by the capitalist system of the northern world. This process created an environment of dependency within the system of southern nation states (Handelman, 2003). Dependency theory criticized the modernization model for concealing the relationship between development and under-development, as if modernization happened independently in the developed world without exploitation (Pieterse, 2001). It is a model that emphasizes the un/equal distribution of wealth and social in/justice and is predicated on the understanding that the economic modernization model can only help a minority of people in developing countries (Frank, 1969). In the words of Pieterse (2001):

> dependency theory – which serves by and large as the political economy of Third World nationalism – is stretched to apply to culture: protectionism, dissociation, endogenous development are prescribed for national culture as they have been for the national economy. (pp. 61-62)

Despite its critical contribution to the development debate, dependency theory has failed to offer any meaningful clarification as to why, how and under what circumstances underdevelopment and development transpire. Furthermore, this theory failed to speak of the issue of interaction between power and income within and outside the home. Interestingly, both "modernization theory and Marxism, development thinking and dependency theory have in common is economism, centrism, and teleology" (Pieterse, 2001, p. 25). Similarly, dependency theory ignores the internal dynamics of clan, race, ethnic oppression, and gender at the community level. It also disregards the question/place for non-capitalist modes of production.

Over the years, both theories have not addressed the contribution of people's knowledge, science and culture to local and national development processes (Barua, 2009). By and large, the Eurocentric model of economic development has engendered and discouraged people-centered development in the developing countries (e.g., Bangladesh and Thailand). Shiva (2000) clearly states that, "the priorities of scientific development and R&D (rural development) efforts, guided by a western bias, transformed the plurality of knowledge systems into a hierarchy of knowledge systems" (p. vii). In fact, economic development based on the Eurocentric model could not address the economic crisis of the Asian tigers in 1997 despite its ambitious goal of achieving high economic growth (Laird, 2000; The Nation, 1997).

As the growth model created a crisis in Asia in 1997, it raised critical questions for local thinkers and development planners regarding the survival of rural economy and culture on the Asian continent (Barua, 2009). Despite this fact, the King of Thailand in his annual address stated, "we have to go backwards, have to be careful and have to return to unsophisticated business … We need to go back so that we can go forward" (The Nation, 1997). Despite this, the so-called developed nation states have become more desperate in an effort to transplant their knowledge and implement their model without acknowledging 'local-specific knowledge' and 'cultural context' in the developing countries (Norberg-Hodge, 1991). "To ignore people's knowledge (and culture) is almost to ensure failure in development" (Agrawal, 1995, p. 2; Barua & Wilson, 2005). Thus, development must be orientated towards the social, cultural, spiritual and political conditions of people. In other words, ideas/interventions "cannot simply be transplanted" (Freire, 1970, p. 4). In truth, external impositions are incompatible with the approach emphasized in ideal Buddhist societies.

People-Centered Development: Towards a People's Science and Knowledge

The people-centered development model is grounded in the principles of social justice, inclusiveness and eco-centric development. It places emphasis on local knowledge, local economics, people's participation, spirituality, and the self-reliance of the community (Barua, 2010; Korten, 1990). "People-centered development does not seek international charity (aid) as the answer to poverty. It seeks the productive use of local resources to meet local needs" (Korten, 1990, p. 18) and it avoids massive expansion, high growth and profit. "There is no self-reliant way of development without primary reliance on peoples' resources including their own knowledge" (Rahman, 1994, p. 70). More importantly, people-centered development encourages people's knowledge, organization, and promotes participatory decision-making processes for achieving sustainable development and biodiversity. Its vision is quite relevant to the Buddhist notion of *eco-centric* development based on simplicity and the preservation of natural resources and towards the promotion of self-reliance and local cultural values. In an ideal Buddhist society, poverty is undesirable as this tends to engross *dhukkha* (ill-being). More importantly, it does not propose to create *pseudo-desires* in order to create delusion within society (Barua, 2009). The Buddhist practice of economic development emphasizes liberation and refinement of human quality in order to control materialistic desires and greed in society for the welfare of all, without discrimination and disparity. The production of local resources for local needs is the most appropriate mode of economic life in a Buddhist society and political-economy. Dependence on imports from a great distance and exports to unknown destinations are uneconomical from the Buddhist point of view. Buddhist economy stresses minimum consumption of natural resources in order to maintain harmony with nature and society. The minimum utilization of resources also helps to sustain a locally self-sufficient economy and to protect the natural environment. It confronts commodification of knowledge, science, and the consumer paradigm (Jones, 1988; Schumacher, 1973). Schumacher (1973) further contends that:

people who live in highly self-sufficient local communities are less likely to get involved in large-scale violence than people whose existence depends on world-wide systems of trade. (p. 49)

Under this perspective, the theory of/approach to development must be of practical relevance to the local context and environment based on compassion and for the benefit of the community (Ariyaratne, 1996; Barua, 2009; Sivaraksa, 1990). In other words, local knowledge, social values and wisdom are considered to be the key elements to the success of development in Buddhist societies. From this perspective, equitable distribution of resources within a community is the central theme of development (Barua & Wilson, 2005) There is no question of property or individual ownership even for the Buddhist monk according to the *Vinaya Pitak* (Niyogi, 1980). It advocates for the equality of all in a society as "people are considered as a treasure" (Ratanapala, 1997, p. 21). The Buddhist notion of development is "based on unity and mutual interdependence" (Matthiessen, 1991, p. xvi) in order to preserve "natural balance, appropriate technology, community life, and economic self-reliance" for eco-centric and people-centered development (Barua & Wilson, 2005, p. 238). It does not take life out (disconnect) of its social, political and economic contexts (Rahula, 1994). It is deeply rooted in the notion of *ahimsa* or non-injury for the welfare of all (Barua & Wilson, 2005). In explaining the Buddhist concept of development, Macy (1994) states that "development is waking up – waking up to our true wealth and true potential as persons and as a society" (p. 149). In this process, development cannot be separated from lands, plants and rivers. In other words, all phenomena are in one way or another conditionally interdependent (Barua &Wilson, 2005). Thus, spiritual practices help to enrich knowledge and wisdom that stresses economic, social, cultural, political and psychological well-being of all (Castellano, 2000).

Having considered some of the major differences between northern modernist discourses and practices of development and a people-centered Buddhist discourse and related practices of development, the following sections take up socio-ecological realities (dislocations) associated with development interventions pertaining to dams and forest-based livelihoods in Bangladesh and Thailand to substantiate the critique of the former and to propose the need for/viability of the latter approach to development in these contexts.

DAMS, DEVELOPMENT, AND DISPLACEMENT OF ETHNIC MINORITIES

While promoting development interventions in developing countries, around 300,000 dams were built by 1997 in order to accelerate the process of industrialization through the scheme of hydropower for more economic growth and development out of which more than 45,000 were large dams. Such projects led to large-scale displacement of rural and indigenous people from their native lands. The construction of large dams, in the name of economic development and modernization, mainly affected ethnic minorities in Asia (Carino, 1999; Hirsch, 1999; Sneddon & Fox, 2008). For example, the building of *Kaptai Hydro Power*

Dam in southeastern Bangladesh in the 1960s displaced the *Chakma* and the *Marma* communities in the hills, including the inundation of some 10 square miles of reserved forest, 54,000 acres of cultivable land, and the displacement of approximately 100,000 ethnic communities of the hills (Bangladesh District Gazetteers, 1975; Dewan, 1990). Furthermore, Moshin and Ahmed (1996) state:

> The construction of the dam had far-reaching consequences for the tribal (ethnic communities) people. ... It made nearly 10,000 *Chakma* ploughing families having proprietary rights, and 8,000 *Chakma jhumia* families comprising more than 10,000 *Chakma* persons landless and homeless. It also affected ... 1,000 *Marmas*. (p. 279)

This dam was constructed in 1964 with the financial assistance of international donor agencies, submerging 250 square miles of prime farming land in the hilly districts, which account for 40 percent of the total cultivable land belonging to ethnic communities. Such dislocation changed the socio-ecology, geography and livelihoods of the people (Barua & Wilson, 2005). Babul, a member of the Chakma community, expresses:

> The dam created an artificial lake in the hills. Our prime agricultural land went under water at the cost of our lives. We also became homeless and landless. Our livelihoods have been displaced and uprooted. Social ties and bonds have been dislocated in a hilly terrain. (Personal Communication, August, 2010)

Because of this dislocation, some members of the *Chakma* and the *Marma* communities are forced to practice *jum* or shifting cultivation due to the scarcity of land in the valley even though many had earlier embraced plough cultivation. Such scarcity resulted mainly from the construction of Kaptai dam for hydropower. The dam itself may become useless because of sedimentation of the Kaptai Lake. Although the dam was supposed to produce 230 MW, it currently generates 50 to 100MW for industry (Gain, 1998).

Similarly, *Park Moon Dam* project of *Ubonrachathani* displaced and dislocated the ethnic minorities in northeast Thailand. Over five million people were relocated by force and thousands of Lao-speaking Isan people have been moved out due to the construction of the dam (Sudham, 2002). The dam was built in 1994 with the financial support of the World Bank. Although the dam was built to produce 316 megawatts of electricity, it produces only 40.93 megawatts (World Commission on Dams [WCD], 2000). Sudham (2007) explicitly states:

> The Dam has been proven to be a disastrous flop since it could not generate sufficient electricity as purported at the expenses of human sufferings and ecological disaster while the World Bank continues to make a handsome return from the loan. (p. 4)

The dam has seriously displaced local communities whose livelihoods traditionally relied on fishing in the Mun River.[2] Moreover, the numbers of fish species and populations have declined.[3] Since the construction of the dam the livelihoods of the people have been adversely affected (Lohmann, 1998).

> In the past, most people of the villages used to go for fishing after working in the rice fields. This has been the culture of the people since the time of our ancestor. Because of this dam, fishing families lost their livelihoods. (Kumsai, Personal Communication, August, 2010)

Such development interventions have destroyed forests, trees, and contaminated rivers in the name of development. Although compensation was offered by the government agencies to the people to relocate, this was seen by the affected communities as being economically unfeasible (Barney, 2007; Dewan, 1993; Kripakorn, 2007). Such rehabilitation programs for the non-ethnic communities created more insecure conditions for the people and led to land disputes in the area (Haque, 1990; Sneddon & Fox, 2008). Amar (cited in Barua, 2010), a member of Chakma community reflects:

> We became refugees in our own land. Our cultivable lands were submerged under water. ... Moreover, the outside people were rehabilitated in our lands. We constantly encounter problems from the settlers. (p. 73)

Similarly, Kiang of northeastern Thailand expresses (cited in Sudham, 2002):

> The dam could not generate electricity in the summer months due to insufficient flow of water. As a result it is left to rust and for taxpayers to pay the debt plus interest, despite immeasurable human suffering and the damage done to the people and the ecology. (p. 106)

Predictably, these destructive development projects triggered violence in southeastern Bangladesh and northern Thailand.[4] Such developmental structural violence (Kripakorn, 2007) has displaced several ethnic communities and destroyed their self-sufficient local economies. The people of these regions have lost access to common property resources. These culturally biased mega projects (Shiva, 1989) undermined people's aspiration, sustainable livelihoods and lifestyles of ethnic communities. In other words, the construction of *dams* neither offered sustainable livelihoods to the ethnic minorities of southeastern Bangladesh and northern Thailand nor have they been ecologically sustainable. Rather, western science-based development projects, in the quest for universalization in the name of progress and development has disregarded people's science and knowledge. Alternatively, the primary quest of a people's science and knowledge is to search and look in to the nature of human beings as being an inseparable part of nature – a search for sustainable development (Barua, 2010). Despite these revelations, western science has been engaged in the promotion of industrial exploitation for growth and profit alone (Ariyaratne, 1996; Norberg-Hodge, 1991). Furthermore, development programs financed by international donors have neither rehabilitated nor addressed the needs and demands of rural ethnic communities in their homeland. These development interventions also encouraged migration and settlement of non-ethnic communities/low land people in the lands of ethnic communities, favoring the settlers over the local inhabitants who have, as a result been further marginalized in their own territories (Brown, 1992; Dewan, 1993; Kripakorn, 2007). The institutionalization of development was in fact a strategic intervention as a counter-measure against the insurgency of the hill people of northeast/northern Thailand and southeastern Bangladesh (Sato, 2000; Tripura, 2000). As a mater of fact, socio-political struggles/cultural resistance for political rights were prevalent and continue to be persistent in northeast/northern Thailand and southeastern Bangladesh (Missingham, 2003; Moshin, 2003).

DEVELOPMENT, FORESTS AND LIVELIHOODS OF ETHNIC COMMUNITIES

The enclosure, encroachment, and reservation of forests and lands were introduced with the assistance of the British colonial administration in southeastern Bangladesh and northern Thailand[5] to commercialize timber and teak (Brown, 1992; Darlington, 1998; Mustafa, 2002; Royal Forest Department, 2001; Sato, 2000). In other words, these encroachments of forests and lands were initiated in the name of scientific management in order to cultivate cash crops (and practice commercial farming in these countries). Ethnic minorities have not only been marginalized and alienated in the process of such economic development through market driven strategies and policies; their traditional customary rights have been overlooked in the hills of southeastern Bangladesh and northeast/northern Thailand (Barney, 2007; Barua, 2010; Mustafa, 2002; Sato, 2000). While introducing these regulations in these countries, the European colonizers never realized that the Buddha was born, became enlightened and died under these very trees in the forest. In Buddhist cultures and societies of South and Southeast Asia, trees, rivers, and forests are valued, honored and worshipped as the Buddha generated his knowledge in this diverse natural setting through meditation (Barua & Wilson, 2005). In other words, the natural environment of the forests and rivers have helped the intellectual evolution that energizes and promotes South and Southeast Asian Buddhist culture (Macy, 1990; Panya & Sirisai, 2003).

> The culture that has arisen from the forest has been influenced by the diverse processes of renewal of life, which are always at play in the forest, varying from species to species, from season to season, in sight and sound and smell. (Tagore,[6] cited in Shiva, 1989, p. 55)

Local knowledge on forest science did not perceive trees as merely wood and market commodities. Rather, it focused on diversity of form and function as the survival of the human species was dependent on the continuation of natural forests (Shiva, 1989). For this reason, the Intergovernmental Panel on Forests (IPE) adopted the element 1.3 program for the development of forests:

> to consider ways and means for the effective protection and use of traditional forest-related knowledge, innovations and practices of forest-dwellers, Indigenous people and local communities, as well as fair and equitable

179

sharing of benefits arising from such knowledge, innovations and practices. (Battiste & Henderson, 2000, p. 260)

Despite this, forest policies have been modified and re-organized in order to displace local forest-dwellers for industrial growth and modernization. The process of modernization and industrialization led to intense deforestation in these regions through the building of dams and the plantations of fast-growing eucalyptus trees, rubber plants, timber or teak and paddy farming for markets and cash that effectively undermined natural forests. As a result, plant life has turned into a nonrenewable resource. Diverse varieties of trees have been replaced by mono-crop cultivation in the forests of northeast/northern Thailand and southeastern Bangladesh (Barua & Wilson, 2005; Barney, 2007; Poffenberger, 2006; Taylor, 1993; Trakarnsuphakorn, 2007). Aung (cited in Barua 2010), a member of the *Marma* community explicitly mentions:

> Unfortunately, the state authority restricted our access to the forest and land. Hence, our livelihoods have been dislocated. Money economy has become dominant. Now people are struggling to survive in our lands. (p. 70)

Likewise, Kiang (cited in Sudham, 2002), a member of Lao-speaking Issan community states:

> Some of these wealthy and influential people (*phum illhiphon*) have awesome power to log the forests, force millions of powerless beings off the land …to plants the harmful and fast growing eucalyputs trees in order to feed pulp and paper mills and exploit us to get rich fast. It is sheer greed that makes them do this. (p. 104)

The extension of commercial plantation has not only restricted community access to the forests, it has also driven away the hill people from their livelihoods (e.g. swidden agriculture/slash-and-burn, raising livestock and natural gardening). Moreover, the migration of lowland/plain land people into the forest lands also instigated deforestation process in the hills of northeast/northern Thailand and southeastern Bangladesh. In the changing socio-ecological environment, these lowlanders tended to destroy more forest areas than required due to their lack of ecological knowledge (Delang, 2002; Gain, 2000).

Aung (cited in Barua 2010), a member of the *Marma* community expresses:

> In the past, villagers lead s simple life through the *jhum* cultivation (swidden agriculture) and plough cultivation. Our economy was deeply rooted in the forest and land. (p. 70)

Although swiddeners are blamed for destruction of forest in both countries, the expansion of logging and cultivation of cash cropping for commercial profit at the cost of forests has accelerated on a massive scale since the Second World War (Delang, 2002; Gain, 2000). This commercialization process has facilitated private ownership by non-ethnic communities from low land areas for the production of cash crops. Such commercialization practically displaced the natural forests in which more than fifty natural species of plants used to grow. Two or three types of trees that were destroyed used to provide fruit or lumber for people while a few other plants protected the surface soil and its fertility (Barney, 2007; Brown, 1992; Khemchalem, 1988). Moreover, the destruction of the forest created economic and environmental hardship for five million forest-dwellers in Thailand (Asian Forest Network, undated). In other words, these development policies initiated the process of "detribalization of tribal lands and forests" through such development encroachments in to tribal areas (Kapoor, 2007, p. 17). Additionally, western-style development interventions also disconnected the ethnic communities from the environment of nature and *siladhamma*.[7] In the view of Pongsak (1992), a Thai forest Monk:

> The balance of nature is achieved and regulated by the functions of the forest. So, the survival of the forest is essential to the survival of *siladhamma* and our environment. It's all interdependent. When we protect our forest, we protect the world. When we destroy the forest, we destroy that balance, causing drastic changes in global weather and soil condition, causing severe hardships to the people. (p. 90)

The loss/deforestation of natural forests and encroachments of lands has further exacerbated the decline of the Buddhist ethical practice of the *dhutanga* (ascetic) of monks in the southeastern Bangladesh and northeast/northern Thailand that provided the foundation for contemplative learning and knowledge in order to help build healthy communities which renounce greed (Barua & Wilson, 2005: Taylor, 1993). This ascetic practice used to provide reflective education for the ordinary members of the community. They were educated to nurture the simple life and preserve the forest for the well being of all creatures without discrimination. As a result, the balance of the natural environment and the spiritual peace of people were lost to economic growth. Despite this, there has been a non-violent socio-cultural engaged activism for preservation of forest through the *Santi Asoka* ecological movement in northeast Thailand (Darlington, 1998).

In Buddhist culture, nature was considered sanctified and sacred (Aariyaratne & Macy, 1992). When nature is degraded, people tend to suffer. Kabilsingh (1990) says that, "when we abuse nature, we abuse ourselves" (p. 8). A human being is likely to make rightful use of nature so that he or she can grow above nature and realize his or her intrinsic spiritual potential. Buddhism promotes a calm and non-violent attitude toward nature. "Nature is the manifestation of truth and of the teachings … when we protect nature, we protect the truth and teachings" (Pongsak, 1992, p. 99). For Buddhists, the forest is the sacred place where the Buddha was enlightened. The Buddha lived with the wild animals in the forest. The preservation of forests and trees always has a place in Buddhist texts. In Buddhist education, nature is not separated from all living beings (Ariyaratne & Macy, 1992; Swearer, 1997). Plants, animals and human beings were considered to have the same inheritance. In other words, the forest is not a place for destruction or plundering but it is there for animals and plants to live, and where human beings can live with animals and plants for ascetic practice (Bloom, 1970).

181

For Buddhists, it is a question of finding the right path of development, the middle way between materialistic illusions and a nonviolent means for achieving the right livelihood in society. In his famous *Mongal Suttas* (Blessing discourse), the Buddha speaks of the "happiness of living in an appropriate environment" (*Patirupa des vasoca*). Thus, the natural environment should not be destroyed. It must be preserved for the benefit of all living beings in the world without disturbing the flora, fauna and rhythm of life (Barua & Wilson, 2005).

CONCLUDING REFLECTIONS

In this chapter, I have critically examined modern development interventions and its impact on the livelihoods of ethnic communities utilizing the discursive framework of Buddhist oriented people-centered development, cultural knowledge and politics in southeastern Bangladesh and northern Thailand. It has been argued that development policies and programs have followed the path of the colonial legacy and market driven model promoting centralized control through the process of imposition and domination. Dams and large-scale plantation schemes have not contributed to poverty alleviation – they have undermined viable alternative approaches and livelihoods of local communities. In fact, "such economic growth may temporarily benefit some humans but in reality disrupts and destroys the whole nature to which we belong" (Hanh, 1988, p. 143). Moreover, these development interventions failed to recognize the psychological, social, cultural and spiritual aspects of local ethnic communities in the region. In other words, this development model disregarded local knowledge, culture and the natural environment. Conventional development actors are neither promoting *people-centered development* nor *nurturing cultural knowledge* for sustainable livelihood of ethnic communities in the hills and forests of Bangladesh and Thailand. Rather, all development interventions tend to promote the *trickle-down approach* to economic growth and progress, which continues to fail the communities in these regions in the name of development.

NOTES

[1] This community lives in upland Chiang Mai, northern Thailand and the members of the community call themselves *Pga K'nyau* (human being).
[2] Despite the protests, the dam was completed. Moreover, the Electricity Authority of Thailand (EGT) had also sought to build the Nam Choam on the upper Kwai River. The Nam Choan dam destroyed Thung Yai reserve and the forced to relocate the Karen minority. As a result of movement, Nam Chon Dam project was abandoned (see Kripakorn, 2007).
[3] The Mekong delta river basin was quite bio-diverse. In the past, the fish species numbered 1,700 (See Sukshri, 2004).
[4] When Thailand stepped into a development process in accordance with the various five-year National Development Plan starting in the late 1950s onward, all natural resources were monopolized by the state for the benefit of economic expansion on its terms (see Kripakorn, 2007).
[5] The Bowring Treaty signed between the United Kingdom and Siam (Thailand) on April 18, 1855 accelerated the western development agenda in Thailand. The western model of forestry was initiated for production of mainly timber and teak as cash crops (see Sato, 2000).

6   The Nobel Laureate, Rabindranath Tagore was noted for his deep respect for Buddhism (see Banerjee, 1973).
7   *Sila* refers to morality/ethics and *Dhamma* refers to truth or justice or teaching.

REFERENCES

Agrawal, A. (1995). Dismantling the divide between indigenous and scientific knowledge. *Development and Change, 26*, 413-439.

Amin, S. (1976). *Unequal development: An essay on the social formation of peripheral capitalism.* Brighton, UK: Harvester Press.

Ariyaratne, A.T. (1996). *Buddhism and Sarvodaya: Sri Lankan experience.* Delhi, India: Sri Satguru Publications.

Ariyaratne, A. T. & Macy, J. (1992). The island of temple and tank: Sarvodaya: Self-help in Sri Lanka. In M. Batchelor & K. Brown (eds.), *Buddhism and ecology.* London: Cassell Publishers.

Asian Forest Network (undated). Sustaining Southeast Asia's Forests, Research Network: Report 1. Retrieved from, http://www.asainforestnetwork. org/pub/pub10.htm.

Banerjee, A. C. (1973). *Buddhism in India and abroad.* Calcutta, India: The World Press Private Ltd.

Bangladesh District Gazetteers (1975). *Chittagong Hill tracts, economic condition* (Chapter VI). Dhaka, Bangladesh.

Barney, K. (2007). A note on forest land concessions, social conflicts, and poverty in the Mekong Region. Conference Proceedings from the *International Conference on Poverty Reduction and Forests,* Bangkok, September.

Barua, B. (2007). Colonialism, education and rural Buddhist communities in Bangladesh. *International Education, 37*(1), 60-76.

Barua, B. (2009). Nonformal education, economic growth and development: Challenges for rural Buddhists in Bangladesh. In A. Abdi & D. Kapoor (eds.), *Global perspective on adult education.* New York: Palgrave Macmillan.

Barua, B. (2010). Ethnic minorities, indigenous knowledge, and livelihoods: Struggle for survival in Southeastern Bangladesh. In D. Kapoor & E. Shizha (eds.), *Indigenous knowledge and learning in Asia/Pacific and Africa: Perspectives on development, education and culture.* New York: Palgrave Macmillan.

Barua, B. & Wilson, M. (2005). Agroforestry and development: displacement of Buddhist values in Bangladesh. *Canadian Journal of Development Studies, XXVI*(2), 233-246.

Battiste, M. & Henderson, J. (2000). *Protecting indigenous knowledge and heritage: A global challenge.* Saskatchewan, Canada: Purich Publishing Ltd.

Bloom, A. (1970). Buddhism, nature and the environment. *The Eastern Buddhists, 5*(1), 115-129.

Brown, K. (1992). In the water there were fish and the fields were full of rice: Reawakening the lost harmony of Thailand. In M. Batchelor & K. Brown (eds.), *Buddhism and ecology.* London: Cassell Publishers Limited.

Buergin, R. (2000). 'Hill tribes' and forests: Minority policies and resource conflicts in Thailand. SEFUT Working Paper No. 7. Freiburg: Albert-Ludwigs-Universitat Freiburg.

Burkey, S. (1993). *People first: A guide to self-reliant, participatory rural development.* London: Zed Books Ltd.

Carino, J. (1999). The World Commission on Dams: A review of hydroelectric projects and the impact on indigenous peoples and ethnic minorities. *Cultural Survival Quarterly, 23*(3), 53-56.

Castellano, M.B. (2000). Updating Aboriginal traditions of knowledge. In G. S. Dei, B. L. Hall, & D. Goldin-Rosenberg (eds.), *Indigenous knowledges in global contexts: Multiple readings of our world.* Toronto, Ontario: University of Toronto Press.

Darlington, S. M. (1998). The ordination of a tree: The Buddhist ecology movement in Thailand. *Ethnology, 37*(1), 1-15.

Delang, C. (2002). Deforestation in northern Thailand: The result of Homong farming practices or Thai development strategies? *Society & Natural Resources, 15*(6), 483-501.

Dewan, A. K. (1990). *Class and ethnicity in the hills of Bangladesh.* Unpublished Doctoral Dissertation, Department of Anthropology, McGill University, Montreal, Quebec, Canada.

Dewan, A. K. (1993). The indigenous people of the Chittagong Hill tracts: Restructuring of political systems. In M. K. Raha & I. A. Khan (eds.), *Polity, political process and social control in South Asia: The tribal and rural perspectives.* New Delhi: Gyan Publishing House.

Frank, A. G. (1969). *Latin America: Underdevelopment or revolution.* New York: Monthly Review Press.

Freire, P. (1970). *Cultural action for freedom.* Cambridge, MA: Harvard Education Review and Center for the Study of Development and Social Change.

Gain, P. (1998). *The last forests of Bangladesh.* Dhaka: Society for Environment and Human Development (SEHD).

Gain, P. (2000). *The Chittagong Hill tracts: Life and nature at risk.* Dhaka: Society for Environment and Human Development (SEHD).

Goulet, D. (1993). Biological diversity and ethical development. In L. Hamilton (ed.), *Ethics, religion and biodiversity: Relations between conservation and cultural values.* Cambridge, UK: The White Horse Press.

Handelman, H. (2003). *The challenge of Third World evelopment: Upper Saddle River* (3rd ed). New Jersey: Pearson Education.

Haque, E. (1990). Tensions in the Chittagong Hill tracts. In S. Haq & E. Haque (eds.), *Disintegrative progress in action: The case of South Asia.* Dhaka: Bangladesh Institute of Law and International Affairs.

Hirsch, P. (1999). Dams in the Mekong region: Scoping social and cultural issues. *Cultural Survival Quarterly, 23*(3), 37-40.

Inglehart, R. (1997). *Modernization and postmodernization: Cultural, economic, and political change in 43 societies.* Princeton, NJ: Princeton University Press.

Jones, K. (1988). Buddhism and social action: An exploration. In F. Eppsteiner (ed.), *The path of compassion: Writings on socially engaged Buddhism.* Berkeley, CA: Parallax Press and Buddhist Fellowship.

Kabilsingh, C. (1990). Early Buddhist views on nature. In A. H. Badiner (ed.), *Dharma Gaia: A harvest of essays in Buddhism and ecology.* Berkeley, CA: Parallax Press.

Kapoor, D. (2007). Subaltern social movement learning and the decolonization of space in India. *International Education, 37*(1), 10-41.

Korten, D. C. (1990). *Getting to the 21st century: Voluntary action and the global agenda.* West Hartford, CT: Kumarian Press.

Kripakorn, D. (2007). Social movement and the natural resource management: A study of the anti Nam Chon Dam movement (1982-1988). *Silpakorn University International Journal, 7,* 112-142.

Laird, J. (2000). *Money politics, globalization and crisis: The case of Thailand: Exploring new towards sustainable development.* Singapore: Graham Brash.

Learner, D. (1958). *The passing of traditional society.* New York: Free Press.

Lohmann, L. (1998). Mekong Dams in the dream of development. Retrieved from, http://www.the cornerhouse.org.uk/resource/mekong-dams-drama-development.

Loy, D. R. (2003). The poverty of development: Buddhist reflections. *Development, 46*(4), 7-14.

Macy, J. (1990). The greening of the self. In A. H. Badiner (ed.), *Dharma Gaia: A harvest of essays in Buddhism and ecology.* Berkeley, CA: Parallax Press.

Macy, J. (1994). Sarvodaya means everybody wakes up. In C. Whitemyer (ed.), *Mindfulness and meaningful work: Explorations in right livelihood.* Berkeley, CA: Parallax Press.

Matthiesen, P (1991). Introduction. In H. Norberg-Hidge (ed.), *Ancient futures: Learning from Ladakh.* San Francisco: Sierra Club Books.

Missingham, B. (2003). *The assembly of the poor in Thailand: From local struggles to national protest movement*. Chiang Mai, Thailand: Silkworm Books.

Moshin, A. (2003). *The Chittagong Hill tracts, Bangladesh: On the difficult road to peace*. Colorado: Lynne Rienner Publishers Inc.

Moshin, A. & Ahmed, I. (1996). Modernity, alienation and the environment: The experience of the Hill people. *Journal of Asiatic Society of Bangladesh, 41*(2), 265-286.

Mustafa, M. (2002). A review of forest policy trends in Bangladesh: Bangladesh forest policy trends. *Policy Trend Report*, 114-121.

Niyogi, P. (1980). *Buddhism in ancient Bengal*. Calcutta, India: JIJNASA.

Norberg-Hodge, H. (1991). *Ancient futures: Learning from Ladakh*. San Francisco: Sierra Club Books.

Panya, O. & Sirisai, S. (2003). Environmental consciousness in Thailand: Contesting maps of eco-conscious minds. *Southeast Asian Studies, 41*(1), 59-75.

Parpart, J. L., Connelly, M. P., & Barriteau, V. E. (2000). *Theoretical perspectives on gender and development*. Ottawa, Canada: International Development Research Centre.

Pieterse, J. N. (2001). *Development theory: Deconstructions/reconstructions*. London: Sage.

Poffenberger, M. (2006). People in the forest: community forestry experiences form Southeast Asia: Community forestry experiences from Southeast Asia. *International Journal of Environment and Sustainable Development, 5*(1), 57-68.

Pongsak, A. (1992). In the water there were fish and the fields were full of rice: Reawakening the lost harmony of Thailand. In M. Batchelor & K. Brown (eds.), *Buddhism and ecology*. London: Cassell Publishers.

Rahula, W. (1994). Buddhism in the real world. In C. Whitemyer (ed.), *Mindfulness and meaningful work: Explorations in right livelihood*. Berkeley, CA: Parallax Press.

Rahman, A. M. (1994). *People's self-development: Perspectives on participatory action research: A journey through experience*. Dhaka, Bangladesh: University Press Limited.

Ratanapala, N. (1997). *Buddhist democratic political theory and practice*. Ramalana, Sri Lanka: Sarvodaya Vishva Lekha.

Rathgerber, E. M. (1990). WID, WAD, GAD: Trends in research and practice. *The Journal of Developing Areas, 24*, 489-502.

Rodney, W. (1982). *How Europe underdeveloped Africa*. Washington, DC: Howard University Press.

Rostow, W. W. (1960). *The stages of economic growth*. Cambridge, UK: Cambridge University Press.

Royal Forest Department (2001). History of Royal Forest Department. Retrieved from http://forest.go.th/rfd/history.html.

Sato, J. (2000). People in between: Conversion and conservation of forest lands in Thailand. *Development and Change, 31*(1), 155-177.

Schumacher, E. F. (1973). *Small is beautiful: Economics as if people mattered*. New York: Harper and Row.

Schultz, T. W. (1961). Investment in human capital. *The American Economic Review, 1*(1), 1-17.

Selener, D. (1997). *Participatory action research and social change*. Ithaca, New York: Cornell University Press.

Shiva, V. (1989). *Staying alive. Women, ecology and development*. London: Zed Books Ltd.

Shiva, V. (2000). Forward: Cultural diversity and the politics of knowledge. In G. J. S. Dei, B. L. Hall, & D. Goldin-Rosenberg (eds.), *Indigenous knowledges in global contexts: Multiple readings of our world*. Toronto, Ontario, Canada: University of Toronto Press.

Sivaraksa, S. (1990). True Development. In A.H. Badiner (ed.), *Dharma gaia: A harvest of essays in Buddhism and ecology*. Berkeley, CA: Paralax Press.

Sneddon, C. & Fox, C. (2008). Struggles over dams as struggles for justice: The World Commission on Dams (WCD) and anti-dam campaigns in Thailand and Mozambique. *Society and Natural Resources, 21*(7), 625-640.

Sudham, P. (2002). *Tales of Thailand*. Bangkok, Thailand: Shire Asia Publishers.

Sudham, P. (2007). Shadowed country. Retrieved from http://www.asian finest.com/forum/index.

Sukhasri, C. (2004). Mekong River Basin: Cooperation towards sustainable development, case study on water & environmental management. In S. Wun'Gaeo (ed.), *Human security now: Strengthening policy networks in Southeast Asia*. Bangkok, Thailand: Chulalongkorn University Printing House.

Swearer, D. K. (1997). The hermeneutics of Buddhist ecology in contemporary Thailand: Buddhadasa and Dhammapitaka. In M. E. Tucker & D. R. Williams (eds.), *Buddhism and ecology: The interconnection of Dharma and deeds*. Cambridge, MA: Harvard University Press.

Taylor, J. L. (1993). *Forest monks and the nation-state: An anthropological and historical study in northeastern Thailand*. Singapore: Institute of Southeast Asian Studies, Singapore National University.

The Nation (1997, December 5). His Majesty urges return to agrarian ideals. *The Nation*, Bangkok, 1.

Trakarnsuphakorn, P, (2007). Space of resistance and place of local knowledge in Karen ecological movement of northern Thailand: The case of Pgaz K'Nyau villages in Mae Lan Kham River Basin. *Southeast Asian Studies, 45*(4), 586-614.

Tripura, P. (2000). Culture, identity and development. In P. Gain (ed.), *The Chittagong Hill tracts: Life and nature at risk*. Dhaka: Society for Environment and Human Development (SEHD).

UNESCO (1995). *The cultural dimension of development: Towards a practical approach*. Paris: Author.

United Nations (1990). *Report of the World summit for social development*. Copenhagen, Denmark: Author.

Wijayartna, M. (1990). *Buddhist monastic life* [Trans, C. Grangier & S. Collins]. Cambridge, UK: Cambridge University Press.

Wilson-Moore, M. (1997). Alas, I am undone for I am a leprosy patient: Applying anthropological methods to planned change. *Canadian Journal of Development Studies, 28*(3), 485-502.

World Commission on Dams [WCD] (2000). *Pak Mun Dam Mekong River Basin Thailand, Final Report*. Cape Town, South Africa: Secretariat of the World Commissions on Dams.

DEVELOPMENT COOPERATION AND LEARNING FROM POWER IN SENEGAL

Blane Harvey, Research Fellow, Institute of Development Studies at the University of Sussex, UK

INTRODUCTION

This chapter draws together lessons learned from research conducted in Senegal in 2007-2008. The research sought to explore how power is exercised through relations of development cooperation and coordinates peoples' activities at various sites within networks of international, regional and local institutions and actors. More specifically, it aimed to provide a concrete illustration of how development practice – imbued with an institutionalised model of operation, largely established extra-locally and disembedded from the context where the development is actually being "done" – has increasingly homogenised its norms and forms of practice. Drawing on these examples of how power has coordinated peoples' activities and aligned their practices with institutionalised norms, the study reflected upon the ways that institutions and collectives in the South might draw upon these experiences to "speak back" to the development process, and the conditions and processes that enabled or constrained them in doing so.

The chapter reflects on this exploration of how inter-institutional power relations, managerial discourses and their associated technologies, and informal learning coalesce within a network of development partners with the aim of: Better understanding how the subjectivity of the development practitioner is constituted through the complex range of networked actors and institutions that he/she must engage with; Considering the scope for transforming the institutionally-driven or mediated initiatives aimed at effecting social change, and; Identifying the conditions and scope for engaging in transformative learning processes from within the development apparatus. In doing so, it aims to draw a conceptual link between ethnographic accounts of the influence of power as it circulates through the development apparatus (cf. Eyben, 2000; Mosse, 2005) and Foley's (2001) call for "contextualised ethnographic accounts of learning in social action that enable us to see the warp and weft of emancipatory and reproductive learning that occurs as people struggle against various forms of oppression" (p. 84).

Drawing on Foley's (1999, 2001) model of learning in counter-hegemonic struggle, I argue that moments of struggle have an instructive dimension that is important to reflect upon. However, the learning these struggles offer is often embedded in the complex processes at hand and is therefore easily overlooked. When reflected upon collectively, however, these moments of informal and

D. Kapoor (ed.), Critical Perspectives on Neoliberal Globalization, Development and Education in Africa and Asia, 187–205.

incidental learning can play an invaluable role in rendering visible relations of power and domination, informing future struggle, strengthening collective strategy and resolve, and ultimately helping to strengthen or reassert peoples' ways (Kapoor, 2004; 2009). I consider specific examples from fieldwork conducted with a progressive Environmental Non Governmental Organisation (ENGO) in Senegal committed to promoting the agency of marginalised peoples, and a farmer's Federation which they support in ways which produced complex and mixed outcomes. In looking at these contexts I explore where these learning opportunities presented themselves and were – or could have been – acted upon, and consider the factors that affected peoples' ability to successfully draw upon learning and critical reflection.

INSTITUTIONS, NETWORKS, AND POWER

Underlying the investigation I have described above is a need to better understand the complex ways that power relations and knowledge production are constructed, transmitted, and put into action across multiple levels of action within a particular setting. Susan Vincent's research on development actors in Peru has drawn similar conclusions to this proposed starting point:

> [U]nderstandings of the political roles of individuals, communities, and governments has changed over the last century, leading to a political contract in which locals are supplicants while outsiders are patrons. The multiple levels of this contract imply that a focus on the local, however complexly contextualized and empowering, cannot fully solve local problems. These problems have at least part of their origin and means of reproduction elsewhere, and I propose that the search for a solution must begin with the form of political relationship or contract between the multiple levels of action. (Vincent, 2004, p. 112)

This has meant using theoretical and methodological approaches that are dynamic and multi-focal, and importantly, that avoid imposing reductionist theoretical frameworks upon a research context that springs from different locales, ideologies, and forms of social and institutional organisation. To address these concerns I have drawn upon a Foucaultian analysis of discourse and power as an analytical starting point, while at the same time drawing upon competing and complementary perspectives to expose other ways of perceiving the issues I have examined.

For Foucault, power is understood as a complex strategic relation which can be both a repressive and productive force; one which induces pleasure and produces discourse, but also enables the domination of one group by another (Foucault, 1980). His interests laid primarily in making visible the *exercise* of power; in the tactics, techniques, and functionings that we impose upon ourselves and on others in a wide range of forms and fields. His investigation of power "in its ultimate destinations, [at] those points where it becomes capillary, that is, in its more regional and local forms and institutions" (p. 96), paired with a *bottom up* analysis of capillary power, from its "infinitesimal mechanisms" as they are displaced and extended into ever more general and global forms of domination – provides a powerful lens with which local articulations of power can be mapped across web-like networks. This form of analysis allows for the association of groups, institutions and actors with the exercise of specific strategies of power without depending upon binary, uniquely structuralist, or exclusively capital-focused frames of analysis, which I argue overlook and even obscure the complexity of these relations (cf. Mosse, 2005). This does not deny the relevance of structural relations and capital to the contexts I have investigated, but rather aims to situate them within a broader web of relations and interdependencies. In analysing power relationships within specific institutional contexts, according to Foucault, one can begin to reveal the *topography* of capillary power and its mechanisms. In the field of international development, where actors implement policy at the level of often isolated and disparate communities while major development policy-making bodies are centralised in a few of the world's major cities, such a form of analysis appears particularly relevant.

While Foucault's analysis of power can help to uncover important insights into the unseen or *normalized* ways in which power shapes the everyday ways of working between actors, it stops short of addressing the question of what specific outcomes resistance and agency might produce in responding to these relations, arguing that the intellectual's role lies in providing instruments of analysis, not defining the project of resistance or its goals. It is here that I feel the linking of a complex analysis of institutional power with approaches to collective *learning in action* (Foley, 1999) or *learning in/through/from struggle* (Foley, 2001; Von Kotze, 2000) can provide a means to extending the analysis through a critical engagement with peoples' experience and learning. Pettit (2006; emphasis in original) notes the value of this form of extension:

> If we accept that power is multidimensional, defined by various forms of agency and socialization, then the learning process should enable us to access, explore and understand as many of these dimensions as possible. [...] [U]nderstanding and addressing power calls for more innovative learning processes, which stimulate not only the *conceptual* and *rational* re-evaluation of one's assumed perspective, but also the more *experiential, embodied, creative, practical* and other *non-dialogical* means of reflection, or making sense of one's experiences of power, and of realising one's capacity to shift power. (pp. 72-73)

Learning and Critical Reflection in Development Practice

It is important to recall that neither *learning* nor *change* are inherently positive concepts. Praxis can itself be understood as either reproductive or revolutionary. As Shaul (as cited in Freire, 1972[1996]), drawing on Freire, has argued

> education either functions as an instrument that is used to facilitate integration ... into the logic of the present system and bring about conformity to it, *or* it becomes the 'practice of freedom,' the means by which men and

women deal critically and creatively with reality and discover how to participate in the transformation of their world. (p. 16)

The discourses of lifelong and experiential learning in the workplace have been amply shown to create a potential avenue toward further socialisation or skilling of adults in line with the dictates of global labour management (flexible, adaptive, transferable, etc.) (Murphy, 2000). Edwards (1998), Fenwick (2001) and others have also highlighted the increasing use of reflective practice as both a 'technology of the self' within modern professional environments. Edwards (1998) notes that "self-management within organization frameworks displaces the forms of autonomous activity which are often associated with professional work. In this sense, reflective practice may be well part of the moral technology and forms of governmentality through which work is intensified and regulated" (p. 387). Even learning termed transformative can be understood as a pathway of personal emancipation rather than collective social change (Finger, 1989), or ultimately disempowering if it fails to actually help people change their situations (Bevins, Moriarty & Taylor, 2009). As a result, it is imperative that we better understand the perspectives on learning which might strengthen collective voice and agency and expand the limits of what is deemed possible at specific sites and instances of struggle and contestation. The concrete impacts (both real and potential) and challenges of engaging in these forms of reflection and analysis are explored through the investigation that below.

SHAPING THE DEVELOPMENT INSTITUTION: THE CASE OF ENDA

As development brokerage has become an increasingly lucrative and professionalized endeavour, the number of NGOs and agencies working in Senegal has grown dramatically, from fewer than twenty in the 1970s, to over 250 NGOs and Community Based Organisations (CBOs) in 1994 (Guèye & Dieng, 1994), and with still more operating today. In the process, the influence of larger international NGOs and Inter-governmental Organisations (IGOs) with country or regional offices in Senegal has shaped the broader landscape of development cooperation (both actors and institutions) and civil society engagement more broadly, in line with the international norms of practice they have established – what Sonia Alvarez (1988) has aptly referred to this transformation as "NGOisation" (cf. Fall, 2004). Uma Kothari (2005) has explored this process at a global level, noting how the professionalization and accelerating expansion of institutionalized development practice after the 1980s "encompass[ed] alternative approaches which were previously marginal to the development mainstream" (p. 438). She notes how radical and alternative discourses were co-opted by mainstream multi- and bilateral development agencies and:

> became increasingly technicalised in order to fit into the more formalized development planning frameworks and models favoured by these organisations. [...] This strategy of appropriation reduced spaces of critique and dissent, since the inclusion and appropriation of ostensibly radical

discourses limited the potential for any challenge from outside the mainstream to orthodox development planning and practices. (Kothari, 2005, p. 439)

In the case of *Environment and Development Action in the Third World* (ENDA-TM), whose work has explicitly sought to develop alternative development models, the pressure (both direct and indirect) that has resulted from this shifting landscape has produced a number of challenges it must confront.

ENDA is an international non-profit organisation, founded in 1972, and headquartered in Dakar, Senegal. Drawing upon the strong post-colonial standpoints of its founding architects, Jacques Bugnicourt, Samir Amin, and Cheikh Hamidou Kane, ENDA committed itself to establishing a clear Southern (and particularly African) focus with a particular attention to the concerns of poor, marginalised populations and the environmental issues that affect them. Bugnicourt described the niche and originality of ENDA's work in the global South as "implementing certain techniques with peasants and slum-dwellers based upon the needs they express ... and, at the same time, publishing works and articles on technology or taking part in the debates of agencies and specialist at the level of the Third World" (Bugnicourt & Mhlanga, 1980, p. 1; translation mine). He adds that a great challenge lies in ensuring that these activities "retain their sense of solidarity and close contact with what is happening in the country sides or the slums, and that the concerns of those who inhabit these areas constitute the defining elements of the range of research, training and action undertaken" (p. 1; translation mine). On this basis, ENDA has developed a theory of change which sees locally-oriented research and popular dynamics as drivers of social, institutional, and personal transformation, encouraging people to deconstruct and reconstruct their identities; grow through creativity, promote change in power relations and collective and personal organisation, and live more sustainably (ENDA Graf, 2005).

Today ENDA has grown into one of the largest Southern-based NGOs worldwide. It collaborates with grassroots groups in search of alternative development models on the basis of the experience, expectations and objectives of marginalised peoples. Accompanying its growth and spreading engagement in the South (particularly in West Africa) has been a growing recognition of the institution as a "centre of excellence" for partnerships with International and Intergovernmental organisations including UN agencies, the World Bank, and others. This has presented an ever-expanding range of new opportunities for partnership and engagement, but has, at the same time, introduced challenges to the retention of its clear and locally-oriented vision for social change amid the growing 'intellectual hegemony' (Chambers & Pettit, 2004) of institutionalised development practice described above. Some of the key challenges which have emerged include engaging and retaining staff members committed to developing transformative approaches to effecting change amid this broader homogenization of practice; maintaining a spirit of collaboration within and between ENDA's teams rather than the free-market-inspired competitiveness that current funding protocols have encouraged; and balancing resistance to dominant development frameworks in favour of locally articulated alternatives while remaining accessible to funders upon whose funding their work depends. It is through their engagement with these networks of differently situated actors and their accompanying protocols that the team both shaped and defended its identity.

Balancing Resistance and Viability

The tensions between external pressures from institutional partners and the institute's own articulation of meaningful social engagement presents challenges, but also opens opportunities for collective reflection and informal learning. In the case of one ENDA team, this has taken the form of weekly meetings to review current and upcoming work; meetings which occasionally evolved into debates over the direction in which particular initiatives or partnerships were taking the team. Numerous examples could be cited here, including collaborative research with Northern institutions which attempted to shift the focus of contracted research toward issues that contravened ENDA's core principles (e.g., promoting nuclear energy as 'clean energy'); partnerships seeking to engage them as a community intermediary for the introduction potentially objectionable initiatives (such as large-scale biofuels projects); and invitations to work with Northern research institutions that have previously engaged in extractive forms of collaboration with ENDA.

Opportunities for relatively open discussion and debate over the broader question of program direction sometimes afforded by the team's weekly meetings served an important and often-unacknowledged purpose. On those occasions when the team was allowed (or allowed itself) to forego the expediency of running through the agenda of to-do items for the week and delve into the messier and less immediate questions of direction and principles, members were able to challenge each other's views, present arguments for their positions based upon their interpretation of ENDA's purpose, on their own experiences, or on their understanding of local needs and concerns. In doing so they reflected upon and began to assert its agency in the face of external pressure, and helped shape the contemporary identity of the team and the institution more broadly. Conversely, it seems that those moments where the opportunity to delve into greater detail about such thorny questions was passed over for the sake of concision or expediency represented lost opportunities for collective learning and strengthening of solidarity within the team.

The institutional challenges noted here represent a site of struggle *within* the institution, where the constancy of external pressure and micro-technologies of institutional power threaten to uproot and de-legitimise the transformative potential of critical and creative social engagement. Driving and giving direction to this resistance within the team is a (sometimes sporadic) critical reflection over the principles and theories that the team wishes to uphold, the threats to these principles and appropriate responses. If, as their principles suggest, one of the institute's aims is to help people bring about changes in power relations through critical reflection and learning about themselves and their environment to better understand the obstacles they face (ENDA Graf, 2005), then it would seem that more dedicated attention on this resistance *within the team* could serve as an important starting point.

Serving as a counterpoint to the internal struggles and debates described above, the second section of this chapter considers the ways that another ENDA team has worked to shape the farming practices of a federation of cotton producers in rural Senegal over a period of approximately 15 years. In this context, where ENDA's perceived roles as facilitator, capacity builder, funding conduit and advocate places them in a position of authority and influence, it becomes possible to see how individuals and groups "are always in the position of simultaneously undergoing and exercising power" (Foucault, 1980, p. 98). It also serves to illustrate how this particular federation struggles to balance the desire for autonomy and self-definition with the perceived security of partnership with NGOs and other external institutions and the models of development they espouse (cf. Marsden, 2004).

Here, I argue, in a community where reliance on outside support is so deeply engrained and articulated through a wide range of processes, the degree to which identities and roles of community members have been shaped by outside forces and institutions is especially high; and this reliance is exacerbated on two fronts, each revealing some of the complexities of development relations. The first I will explore is through the Federation of producers' willingness to subject themselves to new, often complex forms of scrutiny and accountancy in the hope of securing safer and more equitable livelihoods through organic and fairtrade cotton production. The second arises from the fact that locally-active NGOs and development brokers are themselves financially and professionally reliant on facilitating the implementation of aid initiatives at the community level (and thus, of representing the community's needs and potential for 'successful development' within the international development community.

It is important to note that this critique is not necessarily aimed at advocating against organic cotton production in the region. Clearly there are important health, financial and environmental justifications for its pursuit among those who engage in farming for international trade markets as a livelihood activity. Further, given the current situation of conventional cotton markets (globally and nationally) and the current status of conventional cotton farming in Senegal, Federation members, by their own admission, would most likely still be subjected to other forms of external coordination with perhaps even less opportunity for response were they engaged in conventional (rather than fairtrade) production as it is currently structured (cf. Williamson, Ferrigno, & Vodouhe, 2005). Instead, this discussion aims to highlight the ways that the nascent organic and fairtrade cotton markets, established partly under the premise of empowering local producers (through a fairer income, safer working conditions, more democratic decision-making processes, etc.) activates a new and different series of power dynamics that must be better understood when reflecting on its potential impacts and benefits. It also considers how this process is enacted through the Federation's engagement with

193

CHAPTER 12

ENDA, and the implications this has on their capacity to shape a vision of the future.

Community Collaboration

ENDA first began their collaboration with cotton producers about 450km east of Dakar in 1995. They initially helped a small group of peasants produce organic cotton with an aim of responding to environmental and health concerns related to pesticide use in the cotton production process, resulting in the establishment of the first organic cotton project in West Africa. In 1997 a Federation of organic farmers was established, and has since grown to nearly 2000 producers from over 80 villages in the region. In this time it has received both organic and fairtrade certification for its cotton; and has expanded its livelihood activities to include the production alternative indigenous crop varieties, as well as initial ventures into the production of value-added cotton-based products such as thread and clothing.

However, the development of a market and strong production base for organic/fairtrade cotton has proven difficult. Organic agriculture represents a miniscule percentage of agricultural production in Senegal; costs related to training, regular inspection, certification and processing of crops are high; and there is virtually no domestic or West African market willing to pay the additional premiums for organic/fairtrade commodities (cf. Ferrigno, Ratter, Ton, Vodouhê, Williamson, & Wilson, 2005). Thus, the Federation remains highly dependent upon external support, both for finding exporters for their harvests, or, barring that, for paying the difference in price between conventional and organic cotton should they be forced to sell their crops on the conventional market. The need for ENDA's guidance and regular intervention extends beyond the need for financial and marketing support, however, and in fact arises at the level of the day-to-day management and monitoring of farmer's crops in line with the much stricter regulations of organic farming. Farmers opting into organic agriculture find themselves essentially forced to re-learn more traditional approaches to their trade, now re-presented through the scientific/managerial technologies of formally-educated agricultural *specialists*.

Modern-day production of organic cotton is an exacting and highly regulated practice. The degree of control over production processes is, foremost, justified by the need to guarantee that the product has not come into contact with the more commonly-grown conventional cotton or its chemical treatments, sometimes being grown only a few metres away from organic crops. Cotton must be formally certified as organic (and/or fairtrade) to be saleable as such on the global market. These forms of certification and the processes required for obtaining them have been developed in the North, are frequently carried out by Northern institutional representatives, and are not well adapted to the socio-economic contexts found in places like rural Senegal. Producers are expected to abide by strict transparency protocols, providing a meticulous paper-trail documenting the conditions in which the cotton was produced, treatments it received, and the environment in which it was grown. In the case of fairtrade cotton, as is produced by the Federation,

194

producers are also expected to provide documentary proof of the democratic and equitable processes through which they work together (meeting minutes, vote tallies, annual reporting, etc.) (cf. Bassett, 2010). Given high rate of illiteracy among cotton producers in the area, and the costly certification processes, it becomes obvious that the process is nearly impossible without extensive outside support from individuals or organisations accustomed to working within these types of norms (ENDA, 2007).

In examining the standardised precision with which crop treatments, surroundings and history must be recorded, compiled and submitted for inspection, it becomes clear how heavily the process is controlled from outside/above, demanding the compulsory visibility (Foucault, 1978) of producers and their collectives. Bassett (2010), drawing on research in West Africa, also notes that:

> Fairtrade certification largely focuses on the democratic and transparent operations of *producer groups*. The conduct of other actors in the commodity chain (ginning companies, traders, and national producer associations) is not as closely monitored. Although one [...] extension agent found "laughable" the suggestion that cotton companies would be willing to let producers scrutinize their financial records, it is not a laughing matter for cotton growers. (p. 51)

While Bassett's study and others (cf. ENDA, 2007) focus on questions of equity within such international trade arrangements and rightly question to what extent these arrangements actually challenge the marginalising global trade practices of conventional cotton, less has been said on how these processes (and the NGO support that frequently accompanies them) 're-organise' farmers' lives in line with external norms. This point seems highly relevant in considering how this support appeals to ENDA's stated aim of helping people bring about changes in power relations through critical reflection and learning about themselves and their environment. Here, Dorothy Smith's (1984, 2001) work on how replicable texts organise people across space and time proves particularly appropriate in considering the protocols noted above, which are developed in Europe, translated in Dakar, and intervene daily at the level of the local farmer across a whole region of Senegal. Smith (2001) posits that:

> Reproducing the same managerial and accounting procedures across many local settings hooks [people's] local work organization into 'centralized' regulatory and decision processes that are themselves located in particular settings. [...] The multiple replication of exactly the same text that technologies of print made possible enable an organization of social relations independent of local time, place and person suture modes of social action organized extra-locally and co-ordinating multiple local sites of people's work to the local actualities of our necessarily embodied lives. (pp. 174-175)

The result, says Smith (2001), is that "people's doings are no longer just that, but become interpretable as expressions or instances of a higher order organization, independent of particular people" (p. 180). Smith's comments also shed light upon another phenomenon observed within the individual cotton producers that highlights how central ENDA's role is perceived to be; the fact that a great deal of the producers refer to the crop they produce as 'ENDA Cotton'. This points to the degree to which ENDA represents or embodies this 'higher order of organization' and how the processes that regulate their farming practice are seen to come from and be enforced on behalf of them.

The Struggle for Self-Definition

The Federation's dependence upon ENDA's support is well-recognized by its current leaders (themselves farmers), and is a source of concern and frustration. Federation Secretariat members described the challenges they currently face in shaping their own identity, having a greater role in the production, processing and distribution of the crops they produce, and avoiding being themselves "traded" as a development commodity among NGOs and funders. The Federation's President described his ultimate vision of them becoming '75% self-sufficient,' allowing for occasional and limited support from outside agencies. In speaking of the capacities that they need to achieve this desired independence, they noted a need to obtain internet access, and develop capacity in ICTs so that they could begin reaching out on their own to the foreign markets that purchase their cotton. Their capacity to do so thus far has been extremely limited, given the physical distance (two days of travel from Europe) from prospective buyers, their lack of capital (economic, political, social) for developing new markets, and their lack of local infrastructure. As such, international access to the Federation is generally initiated through ENDA's office in Dakar. However, members noted that these issues were rarely given priority in the assessment of their capacities and needs, with focus instead being directed toward enabling them to better meet the inspection requirements mandated through organic/fairtrade protocols.

'Inventing' the Peasant

Funders and cooperants such as ENDA often bring pre-conceived notions about the priorities, values and needs of subsistence farmers and their communities, and how best to help them to improve their lives. These groups, who tend to have clearly-defined political or epistemological orientations toward notions such as progress, development, and the environment can often privilege these orientations (perhaps unsurprisingly), over the agency of the communities with whom they are working. This tendency is particularly pronounced if these communities are perceived as vulnerable, limited in capacity, and of a static identity (e.g. peasants and farmers, not "businessmen" as the assumption appeared to be here). The tendency to pre-suppose the community's lack of interest or aptitude in negotiating the purchase of crops or pre-financing agreements with potential buyers was evident in this relation, and was central to the re-presentation of the Federation's identity to outsiders, and thus served as a vehicle for the construction of their subjectivity. Alvesson (1996), drawing on Foucault, notes that "in the creation of subjectivity, the individual is made into an object for subordination as well as developing (being provided with) a particular identity. [...] Power is thus exercised by binding the subject to a particular identity or form" (p. 102). Here, I would argue, the identities of individuals that made up the Federation's Secretariat and membership are fundamentally shaped by and kept in line with the discursive practices associated to them by the broader development apparatus within which they are embedded.

To be clear, this assertion does not necessarily imply a violent or even overt restriction of the mobility or agency of the Federation's members. Nor is the shaping inherently inaccurate or exclusively constraining. The Federation has, in this case, been cast as a model for successful and empowering rural agricultural development by ENDA and a range of other champions of organic farming and environmental development, and thus as innovative, empowered, democratic, etc. However, the Federation's depiction is always embedded within a broader network of actors, described above, including certification agents, funding agencies, national *sociétiés*, and collaborating NGOs, and the complex patterns of bureaucratic and discursive organisation that assigns each of them their roles and identities. It is here that it seems that these funders, cooperating agencies, and the like have a vested interest in ensuring that individuals, communities and peasants' organisations *do remain* as they have been discursively framed; incrementally improving the quality of their livelihoods and embodying the agreed-upon principles of 'good practice', without evolving to such an extent as to rupture the continuity of their cooperation, or each other's *raison d'être*.

This would be particularly true in cases heralded externally as 'success stories' such as that of the Federation. Development funding in Africa is highly lucrative in comparison to the subsistence activities the majority of these 'vulnerable communities' are involved in, and employs thousands worldwide. In the context of international development practice it may be fair to say that the community itself (or the discursive identity in which it has been cast) has become a resource for (sustainable) exploitation. The question of capital, however, is not the only incentive that explains the need to ensure the discursive construction of these actors remains intact. Rather, as noted at the outset of this chapter, these forms of coordination and subjugation are fundamental to the maintenance of the 'regime of truth' that justifies the entire concept of international development.

While this discussion has sought to demonstrate the forms of dependence that have stemmed from the Federation's compliance with the international protocols on organic/fairtrade agriculture; ENDA, like the Federation, is also subject to the same discursive framing, as are the agencies that fund these initiatives. Thus, both subordinates and those 'in power' (at times, as this chapter has sought to illustrate, one may be both at once) find themselves being bound to discourse and its structures. As such, in order for ENDA to continue being a development NGO, they need communities in need of "developing" and who are responsive to their strategies of action.

One of the questions that arises in considering these dynamics of power is how the Federation and community members can therefore 'speak back' to power, and strengthen their positions as advocates and spokespeople for their own agency.

197

What different arrangement of actors (if any) would facilitate this ability to draw into question the shaping influence of the development apparatus? What strategies or practices might better position them to respond to these outside pressures with a clearly articulated collective vision? In concluding, I turn to the learning dimension of these challenges to consider how collective informal and incidental learning might help to identify and challenge the processes and systems that constrain their abilities to remain "agents of their own histories" (Kapoor, 2004, p. 43). These questions cannot be answered easily or definitely, particularly from a community outsider. Indeed, given the urgency of current pressures upon the community (near-subsistence-level incomes, extreme vulnerability to environmental, political, or social stresses and shocks, etc.) alongside the deeper concerns of autonomy and self-determination, it would seem that one of the key challenges is balancing the short-term urgency of self/community-improvement with a long-time, experimental aim of effecting deeper changes in social order (Lindeman, 1961). This question appears to have been identified by Federation leaders, but they have struggled to create spaces and opportunities where they could consider them collectively and independently of the institutional players whose vested interest in their activities has deeply organised their daily activity and visions of the future. I would argue that collective reflection on these points of contention and struggle could provide an entry point for learning, and re-orientation. This process could inform both the current and longer-term visions of the Federation and its associated communities and open discussion about the impact of 'allied' institutions and global market forces on their livelihood activities.

CHALLENGES TO LEARNING AND COLLECTIVE ACTION

The story of [counter-hegemonic] struggle is one of gains and losses, of progress and retreat, and of a growing recognition of the continually contested, complex, ambiguous and contradictory nature of the struggle between domination and liberation. This struggle also has a learning and educational dimension which emerges when we examine concrete situations. I say 'emerges' advisedly, because the learning is often embedded in other activities and has to be uncovered. (Foley, 2001, p. 77)

Learning and Power

In the cases highlighted by this chapter, a clearer understanding of how relations of power within partnerships shaped the options that were (or were not) being presented, the ease with which certain choices could be made, or the degree to which assistance would be offered for particular forms of action, may have helped participants to make sense of their lived experience and struggles. A more formalised reflection upon the struggles that arose in the course of social action could help to schematise the collective informal and incidental learning that is inherently embedded in these moments of struggle (as noted in the quote from Foley above) and inform future courses of action. In order to appropriately engage with this larger sphere of the development apparatus, as ENDA's own principles of action call upon it to do, or for the cotton producer's Federation to engage with the community and institutions beyond its membership, however, there must first be a clarified understanding of its own relationship with power and capacity to affect change, as well as an appreciation of the internal dynamics and meaning-making processes of those who constitute these collectives.

Pettit's (2006) assertion that understanding and addressing power requires innovative ways to think about learning provides a useful opening to shift this discussion toward a more detailed exploration of how this process can be put into action, and what conditions can either support or constrain it. In reflecting on the actions, inactions, and outcomes that figured in the contexts described above, I am drawn to Klouda's (2004) challenge that the development community's continued attention to critical reflection as a means to stimulating social change has failed to address two key questions: "Why, if people really are capable of doing this, don't they do it more often?" (p. 2). This concluding discussion does not purport to provide a complete answer to Kluda's question, but it does aim to clarify some of the preconditions that played a role in taking those who were involved in this study from recognising the need for change toward feeling equipped and motivated to act accordingly.

Factors which Enable and Constrain Learning in Action

Spaces for Change
The notion of space emerged repeatedly over the course of this study. Its presence, absence, colonisation, and defence, as well as its nature and origin have proven to be fundamental factors in determining the scope for reflection and consultation and, consequently, it shapes peoples' capacity to re-imagine the terms of their engagement with others. Thus, space has a potential productive value as the site where groups can engage in radical rethinking and the acquisition of skills to put this thinking into action, making it at once constitutive and expressive of power relations and people's agency (Cornwall, 2004).

The question of *physical* space emerged in discussions about the potentials and limits of the meeting space at the cotton Federation headquarters, which had previously been shared with ENDA but was now their own. Its value was also visible in the weekly meetings convened in ENDA's offices, where all team members could gather and debate the impacts of the work they were in engaged in. *Temporal* space was constantly at a premium within the ENDA offices, as can be found nearly anywhere that a culture of managerialism has become embedded. This meant that extended discussions on the aims and direction of the team, reflections on new ways to engage with partners, and opportunities to collaborate and dialogue with potential collaborators from within the institution all found themselves in competition with the demands placed upon the team by others. The limited and limiting notions of what constitutes 'productive' time in dominant managerial frameworks (generally utilitarian, capital driven, linear, etc.) often exclude the types of temporal space required for collective reflection and deliberation on change. Perhaps most important, however, is the *conceptual* space for imagining new terms and forms of engagement. On this point, it is important to recognise the intimate link between space and praxis (which is central to our ability to reflect upon change and put it into action). As Mayo (2009) notes, "praxis constitutes the means of gaining critical distance from one's world of action to engage in reflection geared toward transformative action" (p. 100). This was particularly relevant to the Federation's relationship with ENDA, one which was so deeply embedded, that it left little opportunity for members to gain this critical distance and reflect on the options they might have.

Drawing on Gaventa (2006) and Cornwall's (2002) distinction between *closed* (which restrict access to decision making or participation to an elite few), *invited* (which have been regularised or institutionalised, and are open on a restricted basis), and *claimed/created* spaces (which may come from popular mobilisation around sets of common concerns or a rejection of hegemonic spaces) may be useful in further highlighting the link between learning and the struggle for participation. It also recalls Tembo's (2004) assertion that marginalised groups lack space within which they can exercise their images of reality rather than simply affirming the plans established by others. Further, the degree to which invited or claimed spaces are seen as "safe" for those engaged in a learning and reflection process to take on the risk and challenge of being critical of themselves and others (cf. Langdon & Harvey, 2009). It is important to note here that space is a dynamic construct and always subject to transformation. Thus, it can be understood not only as a site where learning, reflection, and planning for change are enabled, but also as a site of incidental learning during struggles over it.

Acknowledgement and Appreciation of Risk

Risk has often been cited as a potential barrier to poor or vulnerable people' willingness to adopt alternative practices in community-based agricultural and environmental adaptation and disaster management (Fafchamps, 2003), and has been explored in literature on action research (Denzin, 2005; Fine, 2006), but its role in collective learning and action within development literature has been less widely recognised. For Kluda (2004) this oversight is fundamental. He argues that:

> It is not critical thinking or even consciousness of reality that is the issue: it is the ability to speak out and act for change in relation to one's own social situation that poses the difficulty. The difficulty is there precisely because an individual has to make an assessment of the level of risk involved in making that challenge. (p. 6)

Risk (or perception of risk) is not uniform across a particular group of actors, as individuals are differently positioned vis-à-vis the change or action under consideration, and differently exposed to the struggle at hand. It is closely related to people's relative ability to dictate their own pathways and the tenuousness with which they hold their current positions, as in the case of the Federation, whose members very livelihoods were in question. It cannot simply be dismissed as conservativeness or a lack of criticality, and must be recognised and addressed in order to enable people to fully engage with processes of learning and change. Doing so is dependent upon the fulfillment of some of the other preconditions noted here, particularly the availability of a space to dialogically explore people's varying interpretations of risk, and the presence of appropriate leadership and support to help people navigate their understanding of risk, and to help attenuate this risk when possible.

Leadership and Support

The notion of leadership and support as a potential enabling or constraining force in transformational learning has been thoroughly debated in the fields of adult education (Brookfield, 2001; Tennant, 1998) and action research (Kapoor, 2009). In relations of leadership and support I would argue, much like education, "the task is to encourage human agency, not mold it in the manner of Pygmalion" (Aronowitz, 1998, p. 10). Where the line must be drawn between encouragement and moulding, however, is a more challenging question; one which recalls Foucault's (1978) question of whether the growth of human capabilities *can* be disconnected from the intensification of power relations, and what forms of supportive arrangement might achieve this effect. Opinions are divergent on two important points here: a) The degree to which leadership can be directive in struggle, and b) the sites from which this leadership can legitimately arise. Rahman, among others (see Kapoor, 2009), argues that it is "absolutely essential that the people develop their own endogenous process of consciousness raising and knowledge generation and this process acquires the social power to assert itself vis-à-vis all elite consciousness and knowledge" (Rahman, 1985, p.15), implying a restrictive view of the scope to which outside leadership and support might be engaged. Holford (1995), by contrast, calls for a stronger leadership role among what he terms "movement intellectuals" in articulating and leading struggle, arguing against seeing educators as merely "equal participants in movements", and sees these leaders as operating at the margins of a particular movement or struggle and the "wider world," but stresses the need for reflexive and self-conscious leadership (or educators) that recognizes the partiality of its own knowledge (p. 106). I find myself aligned with Rahman and others who argue that strategies for struggle must arise from and reflect the lived experience of those engaged in that particular struggle and facing the forms of domination which make that struggle necessary. I do feel, however, building upon Denzin's (2005) notion of the allied other, that there is scope to act in solidarity with that particular struggle and from the locations where our life experience positions us, if we are continuously reflective of our own embeddedness within relations of power and subjugation and the effects that this may be having.

A Common Articulated Vision of Change

Reflecting upon the internal discussions that were initiated within the ENDA team describe earlier in this chapter, I feel that the articulation of a shared vision and theory of change allows groups engaged in struggles with power to come to a common understanding of where they stand and what they hope to achieve, to guard against institutional *drift*, and to better communicate their perspectives outside of the sphere of the group and its allies. 'Non-negotiables' among community groups engaged in development cooperation, for example, can help to demarcate the terms and limits to their engagement with others (Chambers and Pettit, 2004). Hardy, Palmer and Phillips' (2000) depiction of *strategy discourse* as a resource that can be used to construct social reality may also be helpful seeing how the construction of a vision of change (through the production of texts and discursive 'acts'), the practices that arise from this vision and strategy, and the interplay of these with broader societal discourses can ultimately change an organisation and its environment. These impacts are demonstrable not only to those inside the organisation but also to those outside of it. This is not to say that changing reality is as simple as one day changing discursive acts, but rather that discourse can serve as a tool to eventually detach 'truth' from particular relations of power, and that the power to generate new forms of discourse is fundamental to the strategic reversibility of truth regimes.

Equity and Democracy within the Community of Actors

The final point upon which I would like to elaborate on here is the importance of sustained efforts toward equity and democracy within the community of actors. If the articulation of the common vision discussed above must be the product of a dialogical process that leaves space for participation and voice if it is to stimulate a genuine propensity to act, then questions of equity and democracy within this process are fundamental. Further, on the basis of the theory of power upon which I have developed this study, even spaces characterised by a shared vision and sense of identity are subject to relations of power that hold one person or sub-group in a dominant position over another. Equity and democracy in this context are best understood as *processes* rather than fixed endpoints, particularly given a view of power that sees it as continuously in flux. Normative understandings of these concepts can prove difficult and often inappropriate, particularly within post-colonial contexts, and their imposition can become a tool for silencing rather than for the flourishing of dialogue (Brookfield, 1995). Thus, the implications of this precondition will vary according to setting, and will need to be the product of a collective meaning-making that may not necessarily match with the expectations/understandings of outside participants, and must be open to re-evaluation.

CONCLUSIONS

This chapter has highlighted links between an ethnographic account of the influence of power on networks of development actors and institutions, and Foley's (2001) call for "contextualised ethnographic accounts of learning in social action" (p. 84) to explore the opportunities and conditions for drawing on collective learning to contest the subjugating power of development. Using the case an NGO with a stated commitment to challenging relations that marginalise communities in the South, I have sought to illustrate the complexity of negotiating these relations, demonstrating how individuals and institutions are constantly engaged in processes of undergoing and exercising power (Foucault, 1980). On this basis, I argue, it is imperative that people engage in critical reflection about their own agency and the ways in which they have been situated by the development apparatus in order to work toward change. While this aim is laudable, it is no easy task, and better understanding the factors that enable or constrain these forms of reflection and action is a project which must remain central to rethinking development.

REFERENCES

Alvarez, S. (1988). The NGOisation of Latin American feminisms. In S. Alvarez, E. Dagnino & A. Escobar (eds.), *Cultures of politics, politics of cultures: Re-visioning Latin American social movements*. Boulder, CO: Westview.

Alvesson, M. (1996). *Communication, power and organization*. Berlin: Walter de Gruyter.

Aronowitz, S. (1998). Introduction. In P. Freire (ed.), *Pedagogy of freedom*. Lanham, MD: Rowman & Littlefield.

Bassett, T. J. (2010). Slim pickings: Fairtrade cotton in West Africa. *Geoforum, 41*, 44-55.

Bevins, F, Moriarty, K, & Taylor, P, (2009). Transformative education and its potential for changing the lives of children in disempowering contexts. *IDS Bulletin, 40*(1), 97-108.

Brookfield, S. (1995). *Becoming a critically reflective teacher*. San Francisco: Jossey-Bass.

Brookfield, S. (2001). Unmasking power: Foucault and adult learning. *Canadian Journal for the Study of Adult Education, 15*(1), 1.

Bugnicourt, J. & Mhlanga, L. (1980). *Techniques pour le développement rural: L'approche d'ENDA au ras du sol*. Brussels: UNESCO.

Chambers, R. & Pettit, J. (2004). Shifting power to make a difference. In L. Groves & R. Hinton (eds.), *Inclusive aid: Changing power and relationships in international development*. London: Earthscan.

Cornwall, A. (2002). *Making spaces, changing places: Situating participation in development*. Brighton: Institute of Development Studies.

Cornwall, A. (2004). Spaces for transformation? Reflections on issues of power and difference in participation in development. In S. Hickey & G. Mohan (eds.), *Participation: From tyranny to transformation?* London: Zed Books.

Denzin, N. (2005). Emancipatory discourses and the ethics and politics of interpretation. In N. Denzin & Y. Lincoln (eds.), *The Sage handbook of qualitative research*. New York: Sage.

Edwards, R. (1998). Flexibility, reflexivity and reflection in the contemporary workplace. *International Journal of Lifelong Education, 17*, 377-388.

ENDA Graf (2005). *Changement politique et social: Éléments pour la pensée et l'action*. Dakar: Réseau Enda Graf Sahel.

Eyben, R. (2000). Development and anthropology: A view from inside the agency. *Critique of Anthropology, 20*(1), 7-14.

Fafchamps, M. (2003). *Rural poverty, risk and development*. Cheltenham and Northampton: Edward Elgar.

Fall, A. S. (2004). Les ONG au Sénégal, un movement social ascendant. In M. Niang (ed.), *Participation paysanne et développement rural au Sénégal*. Dakar: CODESRIA.

Ferrigno, S., Ratter, S. G., Ton, P., Vodouhê, D. S., Williamson, S., & Wilson, J. (2005). Organic cotton: A new development path for African smallholders? *Gatekeeper Series*. London: International Institute for Environment and Development.

Fenwick, T. (2001). Tides of change: New themes and questions in workplace learning. *New Directions for Adult and Continuing Education, 92*(Winter) 3-17.

Fine, M. (2006). Intimate details: Participatory action research in prison. *Action Research, 4*(3), 253-269.

Finger, M. (1989). New social movements and their implications for adult education. *Adult Education Quarterly, 40*(1), 15-22.

Foley, G. (1999). *Learning in social action: A contribution to understanding education and training*. London: Zed Books.

Foley, G. (2001). Radical adult education and learning. *International Journal of Lifelong Education, 20*(1/2), 71-88.

Foucault, M. (1978). What is enlightenment? In P. Rabinow (ed.), *The Foucault reader*. New York: Pantheon Books.

Foucault, M. (1980). *Power/knowledge: Selected interviews and other writings, 1972-1977*. New York: Pantheon.

Freire, P. (ed.) (1972[1996]). *Pedagogy of the oppressed*. London: Penguin Books.

Gaventa, J. (2006). Finding the spaces for change: A power analysis. *IDS Bulletin, 37*(6), 23-33.

Guèye, A. P., & Dieng, M. (1994). Le diagnostic institutionnel et la méthodologie de développement institutionnel: L'expérience du projet d'appui aux ONGs/USAID au Sénégal. *Bulletin de l'APAD, 8*.

Hardy, C., Palmer, I., & Phillips, N. (2000). Discourse as a strategic resource. *Human Relations, 53*, 1227-1248.

Holford, J. (1995). Why social movements matter: Adult education theory, cognitive praxis, and the creation of knowledge. *Adult Education Quarterly, 45*(2), 95-111.

Kapoor, D. (2004). Indigenous struggles for forests, land and cultural identity in India: Environmental popular education and the democratization of power. In D. Clover (ed.), *Global perspectives in environmental adult education*. New York: Peter Lang.

Kapoor, D. (2009). Participatory academic research (PAR) and people's participatory action research (par): Research, politicization, and subaltern social movements in India. In D. Kapoor & S. Jordan (eds.), *International perspectives on education, participatory action research (PAR) and social change*. New York: Palgrave.

Klouda, T. (2004). Thinking critically, speaking critically. Retrieved from http://www.tonyklouda.pwp.blueyonder.co.uk/

Kothari, U. (2005). Authority and expertise: The professionalisation of international development and the ordering of dissent. *Antipode, 37*(3), 425-446.

Langdon, J., & Harvey, B. (2009). Building anticolonial spaces for global education: Challenges and reflections. In A. Kempf (ed.), *Breaching the colonial contract: Anti-colonialism in the US and Canada*. Toronto: Springer.

Lindeman, E. C. (1961). *The meaning of adult education* (2nd ed). Montreal: Harvest House.

Marsden, R. (2004). Exploring power and relationships: A perspective from Nepal. In L. Groves & R. Hinton (eds.), *Inclusive aid: Changing power and relationships in international development*. London: Earthscan.

Mayo, P. (2009). Paulo Freire and adult education. In A. Abdi & D. Kapoor (eds.), *Global perspectives on adult education*. New York: Palgrave.

Mosse, D. (2005). *Cultivating development: An ethnography of aid policy and practice*. London: Pluto Press.

Murphy, M. (2000). Adult education, lifelong learning and the end of political economy. *Studies in the Education of Adults, 32*(2), 166-180.

Pettit, J. (2006). Power and pedagogy: Learning for reflective development practice. *IDS Bulletin, 37*(6), 69-78.

Rahman, A. (1985). The theory and practice of participatory research. In O. Fals Borda (ed.), *The challenge of social change*. London: Sage.

Smith, D. (1984). Textually mediated social organization. *International Social Science Journal, 36*(1), 59-75.

Smith, D. (2001). Texts and the ontology of organizations and institutions. *Studies in Cultures, Organizations and Societies, 7*(2), 159-198.

Tembo, F. (2004). NGDO's role in building poor people's capacity to benefit from globalization. *Journal of International Development, 16*(7), 1023-1037.

Tennant, M. (1998). Adult education as a technology of the self. *International Journal of Lifelong Education, 17*(6), 364-376.

Vincent, S. (2004). Participation, resistance and problems with the 'local' in Peru: Towards a new political contract? In S. Hickey & G. Mohan (eds.), *Participation: From tyranny to transformation?* London: Zed Books.

Von Kotze, A. (2000). *Learning in/through/with struggle*. University of Technology Sydney Research Centre Vocational Education and Training (Working paper no. 61). Conference *Working Knowledge: Productive learning at work*. University of Technology Sydney, Australia.

Williamson, S., Ferrigno, S., Vodouhe, S. D. (2005). Needs-based decision-making for cotton problems in Africa: A response to Hillocks. *International Journal of Pest Management, 51*(4), 219-224.

AUTHOR BIOGRAPHIES

Dr. Gloria T. Emeagwali is the chief editor of *Africa Update* and the author of several websites, including the UNESCO award winning resource www.africahistory.net. She has authored and edited seven books and sixty journal and book articles. She has taught at several universities including Ahmadu Bello University and the University of Ilorin, Nigeria and Central Connecticut State University (CCSU) where she has taught for the last twenty years. Her research interests include Globalization and its effects on African economies and African Indigenous Knowledge Systems. Dr. Emeagwali is Professor of History and African Studies at CCSU.

Dr. Edward Shizha is Assistant Professor in Contemporary Studies and Children's Education and Development at Wilfrid Laurier University (Brantford) in Canada. His academic interests are in contemporary social problems and education including: globalization, post-colonialism, and indigenous knowledges in Africa. He has published; refereed articles that have appeared in international journals such as *International Education, The Alberta Journal of Educational Research, AlterNative: An International Journal for Indigenous Scholarship*, and the *Australian Journal of Indigenous Education* while his book chapters have been published in *Issues in African Education: Sociological Perspectives* (Palgrave, 2005), *African Education and Globalization: Critical Perspectives* (Lexington, 2006), *Global Perspectives on Adult Education* (Palgrave, 2008), *Education and Social Development: Global Issues and Analysis* (Sense, 2008) and *International Perspectives on Education, PAR and Social Change* (Palgrave, 2009). He has co-authored *Citizenship Education and Social Development in Zambia* (Information Age Publishing Inc (2010) and co-edited *Indigenous Knowledge and Learning in Asia/Pacific and Africa: Perspectives on Development, Education and Culture* (2010).

Dr. Aziz Choudry is Assistant Professor in the Department of Integrated Studies in Education, McGill University, Canada. He has over two decades experience working in activist groups, NGOs, and social movements in the Asia-Pacific and North America. A longtime organizer, educator, and researcher with Aotearoa/New Zealand activist group, GATT Watchdog, he also served on the board of convenors of the Asia-Pacific Research Network from 2002-2004. Currently he sits on the boards of the Immigrant Workers Centre, Montreal, the US-based Global Justice Ecology Project, and is a co-initiator and member of the editorial team of the collaborative website www.bilaterals.org supporting critical analysis of, and resistance against, bilateral free trade and investment agreements. He is co-author of *Fight Back: Workplace Justice for Immigrants* (2009), and co-editor of *Learning from the Ground Up: Global Perspectives on Social Movements and Knowledge Production* (2010).

D. Kapoor (ed.), Critical Perspectives on Neoliberal Globalization, Development and Education in Africa and Asia, 207–210.

Dr. Sourayan Mookerjea's research addresses contradictions of globalization, migration, urbanization, subaltern social movements, popular culture and class politics. Recent publications include *Canadian Cultural Studies: A Reader*, co-edited with Dr. I. Szeman and G. Faurschou, (Duke University Press, 2009). He is Associate Professor of Sociology at the University of Alberta, Canada.

Dr. Dip Kapoor is Associate Professor in Theoretical, Cultural and International Studies in Education at the University of Albert, Canada and Research Associate, Center for Research and Development Solidarity (CRDS), an Adivasi-Dalit organization in South Orissa, India supporting land, forest and water related Adivasi-Dalit movements in the state. His articles have appeared in journals like the *McGill Journal of Education, Adult Education & Development, International Education, Development in Practice, Journal of Postcolonial Education* and *Convergence*. His recent co/edited book collections include: *Indigenous Knowledge and Learning in Asia/Pacific and Africa: Perspectives on Development, Education and Culture* (2010), *Learning from the Ground Up: Global Perspectives on Social Movements and Knowledge Production* (2010), *Education, Development and Decolonization: Perspectives from Asia, Africa and the Americas* (2009), *Education, Participatory Action Research and Social Change: International Perspectives* (2009) and *Global Perspectives on Adult Education* (2009).

Dr. Sidonia Alenuma-Nimoh teaches at Gustavus Adolphus College in the USA. She has an honour BA in Sociology and Russian from the University of Ghana; an MA in International Development Studies from Saint Mary's University, Halifax, Canada; and a PhD in Cultural Studies in Education from the University of Tennessee, Knoxville. Her interests include: international development studies; multicultural anti-racism education; social foundations of education; and educational reform. Some of her publications include: Race, Urban Schools, and Educational Reform (*Teaching City Kids: Understanding and Appreciating Them*, Peter Lang, 2007); Downtown Elementary School (DES): The Unique School that Juxtaposes both Magnet and Professional Development School Programs (*US-China Education Review*, 6(7), 2009); and Making Some Modest Strides: The Story of Downtown Elementary School (DES) (*International Electronic Journal of Elementary Education (IEJEE)*, 1(3), 2009). Dr. Alenuma-Nimoh's book, *Race and Educational Reform in America: History, Strategies and Ethnography*, was published in 2009.

Dr. Loramy Gerstbauer is associate professor of political science and director of peace studies at Gustavus Adolphus College in St. Peter, Minneapolis. Her research interests are forgiveness in international relations and peace building NGOs. She has published articles in: *The Nonprofit and Voluntary Sector Quarterly, Development in Practice, Peace Review* and other journals. She is currently working on a manuscript examining the policy of the United States towards former enemy nations. She teaches international relations courses as well as Latin American politics, politics of developing nations, and peace studies. She received her Ph.D. in Government as well as an M.A. in Peace Studies from the University of Notre Dame.

Munyaradzi Hwami is a PhD candidate and Instructor in the Department of Educational Policy Studies, University of Alberta, Canada and Lecturer, Great Zimbabwe University, Zimbabwe. He has an MEd in the sociology of education from Zimbabwe and has taught history in high school and sociology of education at teachers' college and at the university level in Zimbabwe. His current research interests include: political-sociology of higher education; neoliberal globalization, nationalism and higher education; and critical colonial perspectives/analysis in education. He is particularly interested in higher education in post-independence Africa and Zimbabwe. His articles have appeared in the *Journal of Educational Studies* and the *Zimbabwe Journal of Educational Research*.

Dr. Faisal Islam Faisal Islam has recently received his Ph.D. from the Department of Integrated Studies in Education at McGill University, Montreal, Canada. His research areas focus on participatory research, school-university partnerships, community-based engagements and international development. He also has extensive experience in working with international non-government organizations and is an independent researcher and consultant.

Dr. Claudia Mitchell is a James McGill Professor in the Faculty of Education of McGill University, Montreal, Canada, and an Honorary Professor in the School of Language, Literacies, Media and Drama Education at the University of KwaZulu-Natal. Her research looks at youth and sexuality in the age of AIDS, children's popular culture, girlhood, teacher identity, participatory visual and other methodologies, and strategic areas of gender and HIV&AIDS in social development contexts in South Africa, Rwanda, and Ethiopia. She has published extensively these areas of research. She is also the co-founder and co-editor of *Girlhood Studies: An Interdisciplinary Journal*.

Dr. Al-Karim Datoo is a sociologist of education and an Assistant Professor at the Aga Khan University Institute for Educational Development (AKU-IED) in Pakistan where he heads initiatives related to the social science education programs and does research and teaches graduate level courses in development and education and social studies. He is also a founding member of a multidisciplinary research group working in area of globalization and cultural studies at AKU-IED. His primary research interest is in studying the nexus between globalization, culture and education. Dr Datoo has a PhD in the cultural-sociology of globalization and education from McGill University, Canada. His doctoral thesis/research is a pioneering effort in conducting a critical ethnography of schooling in the Pakistani context. He has an MSc in Educational Research Methodology from the University of Oxford, UK, and the graduate program in Islamic Studies and Humanities from the Institute of Ismaili Studies (IIS), London, UK.

Dr. Jonathan Langdon is Assistant Professor of Development Studies at St. Francis Xavier University, Canada. His doctoral work at McGill University used a participatory research approach to bring together Ghanaian activist-educators to examine social movement dynamics and learning in Ghana since the country's return to democracy in 1992. This work has emerged from relationships developed over a decade with local organizations, communities and movements in Ghana. His recent publications have appeared in the *Canadian Journal of Development Studies*, the *IDS Bulletin* and the *McGill Journal of Education*. He is also the editor of *Indigenous Knowledges, Development and Education* (Sense, 2009).

Dr. Bijoy P. Barua is a Faculty member in the Department of Social Sciences at East West University, Bangladesh. He is also a Senior Fellow of the *Journal of Alternative Perspectives in the Social Sciences*, USA and former Associate Fellow of the Centre for Developing Area Studies (CDAS), McGill University, Canada. He has contributed to scholarly journals, such as *Canadian Journal of Development Studies, International Education* (USA) and edited book collections: *Global Perspectives on Adult Education* (2009), *Education, Decolonization, and Development* (2009), and *Education, Participatory Action Research and Social Change: International Perspectives* (2009), and *Indigenous Knowledge and Learning in Asia/Pacific and Africa* (2010). He is the author of the book, *Western Education and Modernization in a Buddhist Village: A Case Study of the Barua Community in Bangladesh* (2009). He is a member of the International Advisory Board, First Academic International Conference on Exploring Leadership and Learning Theories in Asia, to be held in Kuala Lumpur, Malaysia in February, 2011.

Dr. Blane Harvey is a Research Fellow in Climate Change and Development with the Institute of Development Studies at the University of Sussex, UK. Prior to joining IDS he completed a PhD in Education and International Development at McGill University and worked with the Climate Change Programme at the United Nations Institute for Training and Research (UNITAR). His current work critically examines knowledge production, validation and dissemination processes within climate change and environmental governance, with a focus on how power shapes these processes in North-South partnerships and inter-institutional cooperation. The contribution to this collection draws on his doctoral research conducted in Senegal in 2007 and 2008. He continues to work closely with partner institutes in Senegal, and recently conducted follow-up research on the social impact of organic and fair trade cotton in Senegal and Mali.